AF251978

CHINA

GLOBAL SECURITY WATCH

CHINA

Richard Weitz

AN IMPRINT OF ABC-CLIO, LLC
Santa Barbara, California • Denver, Colorado • Oxford, England

Library of Congress Cataloging-in-Publication Data

Weitz, Richard.
  Global security watch—China / Richard Weitz.
    pages cm. — (Global security watch)
  Includes bibliographical references and index.
    ISBN 978–0–313–38482–0 (hardcopy : alk. paper) — ISBN 978–0–313–38483–7 (ebook)
    1. China—Foreign relations. 2. China—Strategic aspects. 3. China—Military policy. 4. National security—China. I. Title. II. Title: China.
DS518.15.W45   2013
355′.033051—dc23   2013008123

ISBN: 978–0–313–38482–0
EISBN: 978–0–313–38483–7

17 16 15 14 13   1 2 3 4 5

This book is also available on the World Wide Web as an eBook.
Visit www.abc-clio.com for details.

Praeger
An Imprint of ABC-CLIO, LLC

ABC-CLIO, LLC
130 Cremona Drive, P.O. Box 1911
Santa Barbara, California 93116-1911

This book is printed on acid-free paper ∞

Manufactured in the United States of America

Contents

Preface

The People's Republic of China (PRC) has become, after the United States, the world's most important country because of its enormous population, growing economic and military power, and newly assertive foreign policies. Whereas during the Cold War, China was largely isolated and alienated from world politics, the PRC has become a major global security actor. Today, no major security issue, in any region, can be decided without considering Beijing's position. China's influence in Africa, Latin America, and other regions has been expanding along with the PRC's power in Asia. China is following the path of earlier rising economic powers such as Great Britain and the United States in converting its economic potential into military strength. Beijing is also developing increasingly powerful military tools, ranging from nuclear weapons to innovative cyber and space strike weapons. Despite these growing economic and military powers, China has not engaged in a major war since 1953. Western leaders still hope that China will become a responsible global stakeholder and uphold existing international security arrangements.

This volume in the PSI Global Security Watch series reviews the foreign and defense policies of China, with emphasis on developments since the 1989 Tiananmen Square incident. It provides a comprehensive but relatively short and accessible text for students, journalists, and policy makers eager to better understand the implications of China's ascending trajectory. The biographies, chronology, and core documents in the appendices also make the book a handy reference to the general reader as well as academic audiences.

The first chapter describes China's main foreign-policy goals and decision makers. China's economy has been experiencing tremendous growth in recent years but must now transform to escape the "middle-income trap" that has ensnarled so many other developing states whose growth plateaus after they can no longer achieve easy gains from adding low-cost labor inputs to production. In addition, China's authoritarian political system struggles to find legitimacy in an era of democratic change. Chapter two assesses China's military power. The People's Liberation Army has become more professional and capable during the past decade, but it lacks major power projection capabilities such as aircraft carrier fleets and long-range bombers. To compensate, Chinese strategists are developing innovative asymmetric tactics and capabilities, especially in the cyber domain. The third chapter surveys China's foreign policy toward key East, South, and Central Asian countries as well as Taiwan and Russia. Chapter four reviews China's policies toward the United States, Europe, Sub-Saharan Africa, and South America.

I would like to thank my colleagues for the numerous insights they have offered on the issues addressed in this book. Michael Aiken and Andrew Haggard were especially helpful in helping me prepare the manuscript for publication. I wish to thank the Carnegie Corporation, the Smith-Richardson Foundation, the MacArthur Foundation, and other institutions for supporting my research on Chinese foreign and defense policy over the years. Although listing all the China-related discussions and briefings I have participated in during recent years would be impossible, special thanks goes to the experts at the Hudson Institute, the World Politics Review, the Diplomat, and the Second Line of Defense for commenting on various ideas contained in this volume on a topic as important as China's evolving global security role.

China
Karamay
Urumqi
Korla
Kashi
Hami
Hotan
Qiemo
Yumen
Hohhot
Baotou
Beijing
Qiqihar
Jixi
Harbin
Jilin
Changchung
Fuxin
Shenyang
Benxi
Tianjin
Dalian
Yinchuan
Taiyuan
Shijiazhuang
Jinan
Qingdao
Golmud
Xining
Lanzhou
Taian
Zhengzhou
Kaifeng
Xian
Nanjing
Hefei
Mianyang
Chengdu
Wuhan
Hangzhou
Ningbo
Zigong
Chongqing
Yueyang
Nanchang
Wenzhou
Changsha
Lhasa
Fuzhou
Dukou
Guiyang
Taipei
Xiamen
T'ai-chung
T'ai-nan
Kunming
Shantou
Kao-Hsiung
Nanning
Guangzhou
Hong Kong
Haikou
N

CHAPTER 1

China Ascending

Few countries in the world have changed as dramatically as the People's Republic of China (PRC). During the past three decades, China has transformed from a revolutionary state, whose government advocated global communism and the overthrow of the Western-dominated international system, into a "status quo" power with a strategy of integrating into and supporting the current world order. Whereas China before 1979 was an "outsider" that actively opposed most existing international institutions, today's PRC has, for now, become a major global stakeholder in the existing international system, assuming a leadership role in many security and economic institutions. In addition, whereas the Soviet Union and its satellite states experienced massive upheavals during the late 1980s and early 1990s—in which their Communist regimes irretrievably collapsed—China's authoritarian political system successfully managed the 1989 mass protests at Tiananmen Square through a combination of selective political repression and subsequent economic reforms that generated unprecedented prosperity. PRC leaders then skillfully leveraged China's many assets to break out of its post-Tiananmen isolation and escape many sanctions in only a few years. Meanwhile, since the 1980s, China has become a much more complex international actor. Whereas three decades earlier, the PRC might have been described as a largely monolithic society governed by an omnipotent regime, China now represents a more diverse and multifaceted society with many players who could potentially influence the country's foreign and domestic policies. Today's China presents a complicated mix of potential challenges and opportunities for other countries.

China's most visible impact today is the weight of its economic influence on global affairs. Across any number of indicators, the PRC's success during the past three decades has been staggering. Since Deng Xiaoping's economic reforms in the late 1970s, China has averaged more than 9 percent annual growth in its gross domestic product (GDP). Whereas in 1978, the PRC accounted for less than 1 percent of world GDP, today it represents more than 4 percent of the world economy. In 2010, China became the second largest economy (surpassing Japan), the fifth largest source of foreign direct investment, and the world's largest exporter. Because of its large internal market and attractive domestic investment climate, China has managed to attract enormous interest among global investors. In 2002, the PRC surpassed the United States as the largest recipient of foreign direct investment (FDI), attracting nearly $53 billion that year.[1] By 2011, FDI had reached $116 billion.[2] Several new laws have strengthened the attractiveness of China's investment framework. In accordance with the recommendations of the Organization for Economic Co-operation and Development (OECD), the PRC has attempted to establish a stable, transparent framework for regulation instead of offering fiscal and other preferential incentives to investors; the new laws are expected to simplify the tax process for investors, increase tax revenue through better regulation, and attract more foreign investment.[3]

China's policymakers readily apply economic power in bilateral relations with other countries, such as by lending money to the United States and Europe, giving aid to North Korea, and trying to suborn the Taiwanese and their allies. The PRC has attracted hundreds of billions of dollars of foreign investment while loaning comparatively vast sums to the United States as well as to other countries. Double-digit economic growth over the past two decades has also given China a greater voice in international organizations. For example, China will become the third largest shareholder of the International Monetary Fund, with a 6 percent share of the fund by 2014.[4] Meanwhile, similar adjustments are occurring in other international institutions, such as the elevated influence of the G-20 (which includes China) relative to the G-8 (which does not). The U.S. intelligence community sees China as becoming perhaps the most important global actor in coming decades because of its rising economic power. In its 2008 and 2012 Global Trends reports, the National Intelligence Council (NIC) anticipated that the PRC's relative economic strength would increase markedly relative to that of the United States and many key U.S. allies in Europe and Asia.[5]

China's tremendous economic growth has enabled its government to allot more resources to developing the PRC's military power. The People's Liberation Army (PLA) has increased its capabilities in many areas, acquiring more powerful warships, warplanes, and unconventional space and cybercapabilities. Chinese analysts often complain that the PRC is held to an exceptionally high standard regarding its military activities, pointing out that other countries engage in ambitious military activities without evoking international alarm. Although the growth of the PRC's military power is to be expected, China is often treated differently precisely because many people see the PRC as the world's next superpower. The United States, the United Kingdom, and other countries marked their ascent to global economic preeminence with a corresponding growth of their military capabilities. Historians and other scholars have noted how, at the level of the international system, the rise and fall of great powers typically entails major tensions and often major wars.[6] Ascending powers seek to alter international institutions, rules, and norms to their advantage as well as to pursue territorial and other concrete goals by converting some of their growing wealth into military capabilities. Declining great powers often resist these challenges. Unresolved border disputes, competition for scarce resources, and status and prestige considerations can precipitate an armed conflict.

Like earlier rising great powers, the PRC might use its growing economic and military power to uphold common interests, such as freedom of the seas against pirates, political reconciliation, and economic development in the Afghanistan-Pakistan region, or nuclear nonproliferation in the Middle East and East Asia. However, most rising powers seek to reshape the world to better advance their own interests, provoking a countervailing response from the established states. A peaceful power transition is rare and it certainly cannot be presumed that a rising great power will remain a genuine global stakeholder, continuing to defend the values and institutions established by its predecessor. Some recent PRC policies, such as Beijing's increasingly assertive efforts to enforce its maritime claims in the East and South China Seas, are already displaying signs of a revisionist hegemon in the making. As illustrated by the recent controversy over the maps depicting China's larger than recognized borders in the latest version of PRC passports, Beijing's case is more menacing because so many of its land and sea borders are contested with other states. The fundamental question is whether this Chinese-driven power transition will engender major wars—as has often occurred in the past—or whether the transition can be managed in a way that avoids unnecessary loss of life, time, and resources. When confronted by rising powers, the established state can respond in many ways, from graceful retrenchment as occurred during the transition from British to U.S. leadership, to preemptive war, which occurred when several powers responded to the growing power of Germany. As China's economic and military power increases relative to other great powers, PRC leaders are likely to demand more influence over the world's key international institutions and norms. In some cases these demands should be embraced, while in others they should be resisted, which raises the issue over how Beijing will enforce its claims given that the existing power, the United States, will likely support China's neighbors.

Is China destined to become the next peer rival of the United States in the twenty-first century? The NIC depicts the most likely outcome as the continued growth of China's economic and military strength, in conjunction with a persistent authoritarian government committed to the state capitalist model of development. But the analysts also discuss the possibility that a lengthy economic slowdown could lead to "virulent and xenophobic forms of Chinese nationalism" if the Chinese government attempts to blame foreigners for China's difficulties.[7] It is questionable whether the past success of China's "state capitalist" development model—in which the government largely directs national economic activity typically left to private sector market forces in traditional liberal democratic states—will continue to yield superior performance. For the past decade, Chinese leaders have acknowledged that their economic model—based on a high rate of growth driven by top-down, state-directed domestic infrastructure investment driven by loans from state-owned banks—"is unstable, unbalanced, uncoordinated and unsustainable."[8] The PRC is replete with contradictions that make the country simultaneously a strong and weak state. Despite its astounding economic growth during recent decades, China resembles many developing countries with unprecedented pollution problems, sprawling urban growth and migration (now more than half the people live in cities), vulnerability to changes in commodity prices and climate conditions, various public health issues, and pervasive social stresses.

Analysts generally agree that the PRC will need to overcome several major political-military and socioeconomic challenges before it achieves global superpower status, though they differ in their assessment of whether the PRC will surmount them. China's growing income inequalities, widespread corruption, pervasive political repression, limited institutional capacity, and other problems could disrupt its impressive economic performance as well as potentially threaten its ascending military power and political stability.[9] China could easily fall in the "middle-income trap" that has ensnarled so many other developing states whose growth plateaus after they can no longer achieve easy gains from adding low cost labor inputs to production. The PRC's annual growth has fallen to below double-digit levels in recent years, with growing inflation and unemployment. In addition, the country suffers from extraordinarily high rates of wealth and income inequality, both between and within regions. The financial system also remains vulnerable to collapse because of the large number of nonperforming loans issued by state-owned banks to unprofitable state-run enterprises. China regularly ranks very far from the top tier in the annual World Bank "Doing Business" reports—92nd in the 2013 report.[10] But the Chinese government has thus far resisted making major reforms such as closing unprofitable government-backed institutions by depriving them of capital, because the resulting massive unemployment would antagonize the regime's core supporters.

To counter negative scenarios, PRC leaders have agreed with their foreign advisers in declaring a commitment, in China's 12th Five-Year Plan (2011–2015) and in their speeches, to rebalance China's economy into one less dependent on exports and public spending and to one aimed more at meeting the need of China's consumers and private enterprises. Rebalancing depends on further unleashing the country's more innovative, efficient, and profitable private sector businesses and increasing consumer demand. China's other economic challenges include its demographic transition to a society of fewer workers and more retirees, as well as the end of easy gains from adding low cost labor and foreign technology borrowing that has allowed the PRC to catch up to world standards. Rising wages and competition from cheaper workers in other countries has led Chinese producers to substitute capital for labor, increasing unemployment. Instead, they need to improve the quality of their labor, expand the service sector (which is incredibly small given the vast size of China's consumer market), strengthen the social safety net (to give people confidence to spend rather than save as much as they can), and generate more innovations at home.

The PRC also has systematic problems of governance. Like all one-party authoritarian systems, the selection of Chinese leaders is opaque and prone to factional infighting, court politics, and rumormongering, as seen in 2012 with the Bo Xilai affair and then the unexplained disappearance of the presumptive next Chinese leader, Xi Jinping, for several weeks. The Chinese Communist Party (CCP) is the largest political organization in the world, with more than 80 million members, many of whom constantly feel empowered to interfere in the affairs of state and business. Yet, the decentralized nature of China's current political system, a major evolution from the hypercentralized Mao era, bestows considerable influence on the PRC's 45 million local and provincial officials. These functionaries enjoy substantial autonomy because they can evade supervision from Beijing-based ministries while escaping popular control, because of the absence of popular elections.[11] The only check on their abuses thus far has been the Chinese broadcast and social media, but its ability to expose abuses remains constrained by the government's continuing censorship of Chinese media freedoms. Their ability to evade central government supervision, combined with provincial officials' regulatory authority over the major economic enterprises in their jurisdiction, makes it difficult for the Beijing government to enforce national policies, including international agreements. The empowerment of unelected regional leaders and officials, who often collude with the local business elite to exaggerate their economic accomplishments while ignoring environmental and other national regulations that might infringe on their prosperity, also creates considerable opportunities for corruption and perverts the rule of law. The unaccountable local functionaries can ignore China's weak judiciary, making it impossible to enforce property rights. About the only recourse available to people victimized by local officials is to engage in mass or web-based protests, but these still carry risks in an authoritarian political system that continues to interpret demonstrations and other forms of independent civic activism as potentially subversive.

The Chinese political system has seen "pockets" of progress in its becoming more liberal and democratic, but severe restrictions on political pluralism still exist, which keeps China from moving into the democratic mainstream that has gathered renewed strength since the end of the Cold War and the more recent Arab Spring.[12] The Chinese people have experienced improving social and economic rights because of the rising standard of living; even their freedom of expression has expanded, at least in the sense that private utterances of discontent with local policies usually go unpunished. However, the government continues to deny Chinese citizens basic civil and political rights such as the ability to vote in free and fair elections or avoid arbitrary and excessive punishment at the hands of abusive public officials. In addition, the PRC's foreign policy often supports the repressive policy of other regimes by weakening or blocking international sanctions against them or by loaning them money without requiring them to conform to international human rights standards. The economic success of the PRC's authoritarian model inspires these regimes to emulate Beijing and infringe on their own people's civil rights. The Chinese government's failure to enforce international human rights conventions and agreements also calls into question Beijing's commitment to the rule of law in other spheres, such as its adherence to intellectual property rights and other agreements.[13]

Although the Chinese people seem to have set aside their democratic aspirations of the late 1980s in favor of pursuing individual economic rewards and China's national ambitions, their political compliance with the one-party CCP rule may not persist indefinitely. Growing corruption and national income inequalities, especially between urban and rural dwellers, have aroused considerable popular dissatisfaction. In many other societies, rising national prosperity has led people to demand more political rights to correspond with their new economic power—indeed, they seek political influence precisely to defend their growing economic interests. Conversely, an economic downturn could lead people to hold the CCP government responsible and to seek the ruling elite's replacement.

Finally, China's relations with the outside world—especially with the United States, Europe, Russia, India, Japan, Taiwan, and other Asian states—will affect both its economic and security prospects. In this regard, the PRC is modernizing its military, but the PLA still suffers from serious weaknesses that would constrain its ability to match a coalition of major adversaries. The continued growth of China's power across multiple dimensions could well remain a dominant characteristic of this century, but the PRC's evolutionary trajectory remains profoundly unpredictable.

STRATEGY AND TACTICS

The PRC's international priorities have generally consisted of a mixture of defensive and expansive goals: protecting the country's sovereignty and territorial integrity, preserving the CCP regime's political power, promoting national economic development and prosperity, and advancing the PRC's international power and prestige.[14] Chinese scholars themselves insist that, though the PRC is in some respects a global great power, China should be viewed mostly as a developing country with an economically focused agenda best advanced in a climate of international peace and security.[15] The PRC's continued claims to its developing country status have led Chinese diplomats to side with the nonaligned bloc on many issues, which has complicated climate change negotiations and constrained China's willingness to assume a leadership role in many global institutions.

Several historically determined lenses influence how Chinese policymakers pursue these goals, whose relative emphasis and policy manifestations naturally vary over time.[16] For example, the PRC's recent resurgence is seen in Beijing as China resuming its rightful status as a great power, especially in the East Asia region. PRC representatives remain sensitive to perceived infringements on China's sovereignty and fearful that foreign powers will try to constrain and coerce China by exploiting its internal weaknesses. On the other hand, PRC leaders now perceive the success of the country's current growth model as tightly interconnected with global and regional powers, markets, and institutions. According to the PRC's 2008 national defense white paper, "the future and destiny of China have been increasingly closely connected with the global community . . . China cannot develop in isolation from the rest of the world, nor can the world enjoy prosperity and stability without China."[17] Yet, this same document—like other government-approved publications and statements—underscores the pervasive uncertainty among PRC policymakers and scholars about the range and severity of China's threats and opportunities, describing a mish-mash of favorable and unfavorable trends and scenarios.

In terms of how Beijing views the contemporary international security environment, the 2008 PRC white paper states that "peace and development remain the principal themes of the times," a reaffirmation of the international strategy Beijing has followed for at least the past decade. Equally unsurprising, the paper affirms Beijing's commitment to pursue cooperative relations and "win-win" outcomes with other countries. In the authors' assessment, the "major powers are stepping up their efforts to cooperate with each other and draw on each other's strengths." Other trends, such as increasing economic interdependence, are "keeping low the risk of worldwide, all-out and large-scale wars for a relatively long period of time." On a darker note, the white paper cautions that "global challenges are on the increase, and new security threats keep emerging" such as the "struggle for strategic resources, strategic locations and strategic dominance." In addition, "hegemonism and power politics still exist, regional turmoil keeps spilling over, hot-spot issues are increasing, and local conflicts and wars keep emerging." And the authors see the worldwide economic downturn as "triggered by the U.S. subprime mortgage crisis" that has "highlighted deep-seated contradictions" in the global economy.[18]

Notwithstanding the PLA's improving capabilities and other assets, the PRC leadership's preoccupation with possible domestic and foreign challenges as well as threats to the regime's survival has until recently led Beijing to pursue generally moderate external policies. Chinese leaders worry about U.S. and other efforts to contain Beijing as well as threats to their domestic political legitimacy.[19] In practice, these fears have generally induced Chinese self-containment in that PRC policy makers exercise China's rising power with considerable restraint. For example, the PLA has not fought a war since its short 1979 border incursion against Vietnam. They normally eschew actions that could alarm other countries. Yet, these perceptual constraints are largely self-imposed, so PRC leaders could more easily discard them than they could structural and external impediments on the Chinese power, which have been weakening over time. Such a reversal may have already occurred with respect to the PRC's maritime claims, regarding which Beijing has become much more assertive.

Andrew J. Nathan and Andrew Scobell argue that Chinese national security challenges and priorities can be understood in terms of "four rings" of decreasing relative importance. The most important ring is the territory administered or claimed by China, such as the Chinese mainland, which contains several ethnic minorities of dubious loyalty to Beijing, as well as Taiwan and large swathes of the Pacific Ocean. The second ring includes China's 14 land and 8 maritime neighbors, with which China shares historically contested boundaries. China has frequently fought wars with these powerful countries, which include India, Japan, the Koreas, Russia, and Vietnam. PRC diplomats have had to devote enormous efforts to maintaining tolerable relations with these states, but strains persist even if in some cases they are latent. The third ring consists of six geopolitical regions around China that include these neighboring countries but also noncontingent states. The regions are Northeast Asia, Oceania, continental Southeast Asia, maritime Southeast Asia, South Asia, and Central Asia. The importance of these subsystems means that Chinese diplomats often cannot achieve their goals through bilateral diplomacy but must dilute their influence through multilateral engagements. The fourth ring includes the rest of the world, where China has been active only since the late 1990s, and most often for narrow economic purposes (trade, investment, natural resources, and diplomatic partners). For now, the authors claim, China has adopted a primarily defensive posture to prevent threats in the latter three circles from challenging Beijing's control over the first circle. Regime primacy requires strong economic growth, which is best achieved in a secure international environment that creates a benign environment for China's foreign trade and investment.[20]

Despite Beijing's inner fears, most analysts would perceive China's efforts to "rise," while not provoking a countervailing international balancing coalition, as successful.[21] One reason for this success is that Chinese leaders have taken care to characterize their policies as seeking a "win-win" outcome that benefits all parties.[22] This formula enables the PRC to reduce foreign hostility to China's growing economic presence overseas and deepening penetration of international markets. By enticing foreign countries with announcements of generous economic aid, trade, and investment agreements with no strings attached—unlike Western deals, which typically require stringent standards—the PRC has sought to portray itself as a benevolent rising power that does not threaten other countries' security or economic well-being. By pursuing win-win relationships, the PRC has forged mutually beneficial relationships with numerous countries around the world. The deals not only have improved China's security and prosperity in the short-term, but they have also typically established a favorable framework for more extensive long-term cooperation.[23] Beijing's professed cooperative approach to foreign affairs also manifests itself in China's frequent use of such terms as "common interest" and the "new security concept," which stress the PRC's support for economic interdependence, regional integration, and multilateral security cooperation. For the win-win strategy to be effective, it must downplay contentious issues that divide parties, especially where one side's gain would appear as the other side's loss. Thus, China buys oil from Sudan while refraining from criticizing Khartoum's human rights policies in Darfur. Critics see this approach as a manifestation of the amorality of China's foreign policy, which provides benefits only for the political and economic elites of the partner country, while its people are the losers.[24]

Unfortunately for China, the limits of the effectiveness of this "win-win" strategy have begun to appear. In its bilateral relationships with many countries, as well as regarding some global issues such as climate change, PRC negotiators have frequently found it necessary to defend specific Chinese interests rather than to accept solutions that would result in a net global benefit but at a discrete cost to Beijing. China's rising international prominence has also made it more difficult for PRC diplomats to pursue cooperative relations with pariah regimes that violate human rights and other global norms. Moreover, as China's foreign influence grows, the PRC's responsibility for global stewardship increases. For example, other capitals now place great stake in whether Beijing will support international sanctions against Iran, allow further appreciation of the yuan, or limit China's carbon emissions. China's influence will suffer if other countries look to Beijing for leadership that fails to materialize.

ACTORS AND PROCESSES

Although China's foreign policy decision-making process remains highly centralized, over time the number of actors who influence these decisions has grown. The majority of China's foreign policy decisions still lie in the hands of the CCP Politburo Standing Committee—the most powerful decision-making body in the country. Its key members until the November 2012 18th Party Congress were

Table 1.1 Chinese Leaders (as of late 2012)[1]

	Position(s)	Affiliation(s)	Policy Preference Indicators
Xi Jinping	CPC General Secretary, Central Military Commission Chairman, PRC President (expected)	Princeling, Shanghai; Jiang's network	Simultaneously market-friendly and pro-protectionism; military ties and nationalist
Li Keqiang	Premier (expected)	Communist Youth League; Hu's network	Populist; focused on domestic issues such as employment and regional development
Zhang Dejiang	Vice Premier, Chongqing Party Secretary	Princeling; Jiang-ist	Pro-protectionism; son of former PLA major general
Yu Zhengsheng	Shanghai Party Secretary	Princeling, Shanghai; Jiang-ist	Market-friendly, pro-social reform
Liu Yunshan	Director of CPC Propaganda Department	CYL; Hu-ist	Conservative media control
Wang Qishan	Vice Premier	Princeling; Jiang-ist and protégé of former premier Zhu Rongji	Liberalization of foreign investment and trade
Zhang Gaoli	Tianjin Party Secretary	Princeling; Jiang-ist and protégé of former vice president Zeng Qinghong	Market-friendly

[1]Cheng Li, "China's Top Future Leaders to Watch," http://www.brookings.edu/about/centers/china/top-future-leaders, November 15, 2012). See also "Top CPC Leadership," Xinhua, 2013, http://www.xinhuanet.com/english/special/topcpcleadership/index.htm.

the CCP General Secretary, Hu Jintao; the Premier of the State Council, Wen Jiabao; and the Chairman of the National People's Congress, Wu Bangguo.[25] The new leadership team elected at the 18th CCP Congress and confirmed at the National People's Congress (NPC) and the National Committee of the Chinese People's Political Consultative Conference (CPPCC) in March 2013 consists of:

- CCP General Secretary Xi Jinping
- Premier of the State Council Li Keqiang
- Chairman of the National People's Congress Zhang Dejiang
- Chairman of the Chinese People's Political Consultative Conference Yu Zhengsheng

- Executive Secretariat member Liu Yunshan
- Secretary of the Central Commission for Discipline Inspection Wang Qishan
- Executive Vice Premier Zhang Gaoli

These individuals, who comprise the fifth-generation of CCP leaders and are led by two leaders who were born after the PRC was founded in 1949, could remain in charge of China's foreign policy for the next decade or more—or they could lose power almost overnight like Bo Xilai, a rising CCP media star who ran afoul of a major scandal in early 2012. (The biographies of many of these and other Chinese leaders can be found in the appendix to this book.)

None of the new top leaders have a major background in foreign or defense policy. PRC leaders are bound together more by their factional ties than by their substantive policy preferences.[26] Xi is considered to be the leader of the "princeling" faction in the CCP. The princelings are the children of earlier PRC leaders who have now risen to prominence in the Party, State, and especially the PLA. Most were born in relatively privileged circumstances and come from the prosperous coastal provinces and major cities. This environment caused many to become interested in economic development and business. (In fact, most children of CCP leaders enter into business rather than follow their parents into politics.) Members of the so-called Shanghai group are the allies of former leader Jiang Zemin. They generally represent the views of coastal business interest. These two "elitist" factions are often at odds with Hu Jintao's Communist Youth League (CYL) faction and the "populist" coalition that hails from the rural and economically underdeveloped interior and is concerned with the implications of uneven development and the growing income gap. The princelings are expected to be the main rivals of the ruling CYL faction in the coming years, especially with Xi's ascension to the top leadership position. Despite the factional rivalry, most members of the new fifth-generation of CCP leaders are technocratic pragmatists rather than ideologues who will likely not make major breaks in China's foreign policy. Like most Chinese politicians, they place stability and continued Party rule above all other concerns. The main changes in PRC policy will likely lie in the realm of domestic policy, with increased emphasis on economic liberalization, GDP growth, and the development of east coast business interests, contrasting with the previous Hu-Wen administration's focus on improving social welfare and promoting development of China's rural interior. Xi has also emphasized the fight against corruption, which he said could destroy the Party. Since then, the PLA has been instructed to reduce the lavishness of its dinners and other entertainment. The next step may be to reign in local Party bosses, who rule without major local checks and balances. The Chinese economy, with its unique brand of market state capitalism, also needs much attention because of the high costs of food and housing; the property bubble may burst soon given the large number of empty leases.

The CCP's Foreign Affairs Leading Small Group (LSG), headed by the CCP general secretary-cum-PRC president, is a nonstanding body consisting of around two dozen top foreign affairs experts and bureaucrats from the party, government, and military as well as other international relations specialists.[27] It acts as a liaison body among China's foreign affairs institutions and also advises on foreign policy issues.[28] The Central Military Commission (CMC), which consists of the nation's top military officials and has supreme authority over China's armed forces, is another critical organization that advises the Politburo Standing Committee on important foreign policy decisions, particularly in regards to matters of national security. Although some have compared this body to the U.S. National Security Council (NSC), the CMC does not have the same ability for rapid crisis response. Except for the most critical foreign-policy issues, the Politburo (short for Political Bureau) as a whole has minimal involvement in foreign policy processes, though some individual members have direct oversight over certain foreign and defense policy bureaucracies. The CCP Secretariat, which manages the daily functions of the CCP, plays an even smaller role in forming foreign policy. It mainly serves to legitimize, implement, and supervise decisions made by other foreign-policy organs.[29] The National People's Congress (NPC), which on paper represents the most supreme PRC body, also has a limited role in foreign policy decision-making. Though it occasionally may raise questions and concerns or prepare reports for other institutions, the NPC mostly rubber stamps policies made elsewhere. The State Council, which operates underneath the NPC, has a much larger role in foreign-policy implementation, because it oversees various ministries and commissions, such as the Ministry of Foreign Affairs (MFA). The PRC leadership does however use the experts and materials of these organizations to help determine China's foreign-policy strategy and tactics.[30]

The MFA is the PRC's primary institution responsible for implementing China's foreign policy goals. The Ministry administers China's diplomatic work, including negotiating bilateral and multilateral treaties, working with international institutions, and managing some 150 overseas diplomatic missions. In addition to these administrative functions, the MFA also serves as a critical source of information and advice for senior PRC decision makers.[31] In practice, the MFA reports to the Politburo Standing Committee by way of the Central Foreign Affairs LSG, though it officially falls under the authority of the State Council.[32] Yang Jiechi was PRC foreign minister from 2007 until recently. He had decades of diplomatic experience and is a fluent English speaker with a PhD in history. He began his career with the MFA in 1975 and in 1998 became a vice minister; from 2001 to 2005, Yang served as the PRC's ambassador to the United States.[33] In March 2013, Wang Yi became the new PRC Foreign Minister, while Yang became the state councilor for foreign affairs. Wang served as ambassador to Japan from 2004 to 2007 and subsequently as head of the State

Council's Taiwan Affairs Office.[34] His appointment may have reflected Beijing's concern about the recent deterioration in China-Japan ties.

In terms of organization, the MFA is divided into several different regional and functional departments as well as a General Office, which does not act as a hierarchical authority over the other departments but instead provides general logistical and administrative support for the ministry's operations. This includes facilitating communication between the ministry and other foreign affairs offices throughout China at both the provincial and local levels. The General Office also oversees the Confidential Communications Bureau, the Confidential Traffic Bureau, and the Secretariat. The Confidential Communications Bureau handles diplomatic communication from Chinese embassies and other offices around the globe, the Confidential Traffic Bureau coordinates the delivery of sensitive documents to various PRC officials, and the Secretariat is responsible for maintaining the 24-hour situation room as well as managing the many personal secretaries of the MFA's ministers and vice-ministers. Seven regional departments oversee China's interests and activities in the following geographic areas: Africa, Asia, Western Europe, Eastern Europe and Central Asia, West Asia and North Africa, North America and Oceania, and Latin America. These departments are responsible for managing important duties throughout their respective regions, such as maintaining diplomatic relations, bilateral negotiations, and foreign policy oversight and implementation. In addition, a single regional office handles affairs for Hong Kong, Macao, and Taiwan. (The United Kingdom withdrew from Hong Kong in 1997, transferring the territory to Beijing's jurisdiction under the "one country, two systems" principle, a special status that gives its residents the right to choose their local leaders in free elections and enjoy a free press and the right to demonstrate. In recent years, its residents have complained about the erosion of their press freedoms, constraints on their representative democracy, and tilted history lessons taught in their schools.) The MFA also has a total of 19 functional departments and bureaus that handle a variety of internal and external duties—everything from administrative tasks to public relations to translation to research and analysis. The Policy Planning Department has a lead role in overseeing implementation of China's foreign policy initiatives. It drafts speeches and reports on important issues, submits the Chinese government's annual foreign assistance plan, manages the PRC's diplomatic records, and coordinates the government's research and analysis. [35]

The Information Department provides "processed information" to the PRC's central leadership. It is carefully selected and analyzed with the MFA and PRC leadership in mind, as opposed to the "raw" information provided by the Xinhua News Agency, which is meant for more general public consumption.[36] The Information Department's Fourth Division (ID4D), also known as the New Development Division, is responsible for monitoring international events on a 24-hour basis and provides the ministry with up-to-date information and analysis. It produces a daily written briefing for the MFA leadership as well as two other publications: "Xin Qingkuang" (New Development) and "Xin Qingkuang Jianbao" (New Development Brief). The latter is published every two to three days and is circulated only to the PRC's central leadership as well as the "ministerial leadership of central bureaucracies and provincial/army officials." The document provides concise background information and analysis on the most important current foreign policy events. The former publication provides a longer and more in-depth analysis of the developments and how the MFA is responding. It is available to a slightly wider audience, including senior policy makers in Beijing, provincial officials, and influential academics. This document is mostly written by the MFA regional departments, with the ID4D typically only making relatively minor written contributions and acting mainly in an editorial role.[37]

The MFA's other functional departments handle issues related to the department's internal and external operations. The various departments responsible for external affairs oversee issues related to the MFA's foreign missions, receiving foreign diplomats, arms control and weapons proliferation, international treaties and laws, border issues, immigration and visas, foreign language translation, and China's role in international institutions. The internally focused departments handle matters such as funds procurement, facility construction, interbureaucracy communication, and personnel management.[38] Several other important organizations technically operate underneath the auspices of the MFA; however, many of these organizations have grown to act somewhat independently from the MFA's control and typically operate only under the ministry in the form of loose coordination or—in a few cases—by way of the MFA's human resources offices. These organizations include the Institute of International Studies, the Foreign Affairs College, the World Affairs Publishing House, the Diplomatic Service Bureau, the Angler's Terrace State Guest House, the Chinese People's Association for Friendship with Foreign Countries (CPAFFC), and the Chinese People's Institute of Foreign Affairs.[39]

The People's Liberation Army (PLA) holds a unique position among China's national security organizations. Despite being subordinate to the CCP, the PLA has enjoyed some autonomy since its creation, which, as a revolutionary militia under Mao fighting the Chinese Nationalists and the Japanese occupation, predates the PRC's founding in 1949. Two Central Military Commissions— one for the CCP and one for the state—of duplicate membership supervise the PLA. Below these two commissions, four General Headquarters oversee the PLA's daily functions.

The Ministry of National Defense (MND) is something of a misnomer. Unlike similarly named bureaucracies in other countries that formulate and implement policies, the Ministry has primarily a support and public relations function. During the 1980s, when the Ministry's staff numbered around 50, foreign observers saw the MND as a hollow bureaucracy serving as a public relations front for engaging with foreign militaries and the international media.[40] However, the MND staff and budget have grown during the last decade. The recently retired Minister of National Defense, General Liang Guanglie (2008–2012), is an influential and prominent senior official who, in addition to attending major international conferences, was a member of the CMC, the State Council's inner cabinet, and the CCP Central Committee. General Chang Wanquan, a CMC member and previously director of the PLA General Armaments Department, became the new Minister of National Defense in March 2013.[41] In contrast, the Central Military Commission lies at the apex of China's defense policy formulation and implementation. It provides centralized and unified command authority over the country's military forces in several respects, including regarding strategic principles, organizational doctrine, budget management, recruitment, development of military technology, and force deployment. The CMC controls three important educational institutions for advancing the military's capabilities—the Academy of Military Science (AMS), the National Defense University (NDU), and the National University of Defense Technology (NUDT). The AMS is the PLA's highest-level research institute and center of military science. The NDU and the NUDT are directly under the CMC. The former is mainly responsible for education and training of senior officers and researchers, whereas the latter trains and educates senior scientists, engineers, and specialized commanding officers. The CMC also controls the PLA's garrisons in Hong Kong and Macao. The CMC itself is technically two separate bodies. One CMC body serves under the CCP Central Committee, while the other is under the State Council. However, they have identical membership and do not meet separately or operate any differently from one another. Despite the creation of a state CMC, the PLA is still primarily accountable to the CCP rather than to the State Council. This division into two CMCs is viewed by many in China as more of a symbol of unity between the CCP and the State rather than an attempt to structurally equalize control over the PLA.[42] According to the CCP's 12th Constitution of 1982, the CMC chair is to be selected from the CCP Politburo's Standing Committee members. The position has traditionally been held by whoever serves as both CCP Secretary General and PRC President. The vice-chairmen are usually experienced military leaders and powerful members within the CCP. The remaining members consist of the PRC Defense Minister, the senior officers commanding the Four General Headquarters departments, the commander of the PLA Navy (PLAN), PLA Air Force (PLAAF), and the Second Artillery Corps (in charge of China's nuclear weapons and long-range missiles).[43] The full CMC meets several times a year following a Party Plenum and in December prior to the submission of the annual military budget to the State Council. The inner workings of these meetings, which typically last for several days, are secret.[44] Because the CMC is a small, highly centralized body responsible for high-level policy decisions related to the Chinese military, it delegates administrative control to subordinate bureaucracies so they can handle the PLA's daily functions. These Four General Headquarters are the General Staff Department, the General Political Department, the General Logistics Department, and the General Armaments Department. Given the nature of the Chinese foreign policy decision-making process, any use of force would require authorization by the CCP Politburo Standing Committee.[45]

The General Staff Department (GSD) is the largest and most important of these four bodies. It handles operations, planning, modernization, training, recruitment, intelligence, and force mobilization. The GSD also acts as the military command headquarters for the PLA Ground Forces, which, unlike the PLAN and the PLAAF, does not have its own separate headquarters. The GSD oversees responsibilities for the PLAN and PLAAF as well. The Second Artillery Corps is an exception, presumably because it controls China's nuclear weapons. It operates independently and reports directly to the CMC. The GSD also oversees 15 military education and training institutions in areas such as command tactics, science and engineering, aviation, international relations, and foreign languages. There is limited public information regarding how certain GSD branches operate.[46]

The General Political Department (GPD) is responsible for the political education of armed forces personnel and ensuring that the CCP maintains a dominant ideological presence within the PLA. This is primarily done through the Political Commissar and Party Branch systems that Mao established in 1929. These two systems ensure that CCP representatives are dispersed throughout PLA units to ensure that troops follow the party line. Their presence also seeks to give PLA personnel a more direct connection with the CCP. Other key GPD goals include exercising internal discipline, supervising civil-military projects, boosting PLA morale, propaganda and communication with foreign militaries, and other general "political work" in support of the CCP's military agenda.[47]

The General Logistics Department (GLD) is faced with the daunting task of managing the massive logistical requirements for sustaining the operations of the largest military in the world in terms of personnel. It is responsible for non-combat supplies and services such as food, clothing, health, housing, finances, transportation, auditing, and medical care.[48] The concept of "joint logistics" has driven recent reform efforts. This process began in 2000 with the establishment of a Joint Logistics Department (JLD) for each of the seven military regions (which become "military area commands" in wartime) that would handle general logistics requirements for all the service branches, as opposed to having each branch act individually. In 2003, the PLA established a Theater Joint Logistics Department (TJLD) in each military region that will handle even specialized equipment for the PLA Ground Forces, PLAN, and PLAAF.[49]

Established in April 1998, the General Armaments Department (GAD) is the newest of the Four General Headquarters.[50] This department is responsible for the research, development, production, procurement, and maintenance of the PLA's weapons and equipment across all of its branches, including China's space and nuclear programs. It has departments in charge of planning, service weaponry, equipment and technology cooperation, and related functions. Since 1957, the GSD, GLD, and GPD had been the three premier departments for handling daily operations within the PLA, and the creation of the GAD caused some major organizational adjustments within the PLA. The formation of the GAD also consolidated personnel and resources from the GSD, the GLD, and the Commission of Science, Technology, and Industry for National Defense (COSTIND), a civilian organization that develops China's military defense technology. Most of the manufacturing and research for the PLA is carried out by civilian corporations via contracts supervised by the GAD. Until Premier Zhu Rongji's reforms in July 1999, China's military defense industry was dominated by five major state-owned enterprises (SOEs), known as "the Big Five." Zhu's reforms attempted to curb bureaucratic inefficiencies and to create more competition among the SOEs. Each of "the Big Five" was split into two separate Industrial Enterprise Groups (IEGs), which quickly became known as "the Big Ten." However, problems of reorganization and monopolization among China's military-defense companies remain.[51]

The State Administration for Science, Technology, and Industry (SASTIND) also plays an important role in managing military research and development, overseeing arms production (as well as the import and export of defense items), and supplying the PLA with the equipment through extensive coordination with the GAD and its authority of oversight for "the Big Ten" IEGs. China's Atomic Energy Agency also operates under SASTIND to regulate the proliferation of nuclear material and technology. The National People's Congress established SASTIND in 2008. SASTIND's precursor organization—the Commission of Science, Technology, and Industry for National Defense (COSTIND)—was founded in August 1982 by merging the National Defense Industry Office (NDIO) of the State Council, the Science, Technology, and Equipment Commission (STEC) of the Communist Party CMC and the Defense Science and Technology Commission (DSTC). COSTIND was subordinate to the two CMCs and underwent significant restructuring in 1998 to create a rational and competitive defense procurement system. The new COSTIND became a strictly civilian organization, equivalent in status to that of a ministry, under the State Council. Meanwhile, its military elements were incorporated into the newly established GAD. In 2008 COSTIND was renamed the SASTIND and placed under the newly established "super-bureaucracy" of the Ministry of Industry and Information Technology, though its role has not changed much since the 1998 reforms.[52] SASTIND is still an essential voice in China's national defense industry and the PLA's military development.

The Ministry of Commerce, established in 2003 to replace the Ministry of Foreign Trade and Economic Cooperation, oversees all matters of policy implementation related to China's international trade and economic assistance to foreign countries. This includes oversight on import and export measures, taxes, trade laws and regulations, strategies for attracting foreign investment, bilateral and multilateral trade agreements, and coordination with the Taiwan, Macao, and Hong Kong regions.[53] The Ministry's influence runs through the Central Finance and Economics LSG, which has had a powerful voice in the Politburo Standing Committee, particularly in light of China's staggering economic growth over the past decade.

Xinhua News Agency is the PRC's official news organization and the primary provider of "raw" or "unprocessed" information to China's central foreign policy decision-makers. Although it technically falls under the State Council, Xinhua is in practice most accountable to the CCP's Propaganda Department. Xinhua is one of the world's largest news organizations, with more than 10,000 employees and 100 bureaus located around the globe and reports in print, television, radio, and Internet formats in seven different languages. With regard to China's foreign policy, Xinhua is responsible for producing "Cankao Ziliao" (Reference Material), a daily publication with extensive reporting and analysis on international developments. This publication is distributed to the PRC's central leadership, senior military officials, and a select group of foreign affairs professionals outside the government. If the information is deemed highly sensitive, Xinhua will also occasionally produce a classified document for only the PRC's top officials, entitled "Cankao Ziliao (Qingyang)."[54] Xinhua also has a number of research and analysis groups as well as foreign correspondents throughout the world. These units provide crucial information when they are located in countries where the PRC does not maintain official diplomatic representation. Xinhua correspondents occasionally have acted as de facto official representatives to local leaders on Beijing's behalf.[55] Censorship still exists in China, with legal restrictions and other public controls such as the employment of Internet commenters who work for the government. Nonetheless, the advent of a competitive media environment and the evolution of information technology have changed the face of Chinese public opinion and its influence on politics. For example, nationalistic rhetoric has proved successful at attracting more readers, viewers, and profits. Meanwhile, the Internet has become an outlet not only for Chinese nationalists but also Chinese dissenters because online remarks can be made with some anonymity. Although several Internet filters are used in China to block sensitive words, Chinese "Netizens" use hyponyms to allude to innuendos or comment on specific, sensitive events or initiatives taken by the Chinese government and thus avoid government control of online discussions. The regime struggles to repress this dialogue although it also benefits from the increased information provided by the Internet, especially regarding provincial developments.[56]

INTEGRATION PROBLEMS

The capacity of Chinese actors to influence events abroad has expanded faster than the capacity of PRC institutions to manage their activities.[57] China's international interests have grown because of the globalization of China's economy, Beijing's "going out" strategy, the PRC's expanding foreign footprint resulting from these two developments, and China's growing need for overseas resources. At the same time, China's interests have expanded faster than PRC institutions can manage them. These institutions suffer from "stressed capacity" because of increased demands that often challenge existing structures, procedures, and resources. For example, the MFA's foreign-based staff has had to provide many more consular services because of the growing number of overseas Chinese workers, tourists, students, and others. In 2011, the PRC had to evacuate thousands of Chinese nationals from Libya and to deal with an increased number of kidnappings of overseas Chinese workers. In addition, the PRC's role in antipiracy operations in the Gulf of Aden has expanded in recent years. Tellingly, the MFA recently established a 24-hour crisis management center, following the pattern of other major global powers. PLA writers often complain that they lack the institutional and organizational capacity to deal with the increasing number of missions they are being assigned. This problem is compounded by the fact that PLA officers typically remain more insular and travel less than their party or state equivalents.

The PRC leadership also faces severe policy coordination problems with these institutions, manifested in turf-conscious bureaucracies, stove-piped processes, and poor horizontal communication. Even Chinese observers acknowledge significant bureaucratic infighting between the MFA and the PLA as well as uncertainty over how inter-agency processes resolve differences among bureaucratic actors. It is unclear whether any of the numerous "leading small groups" have the authority to resolve these differences, with the sole exception of the CCP Politburo, the party's supreme policy making institution, whose purview is naturally limited. For years the Chinese have discussed establishing a structure similar to the U.S. National Security Council, but this has not occurred. It appears that the bureaucratic resistance to such a move, which would threaten their autonomy, is too strong.

As a result, China has seen a series of recent instances in which coordination appears to have broken down and the military has taken actions that surprised the civilian authorities. In 2007, the PLA destroyed one of its own satellites, breaking a twenty-year international moratorium on testing antisatellite weapons and, by producing an enormous quantity of space debris, placing the MFA in a difficult position. More recently, the PLA decided to conduct the first test of its new stealth fighter on the same day that U.S. Secretary of Defense Robert Gates was meeting the PRC president in Beijing. Gates, who had taken criticism for cutting back on purchases of the U.S. F-22 by citing U.S. air superiority over others, initially wanted to cancel the meeting, while Hu seemed surprised when Gates later mentioned it to him. Reporters subsequently asked both men whether China was trying to send a warning to the Pentagon. In Africa and other developing regions, China's state-owned companies act in exploitative ways that undermine the MFA's good-will efforts toward those regions. An expanding list of bureaucratic actors is trying to influence national policy or acting under the radar of central authorities. As a result, China now has many bureaucratic bodies with overlapping and competing authorities. This is quite evident in the dozen PRC actors having some say in determining China's maritime policies—in addition to the PLAN and the MFA, they include state-owned corporations and even provincial governments and municipalities that pursue their own foreign policies regarding many issues.

One also sees a growing debate among influential Chinese over what comprises the PRC's national security interests and which ones should take priority in the event of conflict. This situation presents a confusing message to foreign audiences. For example, for the past two years, some Chinese have been using terms that describe the South China Sea as a core national interest, whereas others have challenged this label, which implies that Beijing cannot compromise on its demands. PRC state bodies are producing conflicting speeches and white papers to influence internal policy deliberations, but they present a disharmonious cacophony to outside observers. All these developments—especially China's growing international interests and capabilities—call into question long-accepted maxims regarding the PRC's foreign interests, strategies, and policies. Western analysts find it increasingly difficult to determine which Chinese officials and institutions determine policy in any given area as well as what policies they will pursue.

NOTES

1. Organisation for Economic Co-operation and Development, "Reforms Could Boost China's Ability to Attract Foreign Investment,"*OECD.org*, July 3, 2003. http://www.oecd.org/industry/internationalinvestment/investmentstatisticsandanalysis/reformscouldboostchinasabilitytoattractforeigninvestment.htm.

2. "Foreign Direct Investment in China," The US-China Business Council, https://www.uschina.org/statistics/fdi_cumulative.html.

3. Organisation for Economic Co-operation and Development, "The OECD Welcomes Policy Advances at China's 2007 National People's Congress Session," *OECD.org*, March 27, 2007, http://www.oecd.org/investment/investmentfordevelopment/38309228.pdf.

4. International Monetary Fund, "Factsheet—IMF Quotas," *IMF.org*, March 30, 2012, http://www.imf.org/external/np/exr/facts/quotas.htm; and Abhrajit Gangopadhyay and

Anant Vijay Kala, "Brics Wants World Bank, IMF Reforms," *Wall Street Journal*, March 29, 2012, http://online.wsj.com/article/SB10001424052702303816504577311012331186378 .html.

5. U.S. National Intelligence Council, *Global Trends 2025: A Transformed World* (Washington, DC: U.S. Government Printing Office, 2008), http://www.dni.gov/files/documents/ Newsroom/Reports%20and%20Pubs/2025_Global_Trends_Final_Report.pdf; U.S. National Intelligence Council, *Global Trends 2030: Alternative Worlds* (Washington, DC: U.S. National Intelligence Council, 2012), http://www.dni.gov/files/documents/ GlobalTrends_2030.pdf.

6. See for example: Charles A. Kupchan et al., *Power in Transition: The Peaceful Change of International Order* (Tokyo: United Nations University Press, 2001). Some Chinese analysts share this perspective; see for example: Daniel Lynch, "Chinese Thinking on the Future of International Relations: Realism as the Ti, Rationalism as the Yong?" *The China Quarterly* 197 (March 2009): 87–107.

7. U.S. National Intelligence Council, *Global Trends 2025*.

8. John Lee, "Structural Flaws Will Limit China's Rise," *World Politics Review*, November 10, 2009, http://www.worldpoliticsreview.com/article.aspx?id=4868.

9. Clara A. Hills, Dennis C. Blair, and Frank Sampson Jannuzi, *U.S.-China Relations: An Affirmative Agenda, A Responsible Course* (Council on Foreign Relations Press, April 2007), http://i.cfr.org/content/publications/attachments/ChinaTaskForce.pdf.

10. World Bank, *Doing Business 2013: Smarter Regulations for Small and Medium-Size Enterprises* (Washington, DC: World Bank Group, October 2012), http://www .doingbusiness.org/~/media/GIAWB/Doing%20Business/Documents/Annual-Reports/ English/DB13-full-report.pdf.

11. Hills, Blair, and Jannuzi, *U.S.-China Relations*.

12. Nina Hachigian, Michael Schiffer, and Winny Chen, *A Global Imperative: A Progressive Approach to U.S.-China Relations in the 21st Century* (Washington, DC: Center for American Progress, August 2008), http://www.americanprogress.org/issues/2008/08/china_report.html.

13. William F. Schulz, *Strategic Persistence: How the United States Can Help Improve Human Rights in China* (Washington, DC: Center for American Progress, January 2009), http://www .americanprogress.org/issues/2009/01/pdf/china_human_rights.pdf.

14. Fei-ling Wang, "Preservation, Prosperity and Power: What Motivates China's Foreign Policy?," *Journal of Contemporary China* 14, no. 45 (November 2005): 669.

15. Tianjian Shi, Meredith Wen, "Avoiding Mutual Misunderstanding: Sino-U.S. Relations and the New Administration" (Washington, DC: Carnegie Endowment for International Peace, January 2009), http://carnegieendowment.org/files/china_us_relations.pdf.

16. Evan S. Medeiros, *China's International Behavior: Activism, Opportunism and Diversification* (Santa Monica: RAND Corporation, 2009), xvi.

17. State Council Information Office (PRC), *China's National Defense in 2008* (Beijing: State Council Information Office (PRC), 2009), http://english.gov.cn/official/2009-01/20/ content_1210227.htm.

18. Ibid.

19. Fei-ling Wang, "To Incorporate China: a New Policy for a New Era," *The Washington Quarterly* 21, no. 1 (1998): 67–81.

20. Andrew J. Nathan and Andrew Scobell, *China's Search for Security* (New York: Columbia University Press, 2012).

21. Medeiros, *China's International Behavior*, 43.

22. Xinhua, "China to Adhere to 'Mutual Benefits and Win-Win' Strategy," *Embassy of the People's Republic of China in the Republic of South Africa*, August 24, 2006, http://www.chinese-embassy.org.za/eng/zt/pd/t268890.htm.

23. Xinhua, "FM: China, Major World Powers Ties Growing in Cooperation, Win-Win Direction," *Consulate-General of the People's Republic of China in Vancouver*, March 4, 2008, http://vancouver.china-consulate.org/eng/news/t412078.htm.

24. Devin T. Stewart and Joshua Eisenman, "China's New-Rich and Global Responsibility," Carnegie Council, October 13, 2006, http://www.carnegiecouncil.org/publications/ethics_online/0002.html.

25. Alice L. Miller, "The Politburo Standing Committee Under Hu Jintao," *China Leadership Monitor*, no. 35, 2011, http://media.hoover.org/sites/default/files/documents/CLM35AM.pdf.

26. Willy Lam, "Communist Youth League Clique Maintains Clout Despite Congress Setback," *China Brief* 12, no. 23 (November 30, 2012), http://www.jamestown.org/single/?no_cache=1&tx_ttnews%5Btt_news%5D=40180&tx_ttnews%5BbackPid%5D=589.

27. Ning, "Central Leadership," 45–47.

28. Robert L. Worden, Andrea Matles Savada, and Ronald E. Dolan, *China: A Country Study* (Washington, DC: GPO for the Library of Congress, 1987), chap. Foreign Policy Decision Making and Implementation, http://countrystudies.us/china/126.htm.

29. Ning, "Central Leadership," 42.

30. Robert L. Worden, Andrea Matles Savada, and Ronald E. Dolan, *China: A Country Study*. Foreign Policy Decision Making and Implementation.

31. Ning, "Central Leadership," 50–52.

32. Ibid., 20.

33. Ministry of Foreign Affairs (PRC), "The Minister," accessed February 2, 2013, http://www.fmprc.gov.cn/eng/wjb/wjbz/.; and Xinhua, "Yang Jiechi Appointed China's New Foreign Minister," *Xinhuanet*, April 27, 2007, http://news.xinhuanet.com/english/2007-04/27/content_6034725.htm.

34. Peter Ford, "The New Face of Chinese Diplomacy: Who is Wang Yi?," *Christian Science Monitor*, March 18, 2013, http://csmonitor.com/World/Asia-Pacific/2013/0318/The-new-face-of-Chinese-diplomacy-Who-is-Wang-Yi.

35. Ministry of Foreign Affairs (PRC), "Departments," *Ministry of Foreign Affairs (PRC)*, accessed February 2, 2013, http://www.fmprc.gov.cn/eng/wjb/zzjg/.

36. Ning, "Central Leadership," 52.

37. Ibid., 24–27.

38. Ministry of Foreign Affairs (PRC), "The Ministry: Departments."

39. Ning, "Central Leadership," 22–23.

40. Kenneth Allen, "Introduction to the PLA's Administrative and Operational Structure," in *The People's Liberation Army as Organization*, edited by James C. Mulvenon and Andrew N. D. Yang (Arlington, VA: RAND Corporation, 2002), 39.

41. Roy Kamphausen, "China's New Military Leadership and the Challenges It Faces," interview by Greg Chaffin, January 18, 2013, http://www.nbr.org/research/activity.aspx?id=303.

42. Tai Ming Cheung, "The Influence of the Gun: China's Central Military Commission and Its Relationship with the Military, Party, and State Decision-Making Systems," *The Making of Chinese Foreign and Security Policy in the Era of Reform*, ed. David M. Lampton (Stanford: Stanford University Press, 2001), 103.

43. Ministry of National Defense (PRC), "Central Military Commission of Communist Party of China," *Ministry of National Defense (PRC)*, accessed February 3, 2013, http://eng.mod.gov.cn/Database/Leadership/index.htm.

44. David Shambaugh, "The Pinnacle of the Pyramid: The Central Military Commission," *The People's Liberation Army as Organization*, ed. James C. Mulvenon and Andrew N. D. Yang (Arlington, VA: RAND Corporation, 2002), 102.

45. Ibid., 95–105.

46. Peter Mattis, "New Departments and Research Centers Highlight Military's Concerns for the Future," *China Brief* 12 no. 1 (January 6, 2012), http://www.jamestown.org/single/?no_cache=1&tx_ttnews%5Btt_news%5D=38853.

47. Larry Wortzel, "The General Political Department and the Evolution of the Political Commissar System," *The People's Liberation Army as Organization*, ed. James C. Mulvenon and Andrew N. D. Yang (Arlington, VA: RAND Corporation, 2002), 225–233.

48. GlobalSecurity.org, "General Logistics Department," *GlobalSecurity.org*, accessed February 2, 2013, http://www.globalsecurity.org/military/world/china/gld.htm.

49. Cheng Yunjie and Xu Jinzhang, "PLA Continues Long March of Logistics Reform," *Xinhuanet*, July 29, 2007, http://news.xinhuanet.com/english/2007-07/28/content_6441943.htm.

50. Harlan Jencks, "COSTIND is Dead, Long Live COSTIND! Restructuring China's Defense Scientific, Technical, and Industrial Sector," in James C. Mulvenon and Richard H. Yang, eds., *The People's Liberation Army in the Information Age* (Santa Monica, CA: RAND, 1999), pp. 71–72.

51. Harlan Jencks, "The General Armaments Department," in James C. Mulvenon and Andrew N. D. Yang, eds., *The People's Liberation Army as Organization* (Arlington, VA: RAND Corporation, 2002), 273–279.

52. "State Administration for Science, Technology and Industry for National Defense," *Nuclear Threat Initiative*, July 13, 2012, http://www.nti.org/facilities/781/.

53. Ministry of Commerce, PRC, "Mission," *Ministry of Commerce, PRC*, December 7, 2010, http://english.mofcom.gov.cn/column/mission2010.shtml./.

54. Translated as "Reference Material (Proof)."

55. Ning, "Central Leadership, 53–54.

56. For example, see, Susan L. Shirk, "Changing Media, Changing Foreign Policy in China," *Japanese Journal of Political Science* (2007), 8, no.1, 43–70; and Susan L. Shirk, *China: Fragile Superpower* (New York: Oxford University Press, 2007), 80–82; 86–91.

57. David Finkelstein, presentation at the "2012 China Defense and Security Conference," Jamestown Foundation, Washington, DC, February 16, 2012.

CHAPTER 2

Military Power

China's remarkable economic achievements have been the main source of the country's expanding global power and influence. Since the People's Republic of China (PRC) opened up its economy to foreign investment in the late 1970s, its economy has experienced phenomenal growth—doubling every decade. If present trends continue, China will have the world's largest economy by the middle of this century. The ability of the Chinese leadership to promote rapid economic growth while maintaining domestic stability and increasing the PRC's international clout has further enhanced the regime's domestic and international legitimacy—a virtuous cycle to Beijing's benefit. The PRC has achieved this extraordinary economic growth largely by moving away from its Communist roots. Although the ruling elite still belongs to the Chinese Communist Party, the CCP no longer relies on ideology or a charismatic populist leader to determine its policies or justify its status. Domestically, the CCP has concentrated on maintaining economic growth and promoting a "harmonious society" that—while allowing the average Chinese citizen more economic and social freedom than during the totalitarian era of the 1950s and 1960s—nevertheless reacts aggressively to potential challenges to the one-party authoritarian system, as evidenced by the suppression of even nonviolent dissidents and the Falun Gong spiritual movement. In contrast, the regime has become more accommodating toward limited public expressions of Chinese nationalist voices. The CCP also takes care to keep key interest groups, such as the military and security forces, loyal through targeted government spending programs and other support.[1]

Although the de facto abandonment of the internationalist dimensions of its Communist ideology and the embrace of Chinese nationalism help strengthen the PRC's domestic leadership, it does deprive Beijing of possible "soft power" because other people can see much to admire, but less to emulate, in the uniquely

Chinese-PRC model. In contrast, Maoism presented a direct ideological challenge to Western liberal democracy. That said, China's policy move from Maoism to a blend of state capitalism and political authoritarianism—also referred to as the "Beijing Consensus"—appeals to some foreign dictators seeking to justify their perpetual rule in the name of promoting domestic security and prosperity.

The PRC's economic rise has brought considerable benefits to its people and the wider international community, but China's economic growth has made the PRC more militarily powerful and, in certain cases, more assertive in its foreign policy—increasing tensions between China and other states on various issues. In addition, the PRC's new dependence on international trade and foreign investment has fostered unprecedented Chinese vulnerability to maritime threats. China now relies on foreign exports for growth, access to global sea lanes for trade, and foreign investment, technology, and natural resources.[2] PRC officials have been concerned about the prospect of a naval clash involving the United States over Taiwan, competing maritime claims with other East Asian states, and other regional security issues. Furthermore, the PRC government has emphasized the importance of defending China's maritime supply lines and territorial claims. As a result, the Chinese government has used some of its growing economic resources to fund a major military buildup. Since the end of the Cold War, lavish funding has enabled the People's Liberation Army (PLA) to become more efficient, capable, and professional. For example, the PRC has been developing capabilities designed to negate U.S. technological strengths and exploit its asymmetrical vulnerabilities. PLA military strategists see the growing U.S. reliance on information technology for military operations as a potentially serious U.S. vulnerability. Beijing has therefore prioritized developing cyber and antisatellite capabilities as well as other antiaccess/area-denial weapons along with more traditional conventional forces.

China's political leaders have assigned an increasing range of goals, tasks, roles, and missions to the PLA, augmenting the traditional tasks of maintaining domestic security and winning foreign wars. The PLA's "Diversified Military Tasks" include internal and border security, conquering Taiwan, enforcing China's maritime claims, establishing defensive perimeters in the western Pacific, defending the PRC's overseas commercial and economic interests, and what the Pentagon used to call "Military Operations Other Than War" (MOOTW) such as providing humanitarian assistance and disaster relief. In a landmark December 2004 speech, Hu Jintao, then China's president and commander in chief, assigned the PLA what has come to be known as its four "New Historic Missions":

- guarantee the CCP's "ruling position" by working with other PRC agencies to maintain internal stability

- safeguard China's "national development" from external aggression by reinforcing border security, ensuring strategic "defense in depth" of China's interior, and enforcing Beijing's maritime claims and 200-nautical-mile maritime Exclusive Economic Zone

- protect China's "national interests" through power projection, "antiaccess/area denial" strategies, and preemptive spoiler attacks against adversaries amassing forces near China's borders (as in the 1950 Korean War)
- preserve "world peace" by maintaining an effective nuclear deterrent against the United States and other countries, contributing to international peacekeeping missions, and addressing nontraditional military threats

In contrast to Western militaries, these tasks require China to spend enormous human and financial resources to keep some 70 percent of the PLA's 2.25 million personnel deployed near major cities to serve as a backup force in case domestic instability exceeds the capacity of the paramilitary forces to contain. In addition, the PLA serves as a backup border security force for China's almost 14,000 miles of land borders and 9,000 miles of coastline. Here the PLA Navy backstops the PRC Coast Guard, State Fisheries Administration, State Oceanographic Administration, and Marine Surveillance Service.[3] The PLA is also concentrating on developing the capacity to win short, high-intensity conflicts around China, moving beyond its original mission of territorial defense. The PLA Navy is transforming into a "blue-water" navy, which can operate outside of China's territorial waters in defense of Beijing's maritime interests, while the PLA Air Force can increasingly conduct diverse offensive and defensive missions outside of PRC borders. The PLA not only has increased the quantity of its major weapons systems, but also has improved its logistical capacity, its support networks, and its ability to integrate advanced technological systems into its military strategy. The PLA's focus on asymmetric strategies and disruptive military technologies—as well as the PRC's growing strength in nuclear, outer space, and missile capabilities—point to China's commitment to becoming a major military power.

Whatever its motivation, China's sustained military buildup has serious regional and global implications. Many fear that the PLA will become a destabilizing force in Asia and perhaps beyond. Defeating Taiwan continues to be a primary PLA planning contingency, but China also has active maritime disputes with Japan, Vietnam, and the Philippines along with territorial disputes with India, which is also concerned about an increased Chinese naval presence from Myanmar to Pakistan. PLA strategists have discussed acquiring naval support facilities in the Gulf of Aden region, which would supplement ongoing antipiracy operations off the coast of Somalia. As China's power and influence grows, so will the PLA's global role.

MILITARY HISTORY

Benefitting from the PRC's economic strength, the PLA has undertaken a sustained and impressive modernization drive since the end of the Cold War. The demise of the mutual Soviet threat, which had sustained a de facto security alliance between China and the West during the late 1970s and 1980s, led to a major reorientation in Beijing's strategic concerns. No longer fearing a Soviet ground attack from the north and west, PLA strategists have worried more about maritime clashes involving the United States and other countries on the Pacific Ocean. More recently, as China has become a global trading nation increasingly dependent on overseas energy sources and other key imports, its leaders have stressed the importance of defending China's maritime supply lines and countering other threats to their freedom of the seas. For these reasons, the PRC's military buildup has included strengthening the PLA Navy, previously the weakest Chinese military service.

Despite several phases of downsizing beginning in the 1950s, the PLA is still the world's largest military in terms of manpower. The main branches of the PLA include the Ground Forces, Navy, Air Force, Second Artillery Corps, and the People's Armed Police (PAP). The PLA Ground Forces are by far the largest branch, with approximately 1.6 million active duty personnel, 800,000 reservists, and the theoretical capability to call up millions of militia members. The Ground Forces include various forms of infantry, tanks, armored vehicles, helicopters, and artillery platforms. The PLA Navy (PLAN) has some 200,000 personnel and consists of surface and sub-surface vessels, Naval Aviation, and Naval Infantry personnel (marines). The PLA Air Force (PLAAF) has 400,000 personnel who operate fighter, bomber, transport, and reconnaissance aircraft. The PLAAF also includes 200,000 air and missile defense personnel as well as 24,000 airborne infantry (parachute) personnel. The 10,000-member Second Artillery Corps controls long-range missiles, including China's nuclear-armed missile arsenal. Finally, the 600,000-member People's Armed Police is responsible for internal security. Although the PAP normally operates under the Ministry of Public Security, in a crisis or war it becomes part of the PLA.

The PLA dates to August 1, 1927, following the Nanchang Uprising in which 30,000 CCP members, led primarily by Zhou Enlai and Zhu De, rebelled against the ruling Kuomintang Party of China (KMT) and seized the city of Nanchang for three days before being forced into the Jinggang Mountains. In this border region of Jiangxi and Hunan provinces, the CCP formed the First Workers' and Peasants' Army (better known as the Red Army), which would later become the PLA. Though the Red Army initially consisted of a mere 1,000 men, by 1928 its ranks had expanded to nearly 12,000 soldiers. During the Long March from 1934 to 1935, the Red Army came under the command of Mao Zedong, who quickly gained fame for his brilliant and daring guerilla tactics against the numerically superior and better-equipped KMT forces. Following Japan's invasion of mainland China in 1937, the Red Army and Kuomintang fought mostly against the foreign occupiers. By the end of the Second World War, the Red Army had more than one million men and women in its ranks as well as an additional two million militia members. It soon defeated the KMT and occupied Tibet and Hainan Island. When the PLA was declared as China's official military force following the establishment of the PRC in 1949, its ranks included around five million regular ground troops and an additional 5.5 million man militia.[4]

Throughout the early and mid-1950s, China received significant aid from the Soviet Union to modernize its military forces. The Soviets sent large amounts of equipment and a number of technical advisors to China and the PLA began redesigning its organization, tactics, and methods around the Soviet model. However, the CCP leadership became concerned that a professional army would lose its revolutionary principles, which would threaten the vision of a unified "Party-Army" security structure, and stressed the need for political education. In 1959, Minister of National Defense Peng Dehuai was removed by Mao and replaced with Lin Biao, whose vision for the PLA fell more in line with Mao's goals. Shortly thereafter, the Sino-Soviet split ended Soviet military assistance. The PLA's development plans were further disrupted when it became a political instrument for advancing Mao's agenda in the Cultural Revolution. PLA troops were tasked with promoting revolutionary ideas at the expense of military professionalism. The nadir occurred in 1971, when Lin Biao was accused by the radical Gang of Four of plotting a coup against Mao and allegedly died in a plane crash while fleeing to the Soviet Union. Eventually, Mao turned to the PLA to help reign in the excesses of the militias during the Cultural Revolution. In the late 1970s and early 1980s, under the "Four Modernizations" slogans, Deng Xiaoping and other Chinese officials pushed for the PLA's professionalization while reducing its size by more than a million active-duty personnel and streamlining its command structure. This PLA reform process has continued, with the military becoming a smaller, more efficient, better equipped, and more professional fighting force.

MILITARY MODERNIZATION

According to the Pentagon's own public assessments, the Chinese military has been receiving additional resources, altering its doctrine, and restructuring its organization to better accomplish these missions. The Defense Department's annual reports on Chinese military power detail the progress made by each PLA branch in improving its capabilities and expanding its range of operations since the first DOD report on China's military power appeared in 2000. The PLA, which previously concentrated on winning a lengthy war of attrition against any possible foreign invader, is now developing the capacity to win short, high-intensity conflicts around China. In terms of aggregate operational capabilities, not only have the Chinese armed forces increased the quantity of many of their major weapons systems, but the PLA is also acquiring more advanced systems and improving its capacity to integrate the key elements of Chinese military power. Furthermore, the PLA has been strengthening its logistics and other support networks for all of its individual services—strategists have placed special emphasis on making C4ISR (Command, Control, Communications, Computers, Intelligence, Surveillance and Reconnaissance) systems more reliable, survivable, and integrated.[5]

The PLA modernization drive has consisted of two components. Following the Soviet Union's collapse and the end of Sino-Soviet hostilities, China began purchasing advanced naval warships, fighter planes, and other weapons systems from Russia's cash-strapped military-industrial complex that China was unable to produce itself. At the same time, the PRC leadership launched a massive program to modernize China's defense industrial capabilities. The government launched many R&D programs for Chinese versions of advanced surface ships, submarines, and antiship missiles. Following the Pentagon's example, the PLA has sought to use information technologies more extensively in computers, satellites, and other technological enablers, with a goal of developing cyber and other capabilities capable of overcoming U.S. conventional military advantages through employing asymmetric tactics.[6]

The PLA Navy's modernization has been especially noteworthy. Since the late 1990s, China has undertaken an ambitious modernization program that has produced approximately one hundred new warships since 2001.[7] If this rate of expansion continues, the PLAN could possess more vessels than the U.S. Navy at some point during the next two decades.[8] The qualitative improvements have been equally stunning and include longer-range maritime planes and antiship missiles, quieter submarines, more sophisticated surface ships, and better educated and trained sailors. Anticipated future PLAN acquisitions include more advanced blue-water power projection capacities including indigenously made aircraft carriers.

A long-standing PLAN priority has been to enhance the capabilities of its submarine fleet, which has carried an increasingly sophisticated portfolio of antiship cruise missiles as well as land-attack cruise missiles. The PLAN has constructed more than a dozen Song-class SSN (Type 039 or Type 039/039G) attack submarines.[9] Most recently, the PLAN has acquired about a dozen indigenously made submarines that have made major achievements in terms of quietness and range. The Jin-class SSBN (Type 094) is armed with 12 JL-2 ballistic missiles with the theoretical range to hit targets in the western half of the United States from strike positions west of Hawaii. The Shang-class SSN (Type 093) nuclear-powered attack submarines and the Yuan-class SSN (Type 041 or Type 039A) diesel-powered attack submarines complement one another because of their diverging power systems. The dozen Russian-made kilo-class diesel electric submarines have also represented a marked advance in the PRC's undersea warfare capabilities. The Kilo's wake-homing torpedoes present a particularly deadly threat to U.S. aircraft carrier battle groups, which emerged as a key concern for PLA strategists following the U.S. carrier intervention in the 1995–1996 Taiwan Straits Crisis.[10] Although many PLAN submarines are outdated, the newest classes are approaching the capabilities found in the other major world navies in sound-dampening technology, naval propulsion, and weapons systems. The Office of Naval Intelligence anticipates that the PLAN will deploy the next-generation Type 095 attack submarine by 2015.[11]

This interest in extending the PLAN's reach has been confirmed by the construction of a major new Chinese navy base near the resort city at Sanya, on Hainan Island, the PRC's southernmost province. The facility, with its enormous, artificially constructed tunnels that shield its interior from overland imagery from airplanes and satellites, is situated closer to the major sea lanes of Asia than are the PLA bases on the Chinese mainland. The PLAN's new second-generation Jin class SSBN, which will serve as the PLA's primary seaborne nuclear deterrent, has been seen at this location. The Jin is equipped with the JuLang-2 (CSS-NX-4) submarine-launched ballistic missile (SLBM) capable of carrying a single one-megaton warhead or up to four smaller warheads, with a yield of 90 kilotons each. Though not as well armed or silent as the SSBNs serving in the fleets of the NATO or Russian navies, the Jin provides the PRC with a survivable nuclear deterrent and is a foundation for China's development of further missile and submarine technology.[12] In the nuclear area, the PRC wants to maintain a deterrent sufficient to survive a first strike by the United States or another nuclear power and still have sufficient forces to overcome any defenses and retaliate effectively. For this reason, the PLA has been investing in mobile land-based intercontinental ballistic missiles and ballistic missile submarines, both of which are harder to locate and destroy than fixed land-based missiles in silos. As the PLAN further develops its blue-water capabilities, the submarine force will remain a priority for additional funding and development.

In addition to modernizing its submarine fleet the PLA Navy has developed increasingly sophisticated surface combatants. Since the early 1990s, the PLAN has put five new types of destroyers and frigates into service, with each successive model featuring new variations and improvements. Taken together, these modern warships represent a substantial improvement over China's aging Luda (Type 051) destroyers that entered service in the 1970s and 1980s. Many of these new warships feature stealthy hull designs; efficient propulsion systems; and enhanced sensors, electronics, and weapons systems.[13] During the 1990s, China purchased two Sovremenny class missile destroyers from Russia. These outclassed any surface combatants fielded by the PLAN at the time, providing improved antisubmarine warfare capabilities, more advanced antiship missiles, and longer expected sea-duty time.[14] Since the original purchase of these four Russian destroyers, the PRC has introduced its own improvements regarding both design and functionality to its indigenously made surface warships. The PLAN also made the important decision to focus on quality over quantity. The last few generations of warships have only seen a few vessels built per model in an attempt to maximize the new functions of each generation without committing considerable resources into constructing a ship type that might soon become obsolete.

The PLAN's fleet of indigenously manufactured destroyers and, to a lesser extent, frigates, has become increasingly more capable because of the longer reach of their platforms, their improved active electronic countermeasures, their advanced anti-submarine warfare (ASW) helicopters, and their newer generations of air-defense and antiship cruise missiles. The Luzhou, the most current version of the Chinese destroyer, serves the role of a fleet air defense ship with the SA-N-20 missile system capable of engaging targets upwards of 150 kilometers away by utilizing an onboard radar guidance system. The slightly older Luyang-II missile destroyer features an indigenously developed radar system similar to the Aegis AN/SPY-1 used by the U.S. Navy, along with advanced ASCM capable of engaging targets at a distance of almost 300 kilometers. Although it does not employ the SA-N-20 missile, the air defense capabilities on the Luyang II offer substantial improvements to earlier models and, coupled with some ASW capabilities, through the use of an onboard all-weather ASW helicopter, provide the PLAN with a solid foundation on which to build additional fleet support surface combatants. The latest PLAN destroyers, the Taizhou and Ningbo, were constructed in 2004. These models offer more advanced onboard weapons systems—in particular, radar as well as command-and-control features—than their predecessors.[15] However, only two ships were constructed because the PLAN seems to be looking to combine the best ASW capabilities, fleet air defense and antiship missiles, all on one ship class.[16] The latest versions of frigates, the Jiangkai I and II, offer similar improvements as the Luyang or Luzhou class destroyers by employing the latest in conjoined radar and air defense technology. Additionally, the Jiangkai II offers an ASW helicopter and advanced sea-skimming antiship cruise missiles capable of engaging targets at almost 200 kilometers. In summary, the PLAN's new surface fleet includes:

- Four Russian-built Sovremenny-class destroyers, two of which possess enhanced air-defense systems and ASCMs
- Two Luyang II-class destroyers equipped with Chinese HHQ-9 surface-to-air missiles (SAM) that have a long-range phased-array radar similar to the U.S. Aegis system
- Two Luzhou-class destroyers designed especially for antiair warfare that feature a phased-array radar system and are armed with Russian SA-N-20 SAMs, which more than double the range of PLAN antiair capabilities
- Jiangkai I-class frigates (soon to be phased out)
- Jiangkai II-class guided missile frigates that feature vertically launched HQ-7 SAM systems and cruise missiles

These ships have conducted long-distance operations, including multiple counter-piracy patrols in the Gulf of Aden since December 2009, a noncombatant evacuation operation of PRC nationals from Libya, and visits to far-off ports, including in the Western Hemisphere. The new Type 920 hospital ship and longer-range PLAN submarines could also be used for these long-range missions. In addition, the PLAN has been developing a large number of smaller vessels, including indigenously made littoral and coastal vessels, gunboats, missile boats, torpedo boats, and countermine warfare ships. These ships can be used for a variety of missions, both offensively and defensively, or in support of larger ships, though many of these vessels are suitable only for coastal combat because of their limited range and size.[17] The dozens of small Houbei-class (Type 022) fast-attack craft, armed with antiship cruise missiles and using stealthy catamaran hulls, might prove the most useful. They perform coastal patrol and defense missions, allowing larger ships to extend their operations elsewhere.[18]

These new warships in both the frigate and destroyer classes offer significant improvements over the Navy's designs of the 1970s and 1980s. The roles of these ships, that of air defense and power projection, provide the beginnings of what could become a fleet battle group.[19] More recently, the PLAN has begun developing aircraft carriers, a vital but more complex element of a blue-water fleet that extends beyond the "first island" chain—commonly linking Okinawa Prefecture, Taiwan, and the Philippines—and perhaps the "second island" chain linking the Bonin (Ogasawarsa) islets, Guam and Indonesia. The PLAN's first ship in this class is a "starter carrier" intended to provide a training platform and a model to teach the Chinese how to manufacture future carriers. The ship will help pilots learn how to fly off carriers and its sailors learn how to operate and maintain them. In 1998, a Hong Kong company purchased the Varyag, an unfinished Soviet-era sloped-deck carrier, from Ukraine for $20 million. The Chinese buyer claimed it would be used as a floating casino off Macao, and Ukraine removed the vessel's engines and armaments before delivering the ship in 2002. After a few years, it became evident that the Chinese were refitting the Varyag into a warship at the Dalian naval shipyard. The repairs included providing the ship with new boilers, electronic systems, radar, and engines as well as refurbishing its hull and deck.

According to the PRC media, the vessel might carry the J-15 fighter, the JT-9 naval trainer, and the Z-8 helicopter. The single-seat J-15, or Flying Shark, is based on Russia's Su-33 carrier plane, which the Russians have declined to sell for fear that the Chinese would copy it, and the land-based Su-27 Flanker, which Russia both sold to the PRC during the 1990s and used as the basis for its later Su-33 carrier plane. The PLA's land-based J-11B might have served as a conduit for the technology transfer, because the J-11B is based on Su-27SK. The large J-15, which could have a combat radius of 500 to 700 kilometers from the carrier, appears capable of conducting air superiority, combat air patrol, ground attack, and electronic countermeasure missions. The J-15's capabilities will depend on the carrier from which it operates. The sloped-deck launching system on the Varyag severely limits the plane's launch weight, but the Chinese may transition to a superior deck-launched system found on U.S. carriers.[20] Speculation also exists that the Chinese are developing their own short takeoff, vertical landing (STOVL) jet, the J-18, but concrete evidence is lacking. Such a Harrier-type plane would also suffer from limitations. The PLA Navy also has a weak portfolio of helicopters, with the best ones imported from Russia. To compensate for this disparity, the PLA has developed many varieties of missiles, including air-to-air, air-to-ground, surface-to-air, and surface-to-surface systems. Recent Chinese statements have also made evident that the PLA Navy intends to deploy several carriers, which would all be indigenously built and armed. On July 30, 2011, PLA General Luo Yuan, a senior researcher with the Academy of Military Sciences, said that, because India and Japan will each have three aircraft carriers by 2014, China should have no "less than three so we can defend our rights and our maritime interests effectively."[21] The PLA evidently considers these countries' large amphibious assault ships, which are capable of launching combat helicopters and STOVL aircraft, as small carriers. The first few aircraft carriers may be conventionally powered, but expectations are that the PRC will soon build nuclear-powered aircraft carriers, as well as associated conventionally powered support ships, which would prove especially valuable for the PLA Navy given its absence of overseas bases.

There is greater uncertainty over the size of the carriers China might build. The Varyag has an estimated full-load displacement of about 58,500 tons, almost the same size of modern British and French carriers. Carriers of this size can operate about three to four dozen aircraft, mostly STOVL airplanes. In contrast, the latest generation of U.S. Navy carriers are larger, displacing as much as 100,000 tons. Their air wings consisted of 70 or more conventional take-off-and-landing planes. The Navy's latest generation of nuclear-powered carriers can operate the same number of planes but can displace about 100,000 tons. If the PLA Navy wants to have a carrier fleet capable of projecting significant combat power, it will want carriers of this size.

The PLA still lacks the sealift and air transport to transfer and sustain a large expeditionary force in a distant region for an extended period, but the PLAN is increasing its amphibious capabilities. China has effectively doubled its force of roughly 20 landing ship tanks (LSTs) by additionally building 10 Yuting-II and 10 Yubei-class LSTs from 2003 to 2005, each with a capacity to carry roughly 250 troops. The PLAN also maintains numerous smaller transports that augment the LSTs. In 2006, the PLAN built a larger landing platform dock that can hold up to 800 troops, providing greater mission flexibility.[22] In total, the PLAN can amphibiously transport a maximum of 15,000 troops in a single wave. But recently China has begun constructing Yuzhao Type 071 amphibious ships, comparable in size to the previous generation U.S. Navy Whidbey Island/Harpers Ferry (LSD-41/49) class ship. There is speculation that even larger Type 081 amphibious assault ships are under design. These could carry more helicopters and perhaps even STVOL-type planes. However, the PLAN Marine Corps is a small contingent of specially trained troops that serve on China's few amphibious transport dock ships, which are based at the Zhanjiang port attached to the South Sea Fleet.[23] Numbering only some 10,000 troops and with outdated equipment, the PLAN Marine Corps would find it difficult to conduct a contested amphibious operation. The Marines also garrison disputed islands under PRC control and have deployed in the Gulf of Aden to fight pirates.

The PLA Naval Air Force (PLANAF), the Navy's ground-based air contingent, currently provides air support from bases on Chinese territory. In the future, they will conduct flights from Chinese carriers. The PLANAF includes hundreds of older short-range J-7E (a Mig-21 variant) and J-8II air superiority fighters, along with the H-6D bomber (based on the Soviet Tu-16 Badger), which carries antiship missiles. The planes, weapons, and other technology found in the PLANAF lags considerably behind those of the more generously funded regular PLA Air Force. The PLANAF does have Su-27s and Su-30MK2 fighters purchased from Russia to provide longer-range support for naval operations. The Su-30MK2 variant has some advanced C4ISR capabilities along with long-range search radar to detect surface ships to engage them with antiship cruise missiles. The Su-30MK2 variant is generally compared to the U.S. F-15E fighter, though it still lags behind newer fifth-generation aircraft such as the F-22 and F-35.[24] In comparison, the Su-27, originally purchased from Russia, was later produced under license in China. The PRC then copied from the Su-27 to make a Chinese variant, the Shenyang J-11, which has undergone several modifications and technological improvements from the original Russian version.[25] The J-11 offers improvements in radar and early warning systems, but most of these warplanes have gone to the regular Air Force.[26]

As partial compensation for the Navy's weak amphibious and naval aviation capabilities, which would significantly hamper any PLA effort to occupy Taiwan or fight against the United States or another modern navy, China has developed a powerful strike capability in its large number of long-range missiles. According to the Pentagon, the PLA has "the most active land-based ballistic and cruise missile program in the world."[27] PRC policymakers hope this capacity would discourage U.S. military intervention on Taiwan's behalf. The missiles also allow the PLA to threaten more distant targets in Asia. China has positioned more than one thousand short-range ballistic missiles (SRBMs) opposite Taiwan to threaten the island. This arsenal is reinforced with a smaller number of medium-range ballistic missiles and land-attack cruise missiles. The PLAN has also acquired a variety of indigenous and foreign-made antiship cruise missiles. Among the most powerful are Russian-made SS-N-22 Sunburn missiles carried aboard China's Sovremenny-class destroyers and SS-N-27 Sizzler missiles found on some of the PLAN's twelve Kilo-class attack submarines. According to the media, the PLA has been researching and developing an advanced antiship/cruise missile, the CH-SS-NX-13, for use on PLAN submarines.[28]

China's attempts to develop the world's first ballistic missile designed to attack moving ships at sea is of special concern to the U.S. Navy. The PLA's DF-21D antiship ballistic missile (ASBM) is based on the mobile, medium-range, surface-to-surface DF-21 (also known as the CSS-5) ballistic missile. The DF-21D has an estimated maximum range of 1,500 kilometers (some 930 miles), enabling it to strike deep into the western Pacific, with a maneuverable reentry vehicle that could allow its warhead to target moving ships without itself being intercepted. A logical mission for such a weapon would be to disable or destroy a U.S. aircraft carrier before it can move its planes within striking range of PLA targets. Although the DF-21D has yet to be tested over the ocean, the Pentagon considers the system to have achieved initial operational capability. What remains uncertain is whether the PLA can achieve the demanding standard of Command, Control, Communications, Computers, Intelligence, Surveillance and Reconnaissance (C4ISR) capacities required to track a moving ship and maneuver the missile in flight to intercept it. The PRC has been launching a number of reconnaissance satellites in recent years, which supplement its land-, sea-, and air-based radars for tracking maritime targets. But the Pentagon is probably working on a number of counterstrategies to defeat the DF-21D, from improved evasive maneuvering by ships, to enhanced point defenses with lasers and other new systems, to upstream countermeasures to degrade the PLA's C4ISR systems.

In this regard, a widening network of shore-based sensors, ship-based radars, unmanned aerial vehicles (UAVs), and space-based surveillance systems support China's growing arsenal of sophisticated guided missiles and increasing battle-field awareness. The Chengdu Aircraft Corporation is currently designing a large UAV similar to the U.S. Global Hawk. Other companies are developing short-range UAVs, including some able to launch air-to-ground missiles, that could operate from PLAN warships.[29] In recent years, the PLAN has also improved its over-the-horizon radar targeting capabilities. When combined with overhead imagery, these radars in theory could enable precise antiship missile targeting, such as by ASBMs. The PRC has been launching about a dozen reconnaissance satellites each year. On the offensive side, the PLA is also developing kinetic and nonkinetic means to cripple enemy satellites. This new capability became evident in January 2007, when the PRC successfully destroyed one of its own satellites using a controlled collision with a ground-launched rocket.

China's space program also continues to progress. In June 2012, the PRC successfully docked the manned Shenzhou-9 with the Tiangong-1, an orbital space laboratory, demonstrating progress toward China's goal of creating a permanent space station.[30] Senior PLA officers have described the militarization of outer space as inevitable and as providing enabling technologies to support PLA operations.[31] This C4ISR network is underpinned by the PRC's improving information and computing capacities, most visible in the country's cyberweapons.

China's domestic defense industry continues to improve, reducing the PLA's need to import weapons and military technologies from abroad, though China is still dependent on foreign-supplied naval and aircraft engines, where Chinese weapons designers still borrow heavily (and sometimes illegally) from foreign designs. The PRC still buys its most advanced ship and plane engines from abroad, as well as key defense electronics, but no longer purchases entire turnkey weapons systems from foreign sources. The PRC government has sought to integrate the military-industrial sector into civilian industries to facilitate the acquisition of so-called dual-use technologies by PRC defense firms, while the PLA has encouraged the reverse engineering of advanced imported equipment for later use in the manufacture of the PRC's own weapons systems. The development of China's domestic defense industry is closely linked to the increased resource availability brought about by the country's general economic growth. The PRC has pursued a multifaceted strategy for growing its indigenous defense industries. First, to avoid stretching its resources too thin—a major pitfall of the Soviet Union's defense buildup—PRC planners have focused on several important areas in which China enjoys some advantage. Second, the government has sought to integrate the military-industrial sector into civilian industries to facilitate the acquisition of dual-use technologies by defense firms and decrease the financial burden of subsidizing them. Finally, the military has encouraged the reverse engineering of advanced imported equipment, with the knowledge then applied to the manufacture of the PRC's own weapons systems.[32]

CURRENT ASSESSMENTS

The U.S.-China Economic and Security Review Commission report notes that China's conventional military buildup is proceeding well. In 2012, the PLA continued to develop more advanced weapons, improve its naval and air capabilities, practice joint-force training, and expand its international activities. China increased its official defense budget by 11.2 percent, to $106 billion, though the publicly disclosed budget excludes critical elements of China's defense spending such as foreign procurement. The Pentagon estimates PLA spending to be between $120 and $180 billion. In September 2012, China commissioned its first aircraft carrier, The Liaoning, which is a converted Soviet KUZNETSOV-class carrier purchased from Ukraine in 1998. It has been refurbished and was tested several times over the last few years. It is now used as a training platform for the development of an air regiment, which is expected to be operational no earlier than 2017. China's carrier is expected to carry J-15 airplanes (based on the Russian Sukhoi-33), but the ski-jump configuration, instead of the catapult style used on U.S. carriers, will limit the weight of the aircraft. The weight limit would in turn also limit fuel, weapon, range, and mission capabilities, and particularly constrain the type of early warning aircraft that could operate on the carrier. The PLA also continued testing the J-20 fighter aircraft, which has stealth characteristics. Loosely resembling the F-35, it is expected to be operational by 2018. Recent information suggests Beijing has another stealth program, the J-31 prototype, which aims to become a premier air superiority plane like the F-22.[33]

The U.S. Department of Defense (DOD) still does not rank China as a global military superpower. In fact, it argues that the PRC will require several more decades to achieve this status. Pentagon assessments note the large quantity of "antiquated hardware" in the PLA's inventory, as well as "gaps in some key areas" and continued "deficiencies in inter-service cooperation and actual experience in joint exercises and combat operations." According to DOD analysts, the PLA is "steadily closing the technological gap with modern armed forces" through lavish spending but only aspires to become "a world-class economic and military power by 2050" rather than in the next few years. Until then, the PLA will need to incorporate the new military platforms it has recently acquired as it trains its troops to use them effectively as an integrated force.[34] Nonetheless, U.S. officials are not concerned about any single weapon system the PRC is developing. Instead, they are alarmed by the comprehensive and sustained nature of the PLA's military buildup, which the Pentagon fears could be a "destabilizing" force in the Asia-Pacific region: "The pace and scope of China's sustained military investment have allowed China to pursue capabilities we believe are potentially destabilizing to regional military balances, increase the risk of misunderstanding and miscalculation and may contribute to regional tensions and anxieties," explained Michael Schiffer, Deputy Assistant Secretary of Defense for East Asia in an August 24, 2011 briefing. Schiffer asserted that, "[such] capabilities could increase Beijing's options to use military force to gain diplomatic advantage, advance its interests or resolve military disputes in its favor."[35]

According to Dennis Blasko, former Army Attaché in Beijing from 1992 to 1995, the PRC authorities acknowledge that the PLA is still unprepared to accomplish all the missions that the PRC leadership has laid before it, such as conducting large joint combat operations. The PLA leadership assesses that they are two to three decades behind the Pentagon in terms of operational capabilities. Chinese analysts understand that some PLA units still have poor training and equipment and that, since China's last war was its brief border conflict with Vietnam in 1979, in which the PLA did poorly, the PRC armed forces lack recent combat experience. Although some Chinese military writings boast of various new capabilities, Blasko believes that they often describe aspirations rather than already achieved capabilities. For instance, a PLA colonel might note the U.S. dependence on space and cybersupport and propose that the PLA attack these vulnerabilities, but the PLA would still need to develop the capabilities to do so.[36]

Similarly, many PLA statements reflect China's defense budget battles. PRC government statements support the PLAN in principle, but have yet to commit the vast resources needed to endow the PLAN with a "blue-water" naval capacity. Rather, the PLA Navy is still focused on winning a conflict involving Taiwan—hence its focus on acquiring conventionally powered submarines—and on protecting the PRC's extensive coastline and its numerous offshore islands from the U.S. Navy. If China started building large at-sea replenishment ships, this step would more likely indicate an emerging Chinese blue-water capacity. Bernard Cole notes that no foreign or PLA analyst has identified a document that outlines an explicit maritime strategy, suggesting that the PLAN does not have one. Instead, the PLAN just has strong mission statements, which often can be misinterpreted. Cole downplayed the famous "Three Islands Chains" strategy as designed for internal lobbying—seeking to secure more resources for the Chinese Navy—rather than as a clear strategic objective. PLAN strategists now speak more sincerely about being able to control the three seas surrounding the PRC: the East China Sea, the South China Sea, and the Yellow Sea. And often it is the PRC Coast Guard, the fisheries patrol, and so on—rather than the PLAN—that routinely enforce China's maritime claims in these areas.[37]

The PLA now has the ability to conduct "combined arms" operations that integrate multiple elements of a single service—such as using the army's infantry and artillery—but not yet "joint operations" that effectively integrate the assets of several military services. Until the PLA achieves this latter capacity, its ability to exploit the full combat potential of all its new equipment will remain inherently limited. The PLA has been experiencing several challenges in attempting to institutionalize joint operations. In terms of concepts, PLA regulations and doctrine during the past decade have reached the level of "coordination"—when one service knows what the others are doing in an area of operations—but not cross-service joint operations. In 2004, the PLA introduced two concepts that would provide the command and technological foundations for joint warfare. The first term, "integrated joint operations," is what the PLA describes as allowing command elements from one service to have command authority over another service. PLA analysts have also established the goal of conducting "systems-of-systems operations," which means connecting combat technologies together regardless of their service or platform. But these concepts have not become widely used. The second challenge is that the only genuine joint command structure in the PLA is at the top. The Central Military Commission, though still army-dominated, includes senior PLAN and PLAAF officers. All the structures below the CMC, including the major PLA Departments like the General Staff Department and the General Armaments Department, are overwhelmingly dominated by the army. The seven geographic military regions (MR, which become "military area commands" in wartime) are also primarily dominated by the ground forces, with an Army officer as the senior MR commander and a Navy or Air Force officer as his deputy. On paper, these seven commands (Shenyang, Beijing, Lanzhou, Jinan, Nanjing, Guangzhou, and Chengdu) would only become joint structures when activated for war, but this is unproven because they are not standing joint combatant commands like those of the U.S. military. The PLA has made some limited success with joint logistics in the last few years, including establishing a Joint Logistics Department, but its overall impact seems unclear. Training represents yet a third challenge. The PLA has established permanent joint training offices in each MR and conducted some joint exercises, but these have been few in number and are most often combined arms exercises. A logical progression would see cross-MR training and exercises in which one MR simulates an invasion of another with more than one service participating. Incompatible technologies present a fourth challenge. The PLA has been successful at vertically linking units, so that commanders can communicate with and control their subordinate units; however, the PLA has struggled with horizontal integration between units belonging to different services and commands. Because each unit receives funds to develop its own communication systems, the commands have had to exchange personnel and equipment, with every other command with which they want to communicate, to fully overcome this problem. The PLA has recently introduced an integrated command platform that is supposed to operate across services in an attempt to overcome this problem. The final problem relates to the PLA mindset. Many commanders place loyalty to their service or unit first and are unenthusiastic about the idea of a "joint force." The PLA acknowledges all these obstacles. For example, its 2008 White Paper states that the PLA is only laying a foundation for future jointness now and does not expect to attain a genuine joint force for another decade or two.[38]

U.S. analysts conclude that the PLA is pursuing "asymmetric strategies to leverage China's advantages while exploiting the perceived vulnerabilities of potential opponents."[39] In particular, the PLA has been developing so-called assassins' mace capabilities designed to negate U.S. strengths and exploit asymmetrical vulnerabilities in U.S. military defenses.[40] For example, PLA leaders are seeking to degrade U.S. global communications and information support networks while increasing China's capabilities in the unconventional domains of warfare—nuclear, outer space, and the electromagnetic spectrum. The PLA has nuclear-armed missile, antisatellite, cyberwarfare, and other programs designed to neutralize adversaries' technological advantages. Elements of China's conventional forces, including missiles, mines, submarines, and other antiaccess/area-denial weapons also help Beijing deny foreign militaries access to areas around the PRC—or at least make it difficult for foreign militaries to operate there.

The PRC's quest for disruptive military technology also became globally visible in January 2007, when the PLA successfully tested an antisatellite (ASAT) weapon by maneuvering a Chinese ground-launched missile to fly into the path of a nonfunctioning Chinese weather satellite. The PRC government was conspicuously silent about the reasons for its actions, which broke a decades-long international moratorium against such experiments.[41] One interpretation—originally developed by Western arms control advocates, but later expounded by some Chinese analysts—is that Beijing may have hoped to shock the George W. Bush administration into supporting additional outer space arms control measures.[42] A more common assessment is that Beijing was seeking the capacity to disrupt U.S. space–based communications and reconnaissance, especially in the case of a future Taiwan contingency.[43] In any case, the PRC succeeded in confirming for itself, in addition to demonstrating to the rest of the world, that the PLA possessed offensive ASAT capabilities that could inflict acute blows on U.S. defenses.[44] Whatever the reasons for the original decision, the PRC government has since signaled that it does not intend to conduct additional ASAT tests. It has also reaffirmed its support for a formal treaty banning the deployment of weapons in outer space.[45]

According to Dean Cheng of the Heritage Foundation, China has been striving for the ability to conduct high-technology and integrated joint operations through space-based Intelligence, Surveillance, and Reconnaissance (ISR) since watching the decisive U.S. victory in Operations Desert Shield/Desert Storm in 1991. This campaign showed PLA experts how military technology could fundamentally change the nature of warfare. The subsequent U.S. military victories in Kosovo in 1998, Afghanistan in 2001, and Iraq in 2003 reinforced this lesson. Before 1991, the PLA had relied on uncoordinated ad hoc efforts by various PLA elements to introduce automated command processes, with no effort at comprehensive modernization or integration of its C4ISR efforts; since then, the Chinese military has undertaken a major effort to develop its C4ISR concepts and capabilities. As a result, the PLA introduced new terms—including information dominance, information operations, information deterrence, information frontier, unified network electronic warfare, and computer network warfare—between 1991 and 2001 as it modernized its C4ISR functions and doctrine. Immediately after Operations Desert Shield/Desert Storm, the PLA undertook an extensive study of these campaigns and sought to incorporate the lessons learned into its own style of war. In 1993, the PLA introduced new high-level guidelines on "local war under modern conditions" that emphasized the value of modern information operations in warfighting. In 1995, President Jiang called for "two transformations" in the PLA: first, a shift of focus from quantity to quality; second, a transition from a military preparing for "local wars under modern conditions" to those of "local wars under modern high-technology conditions." These latter conditions mean that the conflict is marked by high operational tempos, joint operations predominate, the battlefield has become three dimensional, its geographic scope extends farther and deeper into a country's strategic rear areas, and the role of command, control, communications, and intelligence is paramount. Recognizing the importance of the cyberdimension, the PLA's 2004 White Paper replaced the phrase "local wars under modern high-technology conditions" with "local wars under modern informationalized conditions." PLA texts also refer to "active offense," "tight defense," "seizing and preserving local information dominance," and "breaking the enemy's network and disrupting links." These terms suggest the PLA is developing a potential doctrine for "joint campaign information operations." The PLA places considerable emphasis on psychology—seeking to slow down the adversary's decision-making cycles. The PRC is also employing what others call "lawfare" to degrade U.S. C4ISR capabilities. For example, China has joined with Russia to push cyber and space arms control treaties that would exempt their own systems while constraining those of the United States.

The PRC's efforts to develop the C4ISR capabilities required to implement its doctrine originally suffered from a lack of PLA-wide centralized direction. During the past decade, the PLA sought to provide unified guidance to reconcile requirements and achieve information dominance in all five domains of warfare. The PLA has also developed more advanced outer space capabilities to include space-based communications and sensor networks that use increasingly sophisticated communications, reconnaissance, and spy satellites. The PRC's civilian space program is closely associated with its military. Fighting the PLA would present a new challenge for the U.S. military in this regard because all of its previous adversaries possessed only rudimentary C4ISR systems and no outer-space capabilities. The PLA in effect is creating an advanced C4ISR architecture with multiple layers extending into outer space. But China would also face the challenge that, unlike the United States, the PRC has never tested its C4ISR capabilities in a real war. The PLA might perform better if it had already experienced a Grenada-type operation that, as in the Pentagon's case, exposed its C4ISR vulnerabilities in a relatively nonthreatening environment (such as Army soldiers unable to communicate with Navy ships offshore) and spurred subsequent improvements. The PLA unintentionally may have made its own C4ISR systems more vulnerable by relying so heavily on pirated software. For instance, the PLA cannot be sure that its systems have downloaded the latest software patches to close critical vulnerabilities that an adversary might exploit.[46]

PLA leaders are pursuing advanced outer space ISR capabilities for the same reasons that the world's other major militaries are acquiring them. They perceive outer space not only as a domain to support terrestrial operations, but also as an area of warfare. The PLA desires to use space-based ISR to enhance peacetime situational awareness, which includes knowledge of other countries' military activities as well as for early warning of a potential attack. For example, PLA space-based sensors can determine the location and type of U.S. warships. The PLA has used its satellites to help manage its response to earthquakes by surveying the damage. It is likely that the PRC uses its space-based surveillance capabilities for domestic monitoring purposes as well. Another reason for the PLA's pursuit of space ISR is to support mission planning functions such as targeting missiles or air strikes. Finally, advanced ISR capabilities provide general battle damage assessment, allowing commanders to see how well initial strikes performed and what needs to be attacked again. The PLA's outer space capabilities still lag behind those of the United States, but it has improving space-based communications and electronics reconnaissance. The PLA's current ISR objectives probably include having more optical imagery satellites, better UAVs, improved synthetic aperture radar for penetrating under clouds and surveying at night, superior signals intelligence for monitoring and identifying warships, and greater resiliency (hence the PLA interest in easily replaceable microsatellites). The PLA will benefit from the improving capabilities of China's civilian space program; for example, weather satellites can be useful for calibrating over-the-horizon radar or for providing information about maritime conditions—helpful for targeting ships.[47]

The PLA has also sought to improve its capabilities for disaster relief and humanitarian missions, including at home. The 2004 Asian Tsunami and the 2008 earthquake in Sichuan Province demonstrated to the PRC the need to modernize its capacities. In 2005, while U.S. forces were providing devastated Asian communities with abundant supplies and aid workers via air and sea, the PRC was forced to mostly sit on the sidelines, lacking the capability to provide much assistance because of its deficiencies in air and naval technologies.[48] Beijing suffered even greater embarrassment following the devastating Sichuan earthquake. With the entire world watching, the PRC faced a number of difficulties in providing relief to its own citizens in affected areas.[49] The PLA deployed more than 100,000 troops and over 100 helicopters to provide food, medical supplies, and other emergency relief to the devastated region, but observers noted many deficiencies in military capabilities in this area.[50] The PRC eventually decided to allow the U.S. military to collaborate with the PLA in the relief effort, a major shift from past PRC stances in which the government had steadfastly refused outside help in responding to domestic disasters.[51]

Cyberstrikers

Perhaps China's main form of long-range strike lies in the cyberdomain. These have the advantage of being much more usable and anonymous, in line with a Chinese military tradition that emphasizes deception rather than nuclear or conventional strike weapons. The Pentagon notes that China's "developing capabilities for cyberwarfare is consistent with authoritative PLA military writings."

DOD analysts specify three key areas in which PRC military operations could be merged with cyberwarfare capabilities: "First and foremost, they allow data collection through exfiltration. Second, they can be employed to constrain an adversary's actions or slow response time by targeting network-based logistics, communications, and commercial activities . . . Third, they can serve as a force multiplier when coupled with kinetic attacks during times of crisis or conflict."[52] The PLA's growing cyberwarfare capabilities are designed to damage an adversary's technological infrastructure and disrupt its communications and information networks.[53] The PLA's focus ranges from malware and denial-of-service attacks to botnets and hacking. These methods of attack aim to cripple anything from banking systems to power grids.[54] Chinese theorists call their information warfare initiatives "Integrated Network Electronic Warfare."[55] The Pentagon believes that China hopes to achieve "cyber superiority" over its primary competitors by 2050.[56] In addition to its official assets, Chinese capabilities are enhanced by the large number of "patriotic hackers." Because they are formally independent of the Chinese government, they can conduct cyberoperations in support of official policies while allowing PRC officials to deny responsibility for their actions. President Obama's Homeland Security adviser, Joel Brenner, remarked that, "The Chinese operate . . . through government agencies, as we do, but they also operate through sponsoring other organizations that are engaging in this kind of international hacking, whether or not under specific direction . . . It's a kind of cyber militia."[57]

According to the U.S.-China Economic and Security Review Commission, China has some 250 independent hacker groups based in its territory. The Commission's 2008 report suggests that the government tolerates and even encourages these independent groups.[58] In its 2012 report, the U.S.-China Commission detailed how PRC hackers have employed increasingly sophisticated offensive techniques, such as defeating secure authentication (beating two-factor authentication beyond a password), bridging air gaps (targeting physically isolated networks), targeting deployed platforms (gaining access to military platforms in remote areas, including missiles and ground systems), leveraging the cloud (using Web-based services to reduce geographic visibility), compromising mobile devices (inserting malware into smartphones), and deleting directories and compromising news websites. So far, most Chinese intrusions against U.S. government and military systems seem to focus on collecting intelligence rather than launching malicious attacks; however, both of these options involve the same mechanisms and degree of access. If hackers maintain access to compromised systems, as Chinese hackers often aim to do, an incursion that was previously focused on gathering intelligence could switch to follow a disruptive or destructive path, causing significant costs in terms of time and money, or even compromising U.S. military operations in a conflict. Many entities in China are helping develop its cyberoffensive and defensive capabilities:

- The Second Department of the PLA General Staff Department (2PLA), responsible for military intelligence;
- The 3PLA, responsible for collecting signals intelligence, including computer network exploitation using the Technical Reconnaissance Bureaus across the country, and also possibly the PLA's computer network defense;
- The 4PLA, which engages in electronic warfare and is responsible for computer network attack;
- The PLA Navy and Air Force operate Technical Reconnaissance Bureaus, which may participate in computer network operations;
- The Secondary Artillery Forces may also have cyber-related responsibilities in addition to nuclear and conventional missile responsibilities;
- Cyberwarfare militias are a subset of the PLA militia, which is composed mostly of workers with high-tech day jobs that focus on military communications, electronic warfare, and computer network operations;
- Ministry of State Security—its foreign intelligence service may engage in cyberoperations;
- Ministry of Public Security—its domestic security service engages in surveillance, including in cyberspace of Chinese citizens and foreign travelers in China;
- Customs and border units may tamper with travelers' electronics;
- "Hacktivist" groups acting on nationalistic feeling, usually through denial of service attacks or website defacement;
- "For-profit hacker" groups committing espionage on behalf of private sector, state-owned, or government clients; these are sometimes organized as security and consulting firms;
- Criminal hackers who may either be punished or recruited by PRC government entities;
- "Corporate" entities engaging in, supporting, or benefitting from cyberespionage, that may be considered state-sponsored because of their high proportion of state-controlled industry;
- Telecommunications providers—Internet service providers, web services providers, etc. may be involved in malicious cyberactivities;
- Information technology companies such as components and systems manufacturers, assemblers, or support staff may deliberately introduce vulnerabilities into systems given to foreign entities, including back doors for later access to the system.[59]

Nuclear Weapons

The U.S.-China Economic and Security Review Commission has also detailed sustained improvements in China's nuclear forces. The Commission's 2012 report estimates that China is possibly within two years of attaining a genuine nuclear triad consisting of land-based ballistic missiles, submarine-launched ballistic missiles, and air-dropped nuclear bombs. The most developed of these legs is China's land-based ballistic missile program, though the submarine capability is being developed rapidly. New intercontinental ballistic missile (ICBM) programs, including the DF-31A and eventually the DF-41, are projected to contribute significantly to the range, reliability, and overall effectiveness of China's nuclear arms. DOD currently estimates that China has 50-75 ICBMs capable of reaching the continental United States, including some DF-5s (range greater than 13,000 kilometers), DF-31As (greater than 11,200 kilometers range), and DF-31s (greater than 7,200 kilometers range). Furthermore, China successfully tested a DF-41 road-mobile missile on July 24, 2012; this program is generally thought to have a multiple independently targeted reentry vehicle (MIRV) capacity, able to carry and then release one or more warheads against several targets or carry heavier decoys, which would complicate antimissile defenses. With respect to its two other legs of the nuclear triad, China has nearly developed a new JIN-class submarine (Type-094) and JL-2 submarine-launched intercontinental ballistic missile (SLBM) combination. Two of the five planned submarines are already deployed within the PLA Navy, and the JL-2 program remains in development. In mid-August 2012, the PLA flight-tested a JL-2 from a JIN-class submarine. In contrast, China's strategic bomber capability remains undeveloped. The PLA Air Force has at most 20 H-6 bombers, which rely on gravity bombs and possibly nuclear-armed DH-10 air-to-ground cruise missiles. The U.S. Defense Intelligence Agency estimates that the number of Chinese ICBMs that could strike the continental United States may double by 2025. DOD analysts also believe that China is aiming to develop new strategic technologies such as maneuvering reentry vehicles, advanced decoys, thermal shielding, and ASAT capabilities.[60]

China has disclosed very little information regarding its nuclear arsenal, increasing concerns over its strength, size, and composition. Currently, the Second Artillery Corps uses an intricate combination of rail, road, and underground facilities that shield these nuclear assets from a first-strike attack and increase the probability of a retaliatory strike. The Second Artillery also uses underground facilities for command posts, communication facilities, storage for other weapons and equipment, and personnel protection. China's networks of underground nuclear weapons storage and transport tunnels make assessing its capabilities extremely difficult. Estimates regarding its stockpiles vary wildly depending on the sources—from 100–500 (Western assessments) to 1,600–18,000 (Russian estimates). The tunnels could also simply be an attempt to complicate the targeting of China's nuclear arsenal by enemies.[61]

PRC leaders have traditionally proclaimed a "no-first-use" declaratory doctrine regarding when they might employ nuclear weapons—implying they would resort to nuclear weapons only in retaliation to an adversary's first nuclear use. Even so, conflicting messages emanate from other PLA elements, which espouse "gaining the initiative" and "active defense" through the exploitation of first-strike advantages. Chinese officials have repeatedly stressed that they view nuclear weapons primarily as a tool for deterring nuclear war. They also seem to believe that a robust nuclear arsenal gives the PRC international status. The vagueness of Chinese nuclear strategy, compounded with persistent lack of knowledge regarding the nature of its arsenal, makes it difficult for outsiders to gauge when, how, and to what purpose Beijing might use its nuclear weapons. PLA doctrine emphasizes maintaining the safety and security of nuclear stockpiles and sustaining robust nuclear command-and-control systems, but it is difficult to tell which groups are authorized to launch warheads under what conditions (i.e., peacetime versus wartime), how effective existing and planned warhead security measures are, and how civil-military leadership command-and-communications are managed. For example, the highly centralized Second Artillery Corps, an independent branch of the PLA, is mainly in charge of China's nuclear weapons. Because this branch has both conventional and nuclear missions, and the separation of command and control systems between these elements is unclear, fears arise that swift escalation will follow the initiation of conventional strikes. In practice, it is probably the Central Military Commission, to which the Second Artillery Corps directly reports, that would authorize nuclear use. It is unknown if the CMC, technically a department of the Chinese Communist Party Central Committee but also with senior military members, must also authorize conventional missile strikes.[62]

Role of the PLA in Policy Making

Scholars believe that the relationship between the Chinese Communist Party and the Chinese military has become much more complex and multifaceted than it was when the institutions were created almost a century ago. The PLA has become more "professional" in the sense that Chinese soldiers are better educated and trained in modern warfighting, but the PLA is still a political army, which PRC civilian leaders insist on because they fear that the PLA's depoliticization could weaken its loyalty to the CCP. The PLA has become more cognizant of its collective institutional interests and seeks to advance them in PRC decision-making processes. The heads of the party and the military have different perspectives, with fewer and fewer PRC civilian leaders having served in the PLA, ending the previous era of "soldier-statesmen" such as Mao and Deng. Civilian control of the military remains strong because of the system of commissars, the requirement that all PLA officers be CCP members, various interlinking bodies with members from both institutions, and other means of ensuring party penetration of the military. China's senior leader is still the PRC president, who sits at the apex of both the CCP and the PLA as head of the CMC. But the PLA enjoys much autonomy on military matters, with considerable flexibility in implementing policies. Thus, the Politburo and CMC determine the military budget and broad spending categories, but the PLA probably determines what specific conventional weapons systems to prioritize and how best to use them in China's military strategy and tactics. The PLA's spectrum of interests encompasses many objectives common to other militaries—maximizing its budget, prestige, and autonomy. The PLA is not a rogue military, but it can exploit "ambiguous guidance" from this hands-off civilian leadership. This loosening civilian guidance and augmented military guidance has degraded the PRC's ability to manage crises, such as the 2001 EP3 collision, which require rapid decisions and close civil-military coordination and information sharing.[63]

The PLA has become more influential in determining the PRC's national security policy because of its monopoly of expertise in this area and its more narrowly defined, instrumental, and institutionalized policy orientation, which now focuses mostly on military issues rather than on promoting socioeconomic revolution. Many factors have amplified the PLA's influence in recent years over foreign and defense issues. China's national security interests have expanded and its national leaders are demanding more of the military—including sustaining multiyear counterpiracy patrols in the Gulf of Aden, something few Western experts would have expected even a few years ago. The PLA's new capabilities are augmenting its role in Chinese foreign policy. For example, the PLAN's improving capabilities have given the PRC government the option of dispatching a flotilla to the Gulf of Aden to protect Chinese ships from Somali-based pirates. Other factors have meant that the PLA often has the upper hand in confrontations with the Ministry of Foreign Affairs (MFA). The PLA has higher status than the MFA; for example, it has privileged access to PRC party and government leaders. The PLA also has seats on some of the PRC's highest decision-making organs, including on the Politburo. In contrast, the MFA mostly executes rather than determines policy. Furthermore, the military has a monopoly over defense expertise because there are few civilian defense experts—even among PRC government officials—because of demographic changes that are removing the older generations who fought in the Chinese Civil War or the Korean War from top positions. The PLA has become increasingly skilled at media relations; it even owns some large media outlets. This media influence gives the PLA great potential to shape the views of Chinese citizens—but not yet those of many Chinese neighbors made uneasy, among other matters, by China's military buildup.[64]

REGIONAL REACTIONS

As mandated by Congress, the focus of the annual DOD reports on Chinese military power is on the cross-Strait balance. Although tensions between Beijing and Taipei have decreased following the election in 2008 of a new KMT government more committed to improving cross-Strait relations, the Pentagon believes that the PLA is still seeking, through a military buildup, to deter Taiwan from declaring independence and to coerce Taiwan to accept the PRC's terms for the resolution of any cross-Strait dispute. To this end, Beijing is pursuing capabilities to defeat Taiwan in any military confrontation and to "deter, delay, or deny" possible U.S. military intervention on Taipei's behalf. In fact, one of the prime drivers of the PLA's military modernization program is to improve its ability to occupy Taiwan if necessary. Because of the U.S. defense commitment to assist Taiwan, the PRC has been preparing to fight not only Taiwan, but also the United States, in any cross-Strait conflict. The most prominent objective of the PRC's military buildup appears to be developing "access denial" capabilities to inhibit U.S. intervention in the event of conflict with Taiwan. Such a strategy involves deterring through threats, or disrupting by attack, any U.S. naval force coming to Taiwan's aid. The PLAN's emphasis on attack submarines, long-range missiles, and improved fighter planes all increase the risks to any U.S. naval task force sent to defend Taiwan. China's improving antisatellite and cybercapabilities could reinforce this effort. The PLA continues to deploy additional short-range ballistic missiles and now has more than 1,000 ballistic missile launchers within range of Taiwan. In addition, the PLA keeps approximately 400,000 regular troops in Taiwan's vicinity.

Many of China's neighbors besides Taiwan are wary of China's growing military strength. It is not difficult to conceive of scenarios in which the PRC would use its new capabilities to coerce other Asian states. For instance, China has active maritime disputes with Japan, Vietnam, and the Philippines; these contested regions of the East China Sea and the South China Sea have rich fishing grounds as well as valuable undersea natural resources, including deposits of oil and natural gas. Indians worry about the emergence of a possible Chinese "string of pearls" naval strategy, in which the PLA Navy has established coastal support facilities in sea ports from Burma to Pakistan, using them as operational "lily pads."[65] The PRC has leased a maritime reconnaissance and intelligence center on Burma's Coco Islands and is constructing a major deepwater port—designed primarily to support commercial shipping—on the Arabian Sea at Gwadar in Pakistan.[66] Some Chinese strategists are now openly discussing acquiring naval support facilities in the Gulf of Aden region, which would supplement ongoing antipiracy operations off the coast of Somalia.[67] If expanded, these facilities could help the PLAN execute sea-denial and antiaccess strategies, enhance the fleet's power projection capabilities, and ensure the free flow of oil and natural resources through vital sea lines of communications.

The United States and other foreign governments have long pressured Beijing to make its military programs and policies more transparent to help facilitate confidence-building and mutual security reassurance. Since the mid-1990s, the defense communities of the United States and the PRC have negotiated a series of bilateral defense and security agreements and confidence-building measures seeking to reduce mutual tensions and advance their common security interests. These measures have promoted a better understanding of each party's security concerns, but they remain highly constrained and vulnerable to disruption from external shocks. Several factors have impeded their development. The most important obstacle has been the underlying contentious nature of the U.S.-Chinese relationship, which is manifested most acutely by tensions concerning Taiwan. As leaders of the weaker military power, PRC policymakers fear that excessive transparency could provide Americans with insights into their military vulnerabilities. Influenced by a strategic tradition that emphasizes deception, many Chinese strategists also believe that opacity assists in deterring potential adversaries by complicating their military planning. Furthermore, PRC policymakers do not want to draw foreign attention to their continued military buildup. Finally, the defense communities in both countries have generally resisted measures that constrain their military operations and capabilities.

Despite the strides that China has made toward developing a modern military, it is important to recognize the limits of PRC military power, especially compared with the United States. Notwithstanding the rapid modernization of the Chinese military, a significant technological gap continues to exist between the PLA and the U.S. armed forces in almost all important areas of military power. In addition to the persistent disparity between the two countries in terms of air and naval technology, China lags even farther behind the United States in such important areas as the capacity to organize multiservice joint operations or use the kinds of comprehensive and effective C4ISR systems found in the U.S. military. These systems rely on advanced information processing, improved computer networks, high-speed optic cables, and other sophisticated capabilities in an effort to exert "full-spectrum dominance."[68] Despite its ability to maintain a few combat ships off Somalia, the PLAN fleet is still logistically limited compared to Western navies that have access to overseas bases. China's Navy still lacks a fleet of operational aircraft carriers, large amphibious ships, extensive replenishment and refueling vessels, and other capabilities essential for sustaining military operations in distant regions. Because of the PLA's inability to maintain large forces at a distance, coupled with its technological disadvantages compared to the Pentagon, and lack of PLA combat experience since 1979, the PRC remains a strong regional military power rather than a true global power.

NOTES

1. Susan Shirk, *China: Fragile Superpower* (Oxford University Press, 2007), 35–78.

2. Evan S. Medeiros, *China's International Behavior: Activism, Opportunism and Diversification* (Santa Monica: RAND, 2009), 44.

3. Andrew Scobell and Andrew J. Nathan, "China's Overstretched Military," *Washington Quarterly* (Fall 2012): 135–148.

4. GlobalSecurity.org, "PLA History," *GlobalSecurity.org*, August 7, 2007, http://www.globalsecurity.org/military/world/china/pla-history.htm.

5. *U.S. Department of Defense*, "Military and Security Developments Involving the People's Republic of China 2011," *U.S. Department of Defense*, http://www.defense.gov/pubs/pdfs/2011_cmpr_final.pdf.

6. David Shambaugh, *Modernizing China's Military: Progress, Problems and Prospects* (Berkeley: University of California Press, 2004), 69–74.

7. David Axe, "China's Navy—Good For Us All?" *The Diplomat*, February 12, 2010, the-diplomat.com/2010/02/12/china%E2%80%99s-navy-good-for-us-all/.

8. Robert Kaplan, "China's Two-Ocean Strategy," in *China's Arrival: A Strategic Framework for a Global Relationship*, ed. Abraham Denmark and Nirav Patel (Center for a New American Security, 2009), 45, http://www.cnas.org/files/documents/publications/CNAS%20China%27s%20Arrival_Final%20Report.pdf.

9. Ronald O'Rourke, "China Naval Modernization: Implications for U.S. Navy Capabilities: Background and Issues for Congress," *U.S. Congressional Research Service*, April 9, 2010, 7–9, www.fas.org/sgp/crs/row/RL33153.pdf.

10. Christopher Griffin and Dan Blumenthal, "China's Defense White Paper: What It Does (and Doesn't) Tell Us," *China Brief*, 7, no. 2, January 24, 2007. www.jamestown.org/programs/chinabrief/single/?tx_ttnews%5Btt_news%5D=4023&tx_ttnews%5BbackPid%5D=197&no_cache=1.

11. U.S. Navy, Office of Naval Intelligence, *The People's Liberation Army Navy: A Modern Navy with Chinese Characteristics* (Suitland, Maryland: U.S. Navy, August 2009). http://www.fas.org/irp/agency/oni/pla-navy.pdf.

12. Andrew W. Erikson and Michael Chase, "China's SSBN Forces: Transitioning to the Next Generation," *China Brief* 9, no. 12 (June 12, 2009), http://www.jamestown.org/single/?no_cache=1&tx_ttnews[tt_news]=35120; Andrew W. Erikson and Michael Chase, "Information Technology and China's Naval Modernization," *Joint Forces Quarterly*, no. 50 (3rd quarter 2008): 24–30.

13. O'Rourke, "China Naval Modernization," 13.

14. GlobalSecurity.org, "HangZhou Type 956 Sovremenny," *GlobalSecurity.org*, June 6, 2009, www.globalsecurity.org/military/world/china/haizhou.htm.

15. Chinese Defence, "Project 956/EM Sovremenny Class Missile Destroyer," *Chinese Defence*, April 15, 2012, http://www.chinesedefence.com/forums/chinese-navy/2872-project-956-em-sovremenny-class-missile-destroyer.html.

16. O'Rourke, "China Naval Modernization."

17. Richard D. Fisher Jr., "Plan for Growth: China's Surface Fleet Modernization Fits Beijing's Appetite for Sea Power," *Armed Forces Journal*, April 2006, http://www.armedforcesjournal.com/2006/04/1813798/.

18. O'Rourke, "China Naval Modernization," 13–16.

19. Lyle J. Goldstein, "Cold Wars at Sea," *Armed Forces Journal*, April 2008, http://www.armedforcesjournal.com/2008/04/3373649/.

20. Gabe Collins and Andrew Erickson, " 'Flying Shark' Gaining Altitude: How Might New J-15 Strike Fighter Improve China's Maritime Air Warfare Ability?," *China SignPost*, June 8, 2011, http://www.chinasignpost.com/2011/06/flying-shark%E2%80%9D-gaining-altitude-how-might-new-j-15-strike-fighter-improve-china%E2%80%99s-maritime-air-warfare-ability/.

21. Saibal Dasgupta, "China Wants More Aircraft Carriers to Compete with India," *Times of India*, July 30, 2011, http://timesofindia.indiatimes.com/world/china/China-wants-more-aircraft-carriers-to-compete-with-India/articleshow/9423618.cms.

22. Richard Fisher, Jr., "The Implications of China's Naval Modernization for the United States," International Assessment and Strategy Center, June 11, 2009, www.strategycenter .net/research/pubID.199/pub_detail.asp.

23. U.S. Navy, Office of Naval Intelligence, *China's Navy 2007* (U.S. Navy, Office of Naval Intelligence, [2007]), http://www.fas.org/irp/agency/oni/chinanavy2007.pdf.

24. Sukhoi Corporation, "Su-30MK2," Komsomolsk-on-Amur Aircraft Production Association, March 30, 2010. http://www.knaapo.ru/eng/products/su-30mk2/index.wbp.

25. Wendell Minnick, "Russia Admits China Illegally Copied its Fighter," *Defense News,* February 13, 2009, http://minnickarticles.blogspot.com/2009/10/russia-admits-china -illegally-copied.html.

26. "J-11 (Jianjiji-11)," *GlobalSecurity.org,* 2013, http://www.globalsecurity.org/military/ world/china/j-11.htm.

27. U.S. Department of Defense, Office of the Secretary of Defense, *Military and Security Developments Involving the People's Republic of China: 2010* (Washington, DC: U.S. Department of Defense, August 2010), 1, http://www.defense.gov/pubs/pdfs/2010_CMPR_Final .pdf.

28. International Institute for Strategic Studies, "Long March of China's Military Reform," *Real Clear World,* September 19, 2010. http://www.realclearworld.com/articles/2010/09/19/ long_march_of_chinas_military_reform_99189.html.

29. Fisher, "Implications of China's Naval Modernization."

30. U.S.-China Economic and Security Review Commission, *2012 Report to Congress of the U.S.–China Economic and Security Review Commission* (Washington, DC: U.S. Government Printing Office, November 2012), http://origin.www.uscc.gov/sites/default/files/annual _reports/2012-Report-to-Congress.pdf.

31. Bruce W. MacDonald, *China, Space Weapons, and U.S. Security* (Council on Foreign Relations Press, September 2008), 6–10, http://i.cfr.org/content/publications/attachments/ China_Space_CSR38.pdf.

32. Keith Crane et al., *Modernizing China's Military: Opportunities and Constraints* (Santa Monica: RAND Corporation, 2005), 154–156. http://www.rand.org/content/dam/rand/ pubs/monographs/2005/RAND_MG260-1.pdf.

33. Vladimir Karnozov, "Russian Officials Reveal J-31 Engine and Describe Sales to China," *AINonline,* November 23, 2012, http://www.ainonline.com/aviation-news/ ain-defense-perspective/2012-11-23/russian-officials-reveal-j-31-engine-and-describe-sales -china.

34. This language appears in 2008, 2009, and 2010 annual China military power reports, which are available at http://www.defense.gov/pubs/ as U.S. Department of Defense, *Military Power of the People's Republic of China 2008* (Washington, DC: U.S. Department of Defense, 2009), http://www.defense.gov/pubs/pdfs/China_Military_Report_08.pdf; U.S. Department of Defense, *Military Power of the People's Republic of China 2009* (Washington, DC: U.S. Department of Defense, 2010), http://www.defense.gov/pubs/pdfs/China_Military_Power _Report_2009.pdf; U.S. Department of Defense, *Military and Security Developments Involving the People's Republic of China: 2010* (Washington, DC: U.S. Department of Defense, 2011), http://www.defense.gov/pubs/pdfs/2010_CMPR_Final.pdf.

35. U.S. Department of Defense, "DOD Press Briefing on the 2011 Annual Report to Congress: Military and Developments Involving the People's Republic of China," *U.S. Department of Defense,* August 24, 2011. http://www.defense.gov/transcripts/transcript.aspx ?transcriptid=4868.

36. Dennis Blasko, "PLA Self-Assessments and the Direction of Modernization" (presented at the 2012 China Defense and Security Conference, The Jamestown Foundation, Washington, DC, February 16, 2012).

37. Bernard Cole, "China's Evolving Naval Strategy" (presented at the 2012 China Defense and Security Conference, The Jamestown Foundation, Washington, DC, February 16, 2012).

38. Kevin Pollpeter, "Informationization and Joint Operations" (presented at the 2012 China Defense and Security Conference, The Jamestown Foundation, Washington, DC, February 16, 2012).

39. Office of the Secretary of Defense, *Military and Security Developments Involving the People's Republic of China 2011*, n.d., 27, http://www.defense.gov/pubs/pdfs/2011_cmpr _final.pdf.

40. Kurt Campbell, et al., *The Power of Balance* (Washington, DC: Center for a New American Security, 2008), 43–44.

41. David Sanger and Joseph Kahn, "U.S. Tries to Interpret China's Silence Over Test," *New York Times*, January 22, 2007, http://www.nytimes.com/2007/01/22/world/asia/ 22missile.html?_r=1&oref=slogin.

42. Stephen Herzog, "The Dilemma between Deterrence and Disarmament: Moving beyond the Perception of China as a Nuclear Threat," *BASIC Occasional Papers On International Security* no. 57, August 2008. http://www.basicint.org/sites/default/files/BP57 .pdf

43. Ashley J. Tellis, *Punching the U.S. Military's "Soft Ribs": China's Antisatellite Weapon Test in Strategic Perspective*, Policy Brief, Carnegie Endowment for International Peace, June 2007. http://www.carnegieendowment.org/files/pb_51_tellis_final.pdf.

44. Bates Gill and Martin Kleiber, "China's Space Odyssey: What the Antisatellite Test Reveals About Decision-Making in Beijing," *Foreign Affairs* (May/June 2007), http://www .foreignaffairs.org/20070501facomments86301/bates-gill-martin-kleiber/china-s-space -odyssey-what-the-antisatellite-test-reveals-about-decision-making-in-beijing.html.

45. Stephanie Nebehay, "China, Russia to Offer Treaty to Ban Arms in Space," *Reuters*, January 25, 2008, http://www.reuters.com/article/worldNews/idUSL2578979020080125 ?feedType=RSS&feedName=worldNews.

46. Dean Cheng, "China's C4ISR Modernization: Problems, Progress, and Prospects" (presented at the 2012 China Defense and Security Conference, The Jamestown Foundation, Washington, DC, February 16, 2012).

47. Mark Stokes, "China's Space-Based Intelligence, Surveillance and Reconnaissance" (presented at the 2012 China Defense and Security Conference, The Jamestown Foundation, Washington, DC, February 16, 2012).

48. Harvey Feldman et al., "Asia's Security Challenges," *The Heritage Foundation*, April 4, 2005, http://www.heritage.org/research/reports/2005/04/asias-security-challenges/.

49. United Press International, "Chinese Army's Quake Response Said Lacking," *UPI.com*, July 2, 2008, http://www.upi.com/Top_News/2008/07/02/Chinese-armys-quake-response -said-lacking/UPI-43621215001044/.

50. Jake Hooker, "Quake Revealed Deficiencies of China's Military," *New York Times*, July 2, 2008, http://www.nytimes.com/2008/07/02/world/asia/02china.html.

51. Gordon Lubold, "After Earthquake, China Welcomes U.S. Military," *Christian Science Monitor*, May 30, 2008, http://www.csmonitor.com/2008/0530/p02s01-usmi.html.

52. Office of the Secretary of Defense, *Military and Security Developments Involving the People's Republic of China 2011*, 5–6.

53. Tim Reid, "China's Cyber Army is Preparing to March America, Says Pentagon," *Times Online*, September 8, 2007, http://chinadigitaltimes.net/2007/09/chinas-cyber-army-is-preparing-to-march-on-america-says-pentagon-tim-reid/.

54. Shane Harris, "China's Cyber Militia," *National Journal*, May 31, 2008, http://www.nationaljournal.com/njmagazine/cs_20080531_6948.php.

55. Timothy L. Thomas, "Chinese and American Network Warfare," *Joint Force Quarterly* (July 2005), http://www.dtic.mil/cgi-bin/GetTRDoc?AD=ADA530848.

56. Reid, "China's Cyber Army is Preparing to March America, Says Pentagon."

57. Harris, "China's Cyber-Militia."

58. U.S.-China Economic and Security Review Commission, *2008 Report to Congress of the U.S.–China Economic and Security Review Commission* (Washington, DC: U.S. Government Printing Office, November 2008), 164, http://origin.www.uscc.gov/sites/default/files/annual_reports/2008-Report-to-Congress-_0.pdf.

59. U.S.-China Economic and Security Review Commission, *2012 Report to Congress*.

60. Ibid.

61. Ibid.

62. Ibid.

63. Andrew Scobell, "PLA Professionalization and the Civil-Military Gap" (presented at the 2012 China Defense and Security Conference, Jamestown Foundation, Washington, DC, February 16, 2012).

64. Isaac Kardon, "The PLA as an Interest Group in Chinese Politics" (presented at the 2012 China Defense and Security Conference, Jamestown Foundation, Washington, DC, February 16, 2012).

65. Christopher Pehrson, *String of Pearls: Meeting the Challenge of China's Rising Power Across the Asian Littoral* (Carlisle, PA: Strategic Studies Institute, U.S. Army War College, July 2006), 1–2, http://www.strategicstudiesinstitute.army.mil/pdffiles/pub721.pdf.

66. Craig Nelson, "China's Naval Base Proposal May Raise Suspicion," *The National*, January 3, 2010, http://www.thenational.ae/news/world/chinas-naval-base-proposal-may-raise-suspicion.

67. Reuters, "Chinese Admiral Floats Idea of Overseas Naval Bases," *Reuters* (Beijing, December 30, 2008), http://www.reuters.com/article/2009/12/30/us-china-navy-idUSTRE5BT0P020091230.

68. Erikson and Chase, "Information Technology and China's Naval Modernization," 24–30.

CHAPTER 3

China in Its Asian Neighborhood

Although *China's National Defense in 2008* describes the Asian-Pacific security situation as "stable on the whole," it adds that "many factors of uncertainty" prevail in China's neighborhood. These include adverse repercussions from the global economic downturn, ethnic and sectarian tensions, and "conflicting claims over territorial and maritime rights," many of which—though unstated in the text—involve China. Most of China's neighbors view the People's Republic of China (PRC) with caution, but not necessarily with fear. From their perspective, economic cooperation with the PRC is attractive and mutually beneficial. Although other Asian countries try to maintain positive ties with China, many also seek to develop beneficial relations with other great powers—especially the United States, but also Europe and Russia—to balance and hedge against China's growing economic and military potential. The United States is often an ideal offshore balancer because it has powerful military capabilities and vital interests in preserving a balance of power in Asia and globally. U.S. policy makers also lack colonial aspirations and are willing to temper their advocacy of political democracy when that stance could endanger important U.S. national interests.

SOUTHEAST ASIA

In many respects the Association of Southeast Asian Nations (ASEAN), Asia's primary multilateral institution, is an ideal organization for Beijing because the grouping is sufficiently weak to allow the PRC to pursue its preferred divide-and-conquer strategy. ASEAN lacks a collective security provision, joint military forces, or even a foreign policy solidarity clause—the kind of attributes that prevented the Soviet Union from achieving hegemony in Western Europe during the Cold War. ASEAN's main goal is to enhance its members' economic welfare, an objective also shared by the PRC, which can then sell more goods to its members. The "ASEAN Way" philosophy that, though weakening, is still driving the institution stresses respect for state sovereignty and noninterference in internal affairs, a stance that is harmonious with the PRC's philosophy but discomforting for Western democracies that insist on some respect for human rights, free and fair elections, and other liberal democratic principles.

The increase in trade and economic cooperation between China and ASEAN is the principal engine behind the growth of their relationship. Beijing has cleverly used economic enticements and other "win-win" diplomacy methods to deepen its ties with its Southeast Asian neighbors. The November 2002 Framework Agreement on Comprehensive Economic Cooperation between ASEAN and the People's Republic of China created what was then the largest free trade agreement in the world, with almost two billion consumers, a regional gross domestic product (GDP) of about $2 trillion, and a total trade volume estimated at more than $1 trillion. ASEAN governments are eager to keep good relations with Beijing to maintain these economic gains, despite some competition for third-party export markets—particularly in manufactured goods and products from labor-intensive industries—and external foreign direct investment.

The addition of the PRC as a consultative partner of the ASEAN Regional Forum (ARF) in 1994 represented a significant step toward extending this cooperative economic relationship into the diplomatic realm. In addition, Beijing has continually promoted economic, military, and political cooperation schemes that are "Asia only," as a way to cement China's influence at the expense of the United States. For example, the PRC helped construct the "ASEAN Plus Three" (ASEAN, China, Japan, and South Korea) arrangement by exploiting Southeast Asian concerns over the perceived U.S. reluctance to aid ASEAN during the 1997 financial crisis. The PRC has complemented attempts to improve multilateral relations with ASEAN collectively with efforts to develop and sustain good bilateral ties with Southeast Asian countries.

Because of their proximity to the PRC, which entangles them with several regional territorial conflicts, the Southeast Asian nations have thus far suffered more than most countries from China's rising military power and recent diplomatic assertiveness. Like Russia, Southeast Asian governments have generally sought to balance China's rise by embracing it, presuming that such bandwagoning would lead Beijing to pay more attention to their concerns. But ASEAN leaders have also—with varying degrees of enthusiasm—encouraged the United States to maintain an active presence in their region as an external balancer to the PRC.

One major source of tension between Beijing and some of its Pacific neighbors is the contentious issue of overlapping claims to the South China Sea. This 3.5 million-square-kilometer body of water contains islands and maritime passages contested by various littoral states, as well as oil, mineral, and natural gas reserves below the sea. China and Vietnam assert claims to all the small islands in the South China Sea, whereas Brunei, Malaysia, the Philippines, and Taiwan claim some of them. The Spratly and Paracel Island chains are the most prominent of the islands, whose small size and population bely the potential value of the important natural resources thought to lie under their surrounding waters—above all, oil and natural gas. The islands are also surrounded by valuable fishing waters and straddle vital shipping lanes. According to ASEAN Secretary General Surin Pitsuwan, more than 85 percent of the energy resources shipped to the PRC, Japan, and South Korea pass through the South China Sea.[1]

During the 1990s, the PRC declared the entire South China Sea as part of its territorial waters, but lacked the means to enforce these claims; in the early 2000s, Beijing changed course and pursued a strategy of "smile diplomacy" in Southeast Asia designed to reassure ASEAN nations that China's rising power would not threaten them. On November 4, 2002, the PRC and the ASEAN countries signed the Declaration on the Conduct of Parties in the South China Sea. The signatories pledged to resolve their sovereignty disputes peacefully through direct negotiations.[2] The PRC's mild approach succeeded in keeping the sovereignty issue off the agenda of the ARF and other multinational meetings. China naturally wants to prevent the ASEAN states from combining forces and prefers to deal with them individually and bilaterally, a format that maximizes its bargaining leverage.

For reasons that remain unclear, the PRC abandoned its low-key approach in 2010, when some Chinese officials declared the South China Sea to be a "core national interest" of the PRC. In diplomatic language, a "core national interest" normally means an issue a state is willing to use military force to defend. Until then, PRC leaders had applied that term only to Tibet and Taiwan.[3] Furthermore, the PLA Navy (PLAN) has developed the capacity to enforce this claim, building an enormous base on Hainan Island and reinforcing its ship strength in southern China.[4] In July, the PLAN conducted a massive show of force in the South China Sea with at least a dozen warships from its three Navy fleets—which partially aimed to affirm the PRC's maritime claims.[5]

Southeast Asian countries expressed concern about China's newly aggressive stance. In a July 2010 letter to the United Nations, the Indonesian government formally challenged the PRC's claims to the South China Sea for the first time after a PLAN warship forced an Indonesian patrol boat to release a PRC fishing boat. According to Indonesia, the Chinese boat was captured in an area that lied in its Exclusive Economic Zone (EEZ), but Beijing denied the claim.[6] Philippine, Malaysian, and other ASEAN governments also communicated concerns to Washington about the PRC's growing assertiveness in the South China Sea.[7] Furthermore, they have been engaging in their own military buildup, with their imports of foreign arms increasing at exponential rates. Despite their concerns, the ASEAN countries cannot hope to balance China militarily. The PRC significantly outmatches even the combined weight of ASEAN members in manpower, equipment, and spending. The imbalance is exacerbated by the failure of the ASEAN militaries to pool their defense resources and develop a joint military force. Furthermore, unlike South Korea, Japan, or Australia, most Southeast Asian states lack bilateral defense treaties with the United States. Nonetheless, some ASEAN officials have been privately pressing Washington to intervene on the South China Sea issue to discourage Chinese adventurism.

The U.S. government traditionally has sought to avoid taking a public stance on East Asian sovereignty disputes, but the recent assertive moves by China, combined with the quiet pleadings of some prominent ASEAN leaders to get more involved, galvanized the Obama administration into action. At the July 2010 meeting of the ARF in Hanoi, Secretary of State Hillary Clinton broke with U.S. precedent and offered to help launch multilateral talks on disputed South China Sea territories within the ASEAN framework. She also reaffirmed U.S. opposition to the use of coercion or threats of force to enforce conflicting claims. Clinton justified her statement of concern on this occasion by explaining that, "[the] United States, like every nation, has a national interest in freedom of navigation, open access to Asian maritime commons and respect for international law in the South China Sea."[8] PRC officials unsurprisingly denounced Clinton's efforts to "internationalize" the issue—the Chinese government's position was that neither the United States nor ASEAN as an institution had standing in the debate. Nonetheless, one-third of all the world's commercial shipping traverses waters that Chinese policymakers now claim belong to the PRC.[9]

JAPAN

The Japanese have become increasingly concerned with China's military intentions and capabilities. Japan's relationship with China, burdened by history and intermittent geopolitical disputes, is complex, made ever more so by the PRC's meteoric rise in recent years. Coinciding with Japan's "lost decade," China enjoyed rapid industrial growth during the 1990s and recently surpassed Japan as the world's second-largest economy, according to many measurements. Japan's security concerns regarding China include its expanding military budget and Beijing's exclusive claims to the shipping lanes and natural resources of the East China Sea. A Japanese government-sponsored task force in 2002 described Sino-Japanese ties as the "interweaving of 'cooperation and co-existence' with 'competition and friction,'" a characterization that still holds.[10] Many Japanese continue to see China as replete with tremendous commercial opportunities. Sino-Japanese trade has surpassed U.S.-Japan trade, placing China as Japan's top trading partner even excluding goods and service exchanged via Hong Kong.[11] The PRC is also a major destination for Japanese direct investment. Saddled with guilt for its fifteen-year occupation of China, the Japanese government provided the PRC with more than \$23 billion in development assistance from 1979 to 1999—despite Japan running a trade deficit with Beijing.[12]

Chinese leaders warily view Japan's growing military capabilities, expanding security role in East Asia, and efforts to revise the pacifist clauses in the Japanese constitution. In particular, Beijing fears that Tokyo's expanding military cooperation with the United States could lead to the provision of de facto Japanese assistance to Taiwan in a future cross-Strait confrontation. PRC strategists especially worry that Tokyo and Washington could share missile defense technologies with Taiwan, negating Beijing's deterrent strategy of threatening missile strikes in response to Taiwanese assertions of greater autonomy. Over the long term, Chinese security experts fear that Japan could exploit its technological and industrial potential, including the country's latent nuclear weapons capacity, to become a major military power.

Some of these mutual insecurity concerns emanate from the two nations' troubled shared history, with an unhealthy admixture of geopolitical competition and confrontational populist nationalism. Violence first broke out between China and Japan in 1894–1895, when the two states fought for control of the Korean peninsula. The Chinese people believe that the Japanese, who won the war, played a large role in "the century of humiliation," the period between 1838 and 1945 when China's weaknesses were routinely exploited by predatory foreign states.[13] During Japan's occupation of mainland China from 1931 to 1945, Japanese soldiers committed many war crimes against the Chinese population that are widely cited even today. Because of these wartime atrocities, the Chinese population is distrustful of the Japanese and quick to perceive signs of Japanese aggression. An example of this is the controversy surrounding Japanese officials who visit the Yasukuni Shrine, a memorial dedicated to the memory of Japan's war dead. Because this Shrine includes the remains of World War II Class-A war criminals, the PRC government and people interpret these visits as paying homage to these criminals. Another source of tension is Japan's portrayal of World War II in its history textbooks, which the Chinese see as whitewashing Japanese aggression and "an indication that Japan has not learned lessons from its past and [serves] as a dangerous signal that the right-wing groups are gaining power, which will lead to remilitarization of Japan and eventually jeopardize regional peace."[14] The bilateral negotiations that began in 2004 to resolve their conflicting sovereignty and territorial claims over the East China Sea have neither ended the dispute nor established an agreed mechanism for joint exploitation of the energy reserves, which lie within the two countries' overlapping maritime economic zones. As a result of this impasse, Chinese-Japanese energy collaboration remains focused mostly on bilateral conservation and environmental measures.

For almost two decades, Japan's leaders and public alike have expressed alarm at Chinese foreign policy actions. During the March 1996 crisis over Taiwan, the PRC launched missiles within the island's vicinity, threatening regional maritime commerce. Some of the missiles landed less than 100 kilometers from Okinawa.[15] A few months later, the sovereignty dispute between China and Japan over the Senkaku-Diaoyutai Islands in the East China Sea resurfaced. Japanese policy makers have also expressed concern about China's surge in military spending, which has increased by double digits for many years, a level exceeding the country's average annual economic growth rate.[16] The Japan Defense Agency's *Defense of Japan 2005* identified, for the first time, China's military modernization as potentially threatening and called on Beijing to make its defense programs more transparent.[17]

In a further escalation of tensions, the Chinese government suspended high-level summits with Japanese leaders outside the context of multilateral gatherings to protest Prime Minister Junichiro Koizumi's annual visits to the Yasukuni Shrine. Premier Wen Jiabao's April 2007 visit to Japan helped improve Sino-Japanese relations, but Wen and Prime Minister Shinzo Abe failed to achieve discernible progress on the Sino-Japanese dispute over the energy resources under the East China Sea. Even as Wen visited Tokyo, Japanese officials expressed concern about a report that China National Offshore Oil Corporation (CNOOC) Ltd., had begun processing oil and natural gas from the Chunxiao/ Shirakaba gas fields that are currently disputed by the two countries. At the summit, the two governments agreed only to continue bilateral discussions and to review a report on how their countries could jointly develop the undersea natural resources. In the National Defense Program Guidelines announced in December 2010, the Japanese government expressed concern about the PRC's military build-up as well as its increasing maritime activities in waters near Japan's southwest island chain. Japanese and U.S. officials have adopted hedging policies aimed at responding to a situation in which the PRC's rising economic, political, and military power becomes a security threat.[18] To Beijing's annoyance, the Japanese and U.S. foreign and defense ministers participating in the February 2005 SCC session publicly identified for the first time the "peaceful resolution of issues concerning the Taiwan Strait" as a "common strategic objective" in the Asia Pacific region.[19] When China's 2002 Defense white paper expressed disquiet over joint U.S.-Japanese missile defense research, the unstated concern was that the two countries could share their technologies with Taiwan.

Today, the greatest source of tension between China and Japan is the East China Sea, the body of water that separates eastern China from the southern islands of Japan. At its broadest point, the East China Sea is only 360 nautical miles wide; at its narrowest point, it is merely 180 miles wide. The locus of the dispute centers on an island chain, known in Japan as the Senkaku Islands and in China as the Diaoyu Islands. The islands themselves are not much more than rocky crags, but vast energy reserves and natural resources are believed to surround them. In addition to hosting rich fishing areas, the ocean's seabed is thought to hold large deposits of oil and natural gas—estimated at more than 100 billion barrels of oil and seven trillion cubic feet of natural gas.[20]

Since the late 1990s, Chinese ships have conducted unauthorized exploratory research within waters claimed by Japan, exacerbating their bilateral dispute over exploratory drilling rights in undersea natural gas fields in the East China Sea. According to the United Nations Convention on the Law of the Sea (UNCLOS), a state's Exclusive Economic Zone (EEZ) extends two hundred nautical miles from its shoreline. In addition, a country's EEZ could extend to the outer limit of the continental shelf that the state sits on if that outer edge is less than or equal to 350 nautical miles from the country's shoreline. Though this treaty has replaced many outdated treaties, its language remains ambiguous when it comes to determining what countries have the rights to certain islands. Japan adheres to the UN Law of the Sea when defining its EEZ as extending 200 miles from its shore. China asserts that its EEZ begins not at its coast but from the edge of its submerged continental shelf. Recent Chinese drilling at the Chunxiao/Shirakaba gas fields and Japan's response have highlighted the dangers of these conflicting claims. Although the fields lie just inside China's side of the meridian line separating the two countries' claims, Japanese experts believe that exploiting the fields would siphon gas from fields that extend under waters claimed by Japan—a situation disturbingly similar to that which Saddam Hussein cited to justify his invasion of Kuwait in 1990. The ambiguity surrounding the competing claims in the East China Sea has led to decades of conflict over control of the territory.

The conflict may decrease if the contested resources are determined to be much less valuable than expected. But even if the islands prove economically worthless, the strategic logic of Chinese-Japanese competition for maritime primacy is growing in importance. Many Japanese believe that China is trying to control the Western Pacific. In its 2011 white paper, the Japanese government blamed Beijing for its assertive naval activity in the contested waters. The paper repeated earlier criticism about the size and opaqueness of China's military budget. The report marked a conceptual shift, depicting a pattern of Chinese aggressiveness rather than treating recent Sino-Japanese clashes as isolated incidents. Underlying their differences over history, natural resource claims, and military activities is the fundamental problem that East Asia has never experienced a situation in which both Japan and China were powerful and assertive states. Before Japan's 1868 Meiji Restoration, China was the dominant regional power. For the next century, Tokyo enjoyed a superior position, interrupted only for a short period after World War II. As a result of Japan's decade-long economic stagnation and China's remarkably successful economic transformation, East Asia now must make room for two roughly equivalent economic powers, both with expanding security concerns and military capabilities.[21]

TAIWAN

Taiwan became the home of the exiled Republic of China (ROC) in 1949, when the Kuomintang Party (KMT), also known as the Nationalist Party, lost the Chinese civil war to the Chinese Communist Party, and fled to Taiwan (then called Formosa). Although KMT leader Chiang Kai-Shek died in 1975, his son served as ROC premier from 1972 to 1978. He then became president after 1978. Shortly before his death in 1988, he introduced political reforms by ending martial law, allowing for the creation of new political parties, appointing native Taiwanese to prominent political positions, and granting greater media freedoms. The Democratic Progressive Party (DPP), founded in 1986 as an underground political movement, became the major opposition party and advocated Taiwan's independence from Beijing. Lee Teng-Hui, president and KMT leader from 1988 to 2000, introduced more political and economic reforms and also abandoned the original ROC goal of reunifying China under the KMT rule. Many Taiwanese had been shifting their focus from reclaiming the mainland to developing their island. In 1991, the Beijing-based Association for Relations Across the Taiwan Straits (ARATS) and the Taipei-situated Straits Exchange Foundation (SEF) were founded as quasi-governmental entities to allow the PRC and the ROC, which do not recognize each other's governments, to engage in discussions and reach agreements on a semiofficial basis. Both organizations entered into talks that culminated in the so-called 1992 Consensus. Although it remains a contested term, the Consensus essentially means that both governments agree that there is only one China even if they disagree over how to apply the principle. PRC policy makers believe that Beijing is the sole legitimate government of all China, including Taiwan, and that, as a province of the PRC, Taiwan cannot participate as a full-fledged political entity in international organizations such as the United Nations. For many Taiwanese, "one China" refers to the Republic of China or, in the case of ardent DPP supporters, simply recognizes the cultural and historical ties between their island and the mainland while not mandating Taiwan's political subordination to the physically and politically distant regime in Beijing.

The United States and other Asian countries continued to recognize the ROC government for years after the Communist victory in the Chinese Civil War. But by the 1970s, the United States and other countries sought to improve relations with the PRC to counter what was seen as the greater threat of Soviet expansionism. By 1971, Beijing had secured enough support that the UN General Assembly voted to transfer the China seat in the United Nations from the ROC to the PRC. In January 1979, following the signing of several bilateral communiques to govern their future relationship, the U.S. government severed official diplomatic relations with Taiwan, ended its bilateral defense agreement with Taipei, and formally recognized the PRC. Nevertheless, in April 1979, the

U.S. Congress enacted the Taiwan Relations Act (TRA), which reinstated unofficial economic and security ties with Taiwan, including the sale of arms. Among other provisions, the TRA commits the United States to supply Taiwan the weapons it needs to maintain a "sufficient self-defense capability." Denying any attempt to contain China, U.S. officials have justified these weapons sales on the grounds that they help sustain the peaceful status quo in the Strait by balancing the PLA's growing capabilities, thereby discouraging any PRC attempt to conquer Taiwan by force. Washington has worried that declining to assist the Taiwanese military could encourage Beijing to adopt more aggressive policies toward Taipei, increasing the risks of a Sino-American confrontation through miscalculation and inflicting a major economic shock on the PRC, Taiwan, the United States, and other countries. Less publicly, U.S. officials have also feared, particularly during the 1980s, that stopping arms sales or breaking additional security ties with Taiwan could have the unwelcoming effect of prompting a panicky Taipei to pursue nuclear weapons, long-range missiles, or other destabilizing strategic weapons. In contrast, PRC officials believe that the U.S. arms sales to Taiwan encourage the growth of proindependence sentiment on the island, thereby increasing international tensions and the risks of war. Chinese government white papers warn that U.S.-Taiwan relations remain a continuing obstacle to better Sino-American defense ties. They accuse the United States of stoking cross-Strait tensions by continuing "to sell arms to Taiwan in violation of the principles established in the three Sino-US joint communiqués, causing serious harm to Sino-US relations as well as peace and stability across the Taiwan Straits." The island has since the 1970s become an even more attractive partner for Americans since its government instituted political and economic reforms, including the holding of free and competitive elections. Taiwan has joined the East Asian economic "tigers" with high economic growth rates based on continually moving toward the leading edge of advanced technologies, relatively low income inequalities because of the use of small and medium businesses to distribute the benefits of growth widely, and important commercial ties to U.S. companies. In parallel with its signing of various communiques with China, the United States offered reassurances to Taiwan related to the TRA. The most important were the "Six Assurances," made to the ROC government on July 14, 1982, prior to the U.S. government's signing of the August 17, 1982 communique with the PRC, according to which the United States:

1. will not set a date for ending arms sales to the ROC

2. will not hold prior consultations with the PRC on arms sales to the ROC

3. will not play any mediation role between Taipei and Beijing

4. will not unilaterally revise the Taiwan Relations Act

5. has not altered its position regarding sovereignty over Taiwan, and

6. will not exert pressure on the ROC to enter into negotiations with the Chinese Communists.

Another important assurance was added in the 1990s. By then, Taiwan's democratization had preceded sufficiently far that the U.S. government began insisting that Taiwan's reunification into the PRC would require the support of the Taiwanese people, which thus far has been lacking.

Although PRC leaders have tenaciously adhered to the goal of cross-Strait reunification on Beijing's terms, China has employed changing policies to achieve this goal. PRC leaders have been making fewer military threats in recent years and instead have offered more positive inducements to influence Taiwan's policies. In April 1993, ARATS President Wang Daohan and SEF President Koo Chen-Fu held the first nongovernmental talks in Singapore. The Koo-Wang meeting resulted in the signing of four agreements designed to facilitate trade and economic cooperation between the ROC and the PRC. In regard to the sovereignty issue, both sides agreed that "each regards itself as the legitimate Government of the entirety."[22] In 1995 President Jiang Zemin delivered an eight-point speech on PRC-ROC relations that affirmed:

- The "One China" principle as the basis for peaceful reunification.
- Taiwan could have nongovernmental economic and cultural ties with foreign countries.
- China-Taiwan negotiations on a diverse range of issues.
- Beijing would only employ military force against those who impede China's reunification by striving for an independent Taiwan.
- Broadening cross-Strait economic ties.
- The existence of a common Chinese culture.
- China wanted a healthy and stable Taiwan.
- The importance of cross-Strait relations.[23]

That same year, however, Congressional pressure forced the Clinton administration to renege on its assurances to Beijing and let President Lee Teng-hui make a private visit in June 1995 to speak at Cornell University, his alma mater. PRC authorities reacted with anger, seeing it as implying a kind of official U.S. recognition of Lee's government, and recalled their ambassador to the United States, Li Daoyu, from Washington. More seriously, from July 1995 to March 1996, the PLA staged six massive military exercises in the Strait, including firing ballistic missiles close to Taiwan's major seaports in an effort to intimidate the Taiwanese people from supporting moves toward independence. Whatever its reservations about Lee, the Clinton administration by March 1996 felt compelled to react vigorously after the PLA conducted a series of missile launches, amphibious operations, and live-fire demonstrations near Taiwan. Washington deployed two aircraft carrier battle groups near the island to affirm U.S. support for Taiwan as well as to demonstrate Washington's readiness to use limited military force when necessary to uphold American interests. Although PRC authorities denounced the U.S. actions, the PLA soon ceased their threatening activities toward Taiwan. Shortly thereafter, Lee decisively won reelection, continuing strained PRC-ROC ties. On July 9, 1999, in an interview with Deutsche Well, Lee stated that Taiwan would conduct only "special state-to-state" relations with the PRC regime instead of negotiations under the one-China principle.[24] In an article published later that year in *Foreign Affairs*, Lee argued that Taiwan had a distinct national identity and referred to ROC citizens as the "new Taiwanese." He then set three preconditions for unification with mainland China: PRC goodwill toward the people of Taiwan, renunciation of the use of force toward Taiwan, and democratic reforms in the PRC. The following year, Beijing issued a white paper that rejected these conditions.[25]

In 2000, the DPP candidate, Chen Shui-Bian, won the presidency despite several PRC statements before the elections warning the Taiwanese against supporting him.[26] In 2002, Chen delivered an address to the 29th Annual Meeting of the World Federation of Taiwanese Associations in Japan, in which he said that there is "one country on each side of the straits." This statement infuriated the PRC, whose state-run media warned: "If we want to strive for peace, we have to be fully prepared for military action."[27] During the second half of 2003, Chen undertook a series of provocative initiatives such as resurrecting his controversial "one country on each side" statement and proposing referendums to enhance Taiwan's autonomous status in international organizations.[28] Having learned from its counterproductive response in 1995–1996, PRC leaders adopted a lower-key response on this occasion and instead the PRC leadership sought to work quietly with Washington to curb Chen's provocative actions.[29] U.S. policy makers were by then frustrated that Chen's attempts to assert greater autonomy from the mainland risked escalating into another Sino-American clash over Taiwan. In December 2003, PRC Premier Wen Jiabao visited Washington and secured a statement by the Bush administration that it opposed unilateral action that aimed to change the status quo regarding Taiwan.[30]

After Taiwanese voters reelected Chen in 2004 but defeated his referenda, the PRC enacted an Anti-Secession Law in 2005 that sanctioned "non-peaceful means and other necessary measures" should "possibilities for a peaceful reunification be completely exhausted." In 2005, President Hu issued four guidelines that would govern his policies toward the island, including "never sway in adhering to the one-China principle," "never give up efforts to seek peaceful reunification," "never change the principle of placing hope on the Taiwan people," and "never compromise in opposing the 'Taiwan independence' secessionist activities."[31] He repeated these "Four Nevers," which actually was a more positive message than that of previous Chinese presidents, at the 17th Party Congress in October 2007.[32]

In his Chinese New Year address on January 29, 2006, President Chen proposed abolishing the National Unification Guidelines and the National Unification Council, a step he took the following month. The Guidelines for National Unification, adopted by the Executive Yuan Council on February 23, 1991, outlined a three-step process for China's gradual reunification. Beijing attacked the decision. In 2007 Chen and the DPP announced they would hold a referendum on whether to use the name "Taiwan" in applying to join the United Nations at the time of the 2008 presidential elections. Although the referendum was widely seen as an election strategy appealing to DPP's supporters because Taiwan lacked the votes in the United Nations to enter the organization, a measure Beijing would veto in any case, the PRC's Taiwan Affairs Office Spokesman Yang Yi warned that, "The mainland is deeply concerned about the situation, and will not allow Taiwan secessionist forces to separate the island from China by any means, or in any form."[33] U.S. State Department spokesman Sean McCormack joined with Beijing in opposing the UN referendum and "any initiative that appears designed to change Taiwan's status unilaterally."[34] Taiwanese voters eventually rejected the referendum as well as Frank Hsieh Chang-ting, a former prime minister who ran as the DPP presidential candidate. Nationalist Party candidate Ma Ying-Jeou won the May 2008 elections with a resounding 58 percent share of the votes, the largest margin thus far in four Taiwanese presidential elections. Unlike Chen, whose DPP often lacked a majority in the national legislature during his presidency, Ma's KMT held a solid majority in the Legislative Yuan thanks to its victory in the January 2008 in parliamentary elections.

In his inaugural address, Ma stated that there would be "no reunification, no independence, and no use of force."[35] During the campaign, Ma emphasized the need to revive the Taiwanese economy and advocated expanding social and economic ties with the Chinese mainland, including restoring direct communications, postal, and other commercial links that had atrophied under Chen. Although Ma had expressed willingness to sign a formal treaty with the mainland, Ma has declined to embrace Beijing's version of the One China principle, urging instead that both nations set aside ideological issues and concentrate on economic cooperation. After a nine-year hiatus, the ARATS and the SEF resumed formal talks on June 13, 2008. Four months later, ARATS Chairman Chen Yunlin and SEF Chairman Chiang Pin-kun signed agreements that included the "Three Directs" of direct flights, direct shipping, and direct postal services, replacing circuitous routes that often had to go through Hong Kong.[36] In December 2008, at the 4th Cross-Strait Economic, Trade and Cultural Forum, the PRC announced ten measures toward Taiwan designed to enhance economic cooperation. The third round of ARATS-SEF talks took place in April 2009 in Nanjing. Three agreements were signed, which dealt with regular passage/cargo direct flights, financial cooperation, and countering crime. The two countries signed their most important accord, the Economic Cooperation Framework Agreement (ECFA), in June 2010. The ECFA provides for tariff reductions and greater commerce between Taiwan and the mainland. After it took effect in September 2010, both sides made reciprocal tariff reductions, which reduced the costs to businesses and customers on both sides of the Strait. The agreement has also made Taiwan a more attractive place for foreign investors, because they can export some of their goods into China duty free. Taiwanese opponents of the ECFA protested that Beijing sought to entice Taiwan into becoming economically dependent on the mainland.

Ma and the KMT won reelection in 2012, though with a decreased margin of victory in both the presidential and legislative ballots. On balance, relations between Taiwan and the PRC have never been better. There is no immediate threat of war. Conversely, economic, cultural, and quasi-governmental cross-Strait exchanges and ties have flourished. Taiwan-PRC bilateral trade now amounts to more than $150 billion annually. Hundreds of direct flights each day bring more than 100,000 mainland tourists each month to Taiwan and Taiwanese business managers to the PRC. Taiwanese companies have invested more than $100 billion in China, taking advantage of the lower costs of production and the common languages. Cultural exchanges between China and Taiwan have also grown. Although the parties have yet to negotiate political or security agreements, some of their bilateral agreements invariably touch on political issues, with PRC and ROC officials now routinely consulting on noncontroversial questions of implementation rather than relying on the less efficient process of working exclusively through the quasi-governmental associations. The main Taiwanese complaint at present is that the PRC needs to implement some of the cultural agreements more equably—such as letting in more Taiwanese films, books, and so on. Nonetheless, Ma sees a "virtuous circle" at work in which Taiwan's improving ties with the mainland enhance Taiwan's foreign relations, such as with the United States, while deeper international ties make the Taiwanese people more confident about dealing with the PRC. Before the ECFA, only North Korea joined Taiwan in not being well integrated with the network of free trade agreements that linked northeast Asia. Now the deal and better PRC-ROC ties have made other countries more comfortable reaching economic agreements with Taiwan without worrying about Beijing's reaction. Singapore is actively negotiating a free trade agreement with Taiwan, whose trade with many other countries besides China has already increased considerably in recent years. The rhetoric coming from Beijing is of peaceful reunification, not armed liberation. The Taiwanese government no longer engages in provocative actions.

Despite the change of government in Taipei, the PRC is still seeking to deter Taiwan from declaring independence through military coercion combined with other political, social, and economic means. The PLA now has approximately 500 warplanes and more than one thousand ballistic missiles and hundreds of cruise missiles stationed within range of Taiwan. Besides this quantitative dimension, the PLA inventory facing Taiwan is being modernized. Its extended-range, antiaccess/area denial capabilities are also growing and could degrade the U.S. military's ability to rapidly move forces into the western Pacific if the need arose.

To this end, the PLA is pursuing capabilities to both defeat Taiwan in any military confrontation and to deter, delay, or deny potential U.S. military intervention on Taipei's behalf. DPP leaders cite this buildup in arguing that the Nationalist government is embracing the PRC too soon, too fast, and too much. They argue that Taiwanese businesses and workers suffer from competition from lower-cost PRC competitors. They also correctly observe that China is promoting economic integration as a means toward Taiwan's eventual political integration. Even so, compared with the 2008 elections, in 2012 the candidates argued over the relative costs and benefits of various policies rather than over existential questions such as Taiwan's national identity.

Taiwan has continued to develop its military strength. In 2012, the most notable of these were the Han Kuang Military Exercises in April, the Lien Yung Exercises in June, and the Live-Fire Missile Exercises in early July. Taiwan has also moved forward with its acquisition and deployment of new technologies. Taiwan plans to upgrade 56 F–CK–1 indigenous defense fighters between 2014 and 2017. It has also received U.S. approval to retrofit all the 145 F-16A/B fighters in its fleet with advanced electronic warfare suites, radar capabilities, and other upgrades. Taiwan would like to receive the more advanced F–16 C/Ds, and ideally the F-35. Taiwan has recently deployed land attack cruise missiles capable of striking military bases in China and has also developed Hsin-Hai Missile Corvettes, a 12,500-ton platform equipped with eight antiship cruise missiles. This warship is expected to be delivered in 2014, with a life span of 25 years. Furthermore, Taiwan is planning to build its own submarines through an Indigenous Submarine Development Project. Finally, Taiwan is upgrading its air and missile defense systems to the Patriot Advanced Capability–3 configuration.[37]

Nonetheless, the Pentagon believes that the PLA's modernization drive continues to shift the military balance further in Beijing's favor. Taiwan's defense budget has at times fallen below the 3 percent of GDP floor the government has established as its preferred spending level. During the 2000–2011 period, Taiwan's defense budget increased by less than 2 percent annually, on an inflation-adjusted basis, from $8.3 billion in 2000 to $10.1 billion in 2011 (which actually was a decrease from the peak year of 2008, when Taiwan's spending amounted to $10.8 billion, resulting in a 17.7 percent increase over the previous year). But because Taiwan's active-duty force decreased from 370,000 to 290,000 personnel during this period (a 21.6 percent reduction in troop numbers), its per-soldier defense spending rose more than twice as fast, over 4 percent each year. This trend toward a smaller but higher quality force should continue as Taiwan phases out conscription in favor of an all-volunteer professional force. But Taiwan also must spend considerable funds to replace its aging Mirage 2000 and F-5 fighters.[38]

Chinese policy makers try to reinforce their advantage by denying Taiwan access to foreign arms supplies. The PRC again froze U.S.-Chinese defense relations after the Bush administration notified Congress in 2008 of plans to sell

Taiwan $6.5 billion in military equipment. Ties only resumed in earnest when Barack Obama became president. On January 29, 2010, the Obama administration unveiled a $6.4 billion arms deal with Taiwan. The deal included 60 UH-60M Blackhawk helicopters, 114 PAC-3 missiles and their accompanying radar systems, two Osprey-class mine-hunting ships, 12 Harpoon antiship missiles, and an array of advanced communications equipment. Absent from the deal were F-16C/D fighter jets and diesel-fueled submarines, two items of special interest to Taipei, and of special concern to Beijing. In response to the arms deal, the PRC Foreign Ministry said that, "The U.S. move pose[s] grave danger to China's core interests and hurts bilateral ties seriously, which will inevitably affect bilateral cooperation on some major regional and international issues,"[39] though the damage was limited because of U.S. restraint in providing the most sensitive systems and, perhaps, the improvement in cross-Strait ties.

The United States continues its policy of strategic ambiguity, not taking sides on what Taiwan's ultimate fate should be, but insisting that Beijing-Taipei differences should be settled by peaceful means and implying that the United States might take military action to help defend Taiwan. Some realists argue that the United States should decrease its security ties with Taiwan in coming years now that mainland China has become much more important for U.S. security and economic health. But other analysts believe this distancing would be counterproductive because Taiwan contributes to U.S. security in multiple ways, from serving as a key trip wire of how China will use its growing power, to helping reinforce the credibility of other U.S. alliances in the Asia-Pacific region, to serving as a key element of the all-important East Asian security architecture that has provided such peace and prosperity to the Asia-Pacific region, including the United States. Proponents of continuing arms sales maintain that they help provide the reassurance the Taiwanese need to engage with the PRC. They hope that over time PRC policy makers will understand this benefit and that enticing Taiwan closer to the mainland requires that Beijing make more comprehensive economic and political reforms and cease threatening Taiwan.

THE KOREAS

China is North Korea's most important foreign diplomatic, economic, and security partner. Through the Six-Party Talks and other mechanisms, PRC policy makers have sought to induce the Democratic People's Republic of Korea (DPRK) to relinquish its nuclear weapons and moderate its foreign and defense policies in return for security assurances, economic assistance, and diplomatic acceptance by the rest of the international community. Such a benign outcome would avoid the feared consequences of precipitous regime change— humanitarian emergencies, economic reconstruction, arms races, and military conflicts.

The Chinese have long opposed North Korea's acquisition of nuclear weapons, if for no other reason than its advent might induce South Korea, Japan, and even Taiwan to pursue their own nuclear forces, which under some contingencies might be used against Beijing as well as Pyongyang. PRC decision makers presumably would also like to avoid the negative reaction in Washington and other capitals that would arise if it became evident that Pyongyang had retransferred materials and technologies originally provided by China to third countries. There is evidence that North Korea has supported the WMD and ballistic missile programs of Pakistan, Iran, Syria, and other countries of proliferation concern.

PRC leaders also fear that these ostentatious displays of North Korea's improving missile and nuclear capacities will further encourage the United States, Japan, Taiwan, and other states to develop missile defenses that will in turn weaken the effectiveness of Beijing's cherished ballistic missile arsenal. China's increasingly sophisticated missiles represent a core element of its national security strategy. It has deployed over one thousand intermediate-range missiles within distance of Taiwan to deter, and if necessary punish, Taipei from pursuing policies objectionable to Beijing. In addition, PRC strategists see their strengthening missile capabilities as a decisive instrument for executing their antiaccess/area-denial strategy against the United States. The Chinese military seeks the ability to target any U.S. military forces, including aircraft carriers, which attempt to defend Taiwan or otherwise confront Chinese forces. As a last resort, the PRC relies on its long-range strategic ballistic missiles to deter the United States from employing its own nuclear forces against China.

Despite their irritation with the DPRK regime, most Chinese officials appear more concerned about the potential collapse of the North Korean state than about its intransigence on the nuclear and missile questions. PRC policy makers fear that North Korea's disintegration could induce widespread economic disruptions in East Asia; generate large refugee flows across their borders; weaken China's influence in the Koreas by ending their unique status as interlocutors with Pyongyang; allow the U.S. military to concentrate its military potential in other theaters (e.g., Taiwan); and potentially remove a buffer separating their borders from American ground forces (i.e., should the U.S. Army redeploy into northern Korea). At worst, the DPRK's collapse could precipitate military conflict and civil strife on the peninsula—which could spill across into Chinese territory. PRC policy makers have therefore consistently resisted military action, severe economic sanctions, and other developments that could threaten stability on the Korean peninsula.

To prevent these adverse outcomes, PRC policy makers continue to take steps to avert state failure in North Korea and counter other possible sources of chaos on the Korean peninsula. China still provides the DPRK with essential supplies of food, weapons, and other economic and political support. PRC enterprises also maintain substantial investments in North Korea. Although China provides much economic and technological aid to the DPRK, presumably some economic transactions occur because of commercial considerations that provide some benefits to the Chinese partner. Through high-level visits, Chinese leaders have encouraged North Koreans to pursue economic reform, based on the Beijing model. Such lobbying occurred during the visits of North Korean leader Kim Jong-il to China in 2004 and 2006 and of President Hu Jintao to North Korea in 2005. These growing economic ties with the DPRK, as well as the PRC's security and other interests in North Korea, give many Chinese a major stake in averting additional economic sanctions, not antagonizing the DPRK leadership to such an extent that North Korea might retaliate against Chinese economic interests, and above all avoiding regime change in Pyongyang. This desire to avoid antagonizing Pyongyang partly explains why Chinese authorities continue their controversial policy of forcefully repatriating North Korean political and religious refugees back to the DPRK. Official PRC policy treats all North Koreans who enter China without permission as economic migrants, even though some leave for noneconomic reasons. A bilateral treaty requires Chinese authorities to repatriate them to the DPRK. Fear of antagonizing North Korean leaders, along with a natural desire to avoid thinking about unpleasant outcomes, also explains why Chinese officials have declined U.S. proposals to discuss how their two countries might respond to various DPRK contingencies.

To limit external threats to the DPRK, Chinese government representatives have consistently striven to downplay concerns about the extent of North Korea's missile program and nuclear activities, including evidence of the DPRK's involvement in the proliferation of nuclear and other WMD technologies to third parties. They depict Pyongyang less as a nuclear-armed rogue regime than as a potential failed state and humanitarian disaster. They have also argued that the United States and other countries would need to make some concessions to Pyongyang to secure North Korea's denuclearization, rather than expect North Korea to disarm first before discussing the provision of any possible rewards. Along with South Korea and Russia, China has resisted imposing sanctions that could inflict severe harm on the fragile North Korean economy.

The close alignment between Seoul and Washington in recent years has reinforced Beijing's caution about breaking with the DPRK. The PRC and South Korea established formal diplomatic relations in 1992. Since then, their economic exchanges have soared, with China overtaking the United States as the ROK's main trading partner. China has become the main destination for the ROK's foreign direct investment (FDI), which has made South Korea China's third largest source of FDI.[40] Reciprocal military visits and other exchanges have also blossomed. Yet, tight ROK-U.S. ties have reinforced PRC fears that the DPRK's collapse would be swiftly followed by an extension of the ROK-U.S. alliance northward in the same manner as when NATO moved its defenses eastward into the countries that broke free of Moscow's control in the 1990s. Beijing's policy of returning DPRK refugees caught in the PRC to severe punishment, if not death, in the North also remains a source of bilateral tension between China and South Korea.

RUSSIA

For several years now, Chinese and Russian leaders and commentators have described their bilateral relationship as the best it has ever been. In June 2009, Chinese President Hu Jintao visited Russia to celebrate the 60th anniversary of the establishment of diplomatic relations between Moscow—at the time the capital of the Soviet Union rather than the Russian Federation—and the PRC. He discussed high-level exchanges, mutually supportive statements, and other manifestations of Russian-Chinese cooperation—what both governments refer to as a developing strategic partnership. On the day of President Hu's arrival, Russian President Dmitry Medvedev stated in an interview: "Speaking with utmost openness, this is the highest level of ties in the history of Russian-Chinese relations."[41] The presidents, prime ministers, and other senior officials of Russia and China frequently meet at multilateral conferences and at regular visits to one another's countries. Some of the most important products of these encounters are their individual speeches and joint statements; through these declarations, Russian and Chinese officials try to enunciate a shared vision for global affairs. Their joint statements typically call for a multipolar international system in which the United Nations and international law dominate decision making on all important questions, including the possible use of force. Furthermore, they stress the value of traditional interpretations of national sovereignty rather than the promotion of universal democratic values or other ideologies. Russia and China regularly endorse one another's policies and refrain from criticizing one another's controversial actions. In April 2009, Foreign Minister Sergey Lavrov explained that "Russia and China have a common vision of the contemporary world and of its development trends; a common vision of ways to tackle global and regional problems based on international law, a more central role for the UN, and multilateral diplomacy."[42] Lavrov further asserted that Russian and Chinese leaders "always support each other on concrete issues that directly affect the national interests of Russia and China."[43]

The Russian-Chinese Friendship and Cooperation Treaty—signed in July 2001—established a basis for extensive security and defense collaboration between both countries.[44] Its five core principles include "mutual respect of state sovereignty and territorial integrity, mutual non-aggression, mutual non-interference in each other's internal affairs, equality and mutual benefit and peaceful co-existence." Still, a recurring theme of Russian-Chinese joint statements is the call for a "multipolar" world. In such a framework, Russia and China would occupy key positions and no one great power—that is, the United States—would predominate. On May 20, 1997, both countries issued a joint statement that began: "In a spirit of partnership, the Parties shall strive to promote the multipolarization of the world and the establishment of a new international order."[45] Similarly, their March 2007 joint declaration called for a world that "will promote multilateralism and democracy in international relations." [46]

Russian-Chinese joint statements regularly affirm their shared commitment to upholding traditional interpretations of national sovereignty, which severely limit the right of external actors to challenge a state's internal policies. These statements uphold traditional interpretations of national sovereignty that exempt a government's internal policies from foreign criticism. Beijing and Moscow oppose American democracy promotion efforts, U.S. missile defense programs, and Washington's alleged plans to militarize outer space. The two countries strive to uphold the authority of the United Nations, where the Chinese and Russian delegations frequently collaborate to dilute resolutions seeking to impose sanctions on Burma, Iran, Zimbabwe, and other governments they consider friendly. Since 2005, Russia and China have begun holding major joint military exercises. In July 2008, the neighbors finally demarcated the last pieces of their 4,300-kilometer (2,700 mile) frontier—the longest land border in the world—which ended a decades-long dispute. Most Russian analysts, typically based in Moscow, perceive their main security challenges to the west and south as well as in Washington. They discount the emergence of a genuine military threat to Russia from China—for at least the next decade. With their blessing, the Russian defense industry has sold the Chinese military billions of dollars' worth of weapons, though these systems have typically been optimal for fighting a maritime war in the Pacific rather than a land war in the Russian Far East.

Although these assessments that Sino-Russian ties have never been better are probably correct, this metric does not present an especially high hurdle—their relationship has most often been characterized by bloody wars, imperial conquests, and mutual denunciations. It has only been within the last twenty years, when Russian power had been decapitated and China had become a rising economic power that the two countries have managed to reach a harmonious *modus vivendi*. According to various metrics, the PRC now has the world's second largest economy, while Russia lags near the bottom of the top ten and—because of its slower growth rates—is falling further behind China. However, Russia still has a more powerful military—especially in the nuclear realm. This equipoise has resulted in an improvement of bilateral ties, but not in a formal military alliance or even closely paired policies toward regional security developments in Asia or elsewhere.

CENTRAL ASIA

For centuries China has maintained ties with Central Asia, but Russian and Soviet control of the region since the nineteenth century largely severed these contacts. Since the demise of the USSR in 1990, China has reemerged as a major player in the region. In the security realm, Chinese authorities worry about the spread of potentially destabilizing ideologies—such as liberal democracy and Islamic fundamentalism—in Central Asia, both for their direct local effects and for the consequences of potential spillover into Chinese territory. For example, some of the members of the Uighur Diaspora in Central Asia—which numbers approximately half a million people—have been active in groups seeking an independent East Turkistan. The Chinese leadership has exploited the opportunity presented by Central Asians' striving for greater strategic autonomy and economic development, but cautiously, not wishing to antagonize Moscow by giving the impression that Beijing was seeking to displace Russia in a region that had been under Moscow's control for more than a century.

Beijing policymakers are uneasy about relying so heavily on vulnerable Persian Gulf energy sources, as Gulf oil shipments traverse sea-lanes susceptible to interception by the United States or other naval powers. In addition, the Chinese government recognizes that terrorism, military conflicts, and other instability in the Middle East could suddenly disrupt Gulf energy exports. Because Chinese efforts to import additional oil and gas from Russia have encountered problems, Beijing is pushing for the development of land-based oil and gas pipelines that would direct Central Asian energy resources eastward toward China. New inland routes would provide more secure energy supplies to China than existing sea-borne links. China is beginning to develop direct pipelines with its Central Asian neighbors, especially Kazakhstan. Avoiding political instability in these countries is a key concern of Chinese policymakers. Besides securing access to the region's energy resources, PRC officials also seek to enhance commerce between its relatively impoverished northwestern regions and their Central Asian neighbors; this consideration applies particularly to restless Xinjiang, as more than half the province's income derives from trade with Central Asian countries.[47] Trade across China's other borders with Central Asia also has been increasing—albeit starting from very low levels. The Chinese government has granted hundreds of millions of dollars of credit to Central Asian countries for the purchase of Chinese goods. Increased commerce could help promote the economic development of Xinjiang, Tibet, and other regions that have lagged behind China's vibrant eastern cities.

Countering unrest in Xinjiang is a major reason the Shanghai Cooperation Organization (SCO) has become one of the PRC's most important regional security institutions. China, along with Russia and the countries of Central Asia —except for Turkmenistan—established the SCO at an international meeting in Shanghai in 2001, a development that had a major impact on China's Eurasian policies. Whereas the focus of the preceding Shanghai Five group had been establishing stable border relations between the PRC and its four new post-Soviet neighbors, the SCO has pursued a broader and more positive agenda of furthering security, diplomatic, economic, and other types of relations among its Eurasian members and observers. The SCO's broader geographic and functional agenda has helped elevate China's ties with the other Central Asian states to a new level. PRC policymakers made sure that one of the SCO's avowed goals is to fight the "three evils" of "terrorism, separatism, and extremism." Beijing has used this provision and its influence within the SCO to pressure the other members to suppress Uighur opposition to Beijing in Central Asia.

The SCO has established a Regional Anti-Terrorism Center in which the member governments—which includes China, Russia, and all the Central Asian countries except Turkmenistan—share information about possible terrorist threats. The SCO also organizes periodic exercises involving paramilitary and law enforcement agencies to conduct counterterrorism operations. PRC officials have combined explicit and implicit threats with targeted economic and military assistance to induce other SCO governments to curb Uighur communities in Central Asia, to deport Uighur political refugees fleeing PRC persecution back to China, and to not protest Chinese repression in Xinjiang. The fact that Beijing shares SCO leadership with Moscow has generated tension between the two governments when they have advocated divergent policies for the organization. For example, PRC policymakers have warded off Russian attempts to give the SCO a major military dimension—China and some of the Central Asian governments want the SCO to remain primarily an antiterrorist institution that focuses on countering internal threats to members' security. Conversely, Moscow's opposition has blocked Beijing's proposals to establish an SCO-wide free trade zone, which could result in Chinese products driving Russian exporters out of their traditional Central Asian markets.

Besides securing access to energy resources, the Chinese also desire to expand commerce and increase their investment in Central Asia. Meanwhile, Central Asian political and business leaders see China as potentially the region's most important engine of future economic growth, a belief that has led them to embrace the PRC's growing presence and show respect for Beijing's economic and security preferences. China offers Central Asian countries billions of dollars in short-term credits and other loans. Beijing has proposed establishing a new multibillion dollar SCO Development Bank, with China initially lending the proposed institution most of its money. Nevertheless, major increases in Chinese economic exchanges with Central Asia will require substantial improvements in the capacity and security of the region's economic institutions and reductions in barriers to trade and investment. These encompass the strengthening of physical institutions such as east-west transportation links, but also improvements in visa and customs policies, the upgrading of financial and communications networks, and better respect for property rights and the rule of law. The legacy of the formerly integrated Soviet economy in Eurasia also presents a major barrier. At the time of their independence, the major roads, railways, and energy pipelines in the new states of Central Asia all flowed northward toward Russia rather than eastward toward the PRC. During the past decade, China and Central Asia have launched several initiatives to develop direct transportation links, including constructing multiple east-west energy pipelines and high-speed rail and road connections. These initiatives might accelerate should peace return to Afghanistan.

SOUTH ASIA

Relations between China and India have been strained because of long-standing territorial conflicts, economic issues, and reciprocal military modernization programs. The two governments have made little progress in resolving their border dispute. Since 2003, Chinese and Indian representatives have held more than a dozen rounds of formal negotiations by high-level special representatives to resolve the long-standing territorial disagreement, but the only significant achievement from these high-level exchanges—an April 2005 Sino-Indian agreement—simply outlines basic principles for mutual consideration in establishing a framework for resolving the dispute, rather than providing a detailed blueprint. In 2009, the Indian government announced it would deploy 60,000 troops in the disputed border region of Arunachal Pradesh, supported by India's frontline warplanes stationed in the region. Although PRC officials reacted calmly and simply reaffirmed Beijing's desire for a peacefully negotiated solution to their border disputes, the state-run press published several articles criticizing the Indian military buildup and hinting at Chinese retaliation.[48] The PRC became India's largest trading partner in 2008. Much of China's imports from India consist of low-end commodities and raw materials, as opposed to high value-added goods. Both countries complain about barriers to direct investment in the other's markets, though strategic considerations explain their wariness of inviting companies owned by a potential military rival to establish a permanent presence in their home markets. Another source of mutual strains is Indian fears of encirclement by China's cultivation of relations with Bangladesh, Pakistan, Sri Lanka, and other South Asian states. Some Indians see these ties as a Chinese "pincer movement" to contain India and focus New Delhi's strategic concerns on southern Asia rather than against China. Finally, the nuclear arms buildup of both countries has adversely affected regional security dynamics. Nevertheless, Indian analysts have seemed much more concerned with the PRC than Chinese policymakers have been about India. PRC strategists have often described India as a second-ranked power compared to Japan, Russia, and the United States. This perception may change because of India's growing military power and deepening security relationship with Washington.

Beijing has long cultivated close ties with India's archrival, Pakistan. The PRC has provided Pakistan with military equipment and technology, and helped Pakistan develop nuclear weapons and ballistic missiles. When India tested its nuclear weapons in May 1998, its government justified this controversial action by citing the threat posed by China's military ties with Pakistan, as well as Beijing's powerful nuclear capabilities—more so than the threat from Islamabad directly. China and Pakistan have been natural allies from around the time both states were founded in the late 1940s. Since then, while Pakistan and the PRC have developed cultural and economic ties, their shared strategic interests remain the main binding force of their relationship. PRC officials traditionally have considered Pakistan a counterweight to India in South Asia, an important base for enhancing Beijing's influence in Central Asia, and a significant economic partner—both directly and as a transit country. In addition to the economic and strategic benefits of assisting Pakistan, many Chinese strategists also view maintaining good relations with the Islamic Republic of Pakistan as helping boost Beijing's image in other Muslim nations in Asia, Africa, and the Middle East. Throughout the 1950s, China and Pakistan tended to focus their attention in different directions—with Islamabad looking westward and Beijing's leaders focusing inward—but a shared desire to contain India's influence in South Asia brought them together as strategic partners.

Chinese policymakers began to see Pakistan as an important ally against India, while Pakistani strategists conceived China in similar terms. Since then, a core Chinese objective has been to use Pakistan to balance, distract, and constrain India. For the last three decades, the PRC has become one of Pakistan's leading suppliers of conventional arms. PRC strategists believe that they can negate any Indian military threat to China by keeping New Delhi distracted with Pakistan's Beijing-supported military buildup. The PRC's security assistance has also included the training of Pakistani defense personnel, the sharing of military intelligence, and the holding of joint military and counterterrorist exercises. China's extensive assistance in the development of Pakistan's nuclear infrastructure concerns India as well as other countries. The PRC remains the only major nuclear weapons state willing to help Pakistan develop its civilian nuclear energy sector, providing technical and other dual-use assistance that could potentially assist Pakistan's nuclear weapons program. Yet, the PRC has provided only limited economic and security assistance—targeted to help Pakistan meet key needs that also coincide with Chinese interests—but not the kind of comprehensive economic and security assistance that Pakistan desires. Furthermore, PRC leaders remain concerned about Pakistanis' links with international terrorist groups, despite Pakistani government assertions that Islamabad will use its influence to divert Islamist militants away from Chinese targets. Beijing is also eager not to drive India into closer alignment with the United States through overly close ties with Pakistan.

Afghanistan has become an emerging area of security and economic interest for China in recent years. When the Taliban ruled most of Afghanistan and was hosting Al-Qaeda, they both provided substantial assistance to Uighur terrorists seeking to establish an independent Muslim state in Xinjiang. PRC policymakers want to prevent such a recurrence. Another Chinese concern is curbing the narcotics flows from Afghanistan into and through China. Although the PRC is not situated along the "Northern Route"—through which illicit Afghan drugs traditionally have entered Central Asia and Europe—new narcotics trafficking networks have developed since 2005 that transport the drugs from Afghanistan through Pakistan and from Central Asia into China.

After the Afghan government opened its energy, mineral, and raw material sectors to foreign investment in 2008, China rapidly became one of Afghanistan's largest foreign investors when a Chinese firm purchased a controlling stake in the Aynak copper field. The $3.5 billion bid offered by the state-owned China Metallurgical Group for the 30-year lease far exceeded the sums offered by competing Russian, American, and other foreign firms for the world's potentially largest undeveloped copper field.[49] More PRC investment may soon follow because Afghanistan is thought to have unexplored or underdeveloped reserves of oil, natural gas, iron, gold, copper, and other raw materials that China imports in abundance.[50] By acquiring these goods from Afghanistan, the PRC could further diversify its source of imports away from more distant world regions—whose products are transported to China along lengthy ocean shipping routes vulnerable to pirates, foreign navies, and other interruptions. Importing materials from Afghanistan also allows Beijing to pursue a more geographically balanced process of internal economic development. China's western provinces need readily available natural resources to develop. Trade with Afghanistan would accelerate the economic growth of the sensitive region of Xinjiang, which borders Afghanistan as well as Pakistan and the Central Asian republics—other countries that have seen considerable Chinese direct investment in recent years.

PRC representatives have expressed interest in assisting the Afghan government counter the Taliban insurgency and the country's narcotics trade. Yet, China's security ties with Afghanistan remain much less developed than with many other Central and South Asian governments—though they do resemble Beijing's policies in Iraq, which have focused on investing in the Iraqi energy sector while ignoring any major security presence. Chinese policymakers seem ambiguous about the roles of the United States and NATO in both Afghanistan and Iraq. They certainly do not want Islamist extremists to succeed there, because they could then use these territories to spread extremism within China. PRC officials also have traditionally avoided challenging the United States on core security issues—and the Obama administration has clearly identified the Afghan theater as one of them. Having the Americans take the lead in fighting Islamist insurgents in Afghanistan and elsewhere also relieves China of having to fight them directly. Yet, PRC policymakers do not support a long-term Western military presence in Afghanistan or the Central Asian region. Beijing's limited support for the NATO-U.S.-Afghan counterinsurgency campaign has provoked some irritation among Western observers about China's "free riding" on the back of dead European, American, and Afghan soldiers. Even so, the PRC government has continued to reject suggestions that it contribute combat forces to the NATO-led International Security Assistance Force seeking to pacify Afghanistan.

NOTES

1. Voice of America, "US-China Tensions Flare Over South China Sea Dispute," *VOA*, July 28, 2010, http://www.voanews.com/content/us-china-tensions-flare-over-south-china -sea-dispute-99538694/166117.html.

2. Ian Storey, "Trouble and Strife in the South China Sea: Vietnam and China," *China Brief* 8, no. 8 (April 14, 2008), http://www.jamestown.org/single/?no_cache=1&tx_ttnews %5Btt_news%5D=4854.

3. Edward Wong, "China Hedges Over Whether South China Sea Is a 'Core Interest' Worth War," *New York Times*, March 30, 2011, http://www.nytimes.com/2011/03/31/ world/asia/31beijing.html?_r=0.

4. Thomas Harding, "Chinese Nuclear Submarine Base," *The Telegraph,* May 1, 2008, http://www.telegraph.co.uk/news/worldnews/asia/china/1917167/Chinese-nuclear-submarine -base.html.

5. International Institute for Strategic Studies, "China's Three-Point Naval Strategy," *International Institute for Strategic Studies*, October 2010, http://www.iiss.org/publications/ strategic-comments/past-issues/volume-16-2010/october/chinas-three-point-naval-strategy.

6. Robert Sutter and Chin-Hao Huang, "China-Southeast Asia Relations: US Interventions Complicate China's Advances," *Comparative Connections* (October 2010), http://csis .org/files/publication/1003qchina_seasia.pdf.

7. Sheldon Simon, "US-Southeast Asia Relations: Growing Enmeshment in Regional Affairs," *Comparative Connections* (October 2010), http://csis.org/files/publication/1003qus _seasia.pdf.

8. Mark Landler, "Offering to Aid Talks, U.S. Challenges China on Disputed Islands," *New York Times*, July 23, 2010, http://www.nytimes.com/2010/07/24/world/asia/24diplo .html.

9. S. P. Seth, "US-China Strategic Competition," *Daily Times*, August 15, 2010, http://www .dailytimes.com.pk/default.asp?page=2010%5C08%5C15%5Cstory_15-8-2010_pg3_4.

10. Task Force on Foreign Relations for the Prime Minister (Japan), "Basic Strategies for Japan's Foreign Policy in the 21st Century: New Era, New Vision, New Diplomacy," *Prime Minister of Japan*, November 28, 2002, http://www.kantei.go.jp/foreign/policy/2002/ 1128tf_e.html.

11. Asahi Shimbun, "China Surpasses U.S. to Become Japan's Largest Trading Partner," *Asahi Shimbun*, April 26, 2007, http://www.asahi.com/english/Herald-asahi/ TKY200704260104.html.

12. Kenneth Pyle, *Japan Rising: The Resurgence of Japanese Power and Purpose* (New York: Public Affairs, 2007), 327.

13. Peter Hays Gries, "Nationalism, Indignation and China's Japan Policy," *SAIS Review* 25, no. 2 (Summer-Fall 2005), 107–109, http://muse.jhu.edu/login?auth=0&type =summary&url=/journals/sais_review/v025/25.2gries.pdf.

14. Jin Qiu, "The Politics of History and Historical Memory in China-Japan Relations," *Journal of Chinese Political Science* 11, no. 1 (2006), 38.

15. Morton I. Abramowitz, Funabashi Yoichi, and Wang Jisi, *China-Japan-U.S. Relations: Meeting New Challenges* (Tokyo: Japan Center for International Exchange, 2002), 50.

16. An extensive description of China's growing military capabilities appears in the annual U.S. Department of Defense reports to Congress on Chinese military power; see also Michael Armacost, "The Mismatch between Northeast Asian Change and American Distractions," *NBR Analysis*, 18, no. 1 (January 2007), 8, http://www.nbr.org/publications/analysis/pdf/vol18no1.pdf.

17. Japan Defense Agency, Defense of Japan 2005 (Summary/Tentative Translation), (Tokyo: 2005), 13, www.mod.go.jp/e/index_.htm.

18. This perception is shared by former officials of both the Bush and Clinton administrations; see Dan Blumenthal, "America and Japan Approach a Rising China," *AEI Asian Outlook*, no. 4 (December 2006), www.aei.org/docLib/20061208_200612AOg.pdf; and Richard Bush, "Abe Foreign Policy: A Good Start but Challenges Ahead," *Japan Economic Currents*, no. 64 (Winter 2007), 7, www.brook.edu/views/articles/bush/20070221.pdf.

19. U.S. Department of State, "Joint Statement of U.S.-Japan Security Consultative Committee," *Department of State*, February 19, 2005, http://www.state.gov/r/pa/prs/ps/2005/42490.htm.

20. U.S. Department of Defense, *Military Power of the People's Republic of China 2008* (Washington, DC: U.S. Department of Defense, 2008), 11, http://www.defense.gov/pubs/pdfs/China_Military_Report_08.pdf.

21. Some of these issues are addressed in Aaron L. Friedberg, "Ripe for Rivalry: Prospects for Peace in a Multipolar Asia," *International Security* 18, no. 3 (Winter 1993/94), 5–33.

22. Nicholas D. Kristof, "China and Taiwan Have First Talks," *New York Times*, April 28, 1993, http://www.nytimes.com/1993/04/28/world/china-and-taiwan-have-first-talks.html.

23. China Radio International, "Jiang Zemin's Eight-point Proposal," *China Radio International*, January 11, 2007, http://english.cri.cn/4426/2007/01/11/167@184028.htm.

24. Ramon H. Myers, "The Divided China Problem: Conflict Avoidance and Resolution," *Hoover Institution*, June 1, 2000, http://www.hoover.org/publications/monographs/27162.

25. Lee Teng-hui, "Understanding Taiwan: Bridging the Perception Gap," *Foreign Affairs* (November/December 1999), http://www.foreignaffairs.com/articles/55598/lee-teng-hui/understanding-taiwan-bridging-the-perception-gap.

26. Robert L. Suettinger, "Leadership Policy toward Taiwan and the United States in the Wake of Chen Shui-bian's Reelection," *China Leadership Monitor*, no. 11 (2004), http://media.hoover.org/sites/default/files/documents/clm11_rs.pdf.

27. Henry Chu, "In Rebuke of Taiwan, China Raises Specter of Military Clash," *Los Angeles Times*, August 8, 2002, http://articles.latimes.com/2002/aug/08/world/fg-chitai8.

28. The proposed referendum topic changed several times, and at various points dealt with Taiwan's participation in the World Health Organization, the establishment of Taiwan's fourth nuclear plant, to one asking Beijing to remove its missiles opposite Taiwan.

29. Philip P. Pan, "China Warns Taiwan Again on Issue of Independence," *Washington Post*, November 27, 2003.

30. Dana Milbank and Glenn Kessler, "President Warns Taiwan on Independence Efforts," *Washington Post*, December 10, 2003.

31. Xinhua, "Four-point Guidelines on Cross-Straits Relations Set Forth by President Hu (Full Text)," *Xinhuanet*, March 4, 2005, http://news.xinhuanet.com/english/2005-03/04/content_2651270.htm.

32. Hu Jintao, "Hold High the Great Banner of Socialism with Chinese Characteristics and Strive for New Victories in Building a Moderately Prosperous Society in All Respects" (speech presented at the 17th National Congress of the Communist Party of China, Beijing, Great Hall of the People, October 15, 2007), http://www.chinadaily.com.cn/china/2007-10/25/content_6204667_10.htm.

33. CCTV.com, "Chinese Mainland Official Slams Referendum Promoted by Taiwan Separatists," *Xinhuanet*, July 14, 2007, http://news.xinhuanet.com/english/2007-06/14/content_6241730.htm.

34. U.S. Department of State, "Taiwan U.N. Membership Referendum Opposed by United States," *America.gov*, June 25, 2007, http://www.america.gov/st/washfile-english/2007/June/20070625135742zjsredna0.3750421.html.

35. Taipei Times, "Ma's 'No War' Mantra Is Capitulation," *Taipei Times*, October 27, 2008, http://www.taipeitimes.com/News/editorials/archives/2008/10/27/2003427063.

36. "Next Chiang-Chen Meeting Crucial," *China Post*, October 27, 2008, http://www.chinapost.com.tw/taiwan/china-taiwan-relations/2008/10/27/180482/Next-Chiang-Chen.htm.

37. U.S.-China Economic and Security Review Commission, *2012 Report to Congress*.

38. David J. Berteau, Guy Ben-Ari, Joachim Hofbauer, Priscilla Hermann, and Sneha Raghavan, *Asian Defense Spending, 2000–2011* (Washington, DC: Center for Strategic and International Studies, October 2012), http://csis.org/publication/asian-defense-spending-2000-2011.

39. Xinhua, "China Urges U.S. Companies Stop Arms Sales to Taiwan," *People's Daily Online*, February 2, 2010, http://english.peopledaily.com.cn/90001/90776/90883/6885977.html.

40. Scott Snyder and See-won Byun, "China-Korea Relations: China's Post-Kim Jong Il Debate," *Comparative Connections* (January 2012), http://csis.org/files/publication/1103qchina_korea.pdf.

41. RIA Novosti, "President Medvedev's Interview with China Central Television," *RIA Novosti*, June 15, 2009, http://en.rian.ru/analysis/20090615/155252094.html.

42. Ministry of Foreign Affairs (Russia), "Transcript of Remarks and Response to Media Questions by Russian Minister of Foreign Affairs Sergey Lavrov Following Talks with Chinese Minister of Foreign Affairs Yang Jiechi," April 27, 2009, http://www.mid.ru/bdomp/brp_4.nsf/e78a48070f128a7b43256999005bcbb3/9da17eb2ca6711d7c32575a600255d45!OpenDocument.

43. Ibid.

44. Russian Federation and People's Republic of China, "Treaty of Good-Neighborliness and Friendly Cooperation Between the People's Republic of China and the Russian Federation," signed at Moscow, July 16, 2001, http://www.fmprc.gov.cn/eng/wjdt/2649/t15771.htm; Article 2 text: "The contracting parties reaffirm their commitment that they will not be the first to use nuclear weapons against each other nor target strategic nuclear missiles against each other."

45. *United Nations Security Council*, "Russian-Chinese Joint Declaration on a Multipolar World and the Establishment of a New International Order," *United Nations Security Council*, April 23, 1997, http://www.fas.org/news/russia/1997/a52—153en.htm.

46. Ministry of Foreign Affairs (PRC), "Joint Statement Between the People's Republic of China and the Russian Federation," *Ministry of Foreign Affairs (PRC)*, April 6, 2007, http://www.fmprc.gov.cn/eng/wjdt/2649/t309361.shtml.

47. Zhao Huaheng, "China, Russia, and the United States: Prospects for Cooperation in Central Asia," *CEF Quarterly: The Journal of the China-Eurasia Forum* (February 2005), p. 24, http://www.silkroadstudies.org/new/docs/CEF/CEF_Quarterly_Winter_2005.doc.pdf.

48. Damien Tomkins, "China-Indian Relations: An Unresolved Border and 60,000 Troops Deployed," *Atlantic Council*, June 23, 2009, http://www.acus.org/new_atlanticist/china-india-relations-unresolved-border-and-60000-military-personnel-deployed.

49. Ron Synovitz, "Afghanistan: China's Winning Bid For Copper Rights Includes Power Plant, Railroad," *Radio Free Europe/Radio Liberty*, November 24, 2007, http://www.rferl.org/content/article/1079190.html.

50. Nicklas Norling, "The Emerging China-Afghanistan Relationship," *Central Asia-Caucasus Institute Analyst*, May 14, 2008, http://www.cacianalyst.org/?q=node/4858.

CHAPTER 4

China and the Wider World

During the past two decades, the PRC has experienced a remarkable resurgence in international influence. Whereas Beijing was largely isolated and alienated following the June 1989 Tiananmen Square crackdown, today China's policies regularly dominate global affairs. Whenever possible, PRC policymakers have sought to address Western security concerns. Especially in their publicly declared policies, Beijing professes support for achieving mutually beneficial, "win-win" outcomes that advance Chinese, Western, and global interests. This solicitude to Western international interests is understandable—PRC officials and analysts consider the United States and its allies as the most influential global actors in security, economic, and diplomatic realms of vital importance to Beijing. Furthermore, they desire to maintain good bilateral relations with Washington and its allies as part of their general strategy of preserving a benign international environment in which Beijing's power and prosperity can increase unfettered by Western sanctions or other impediments to China's rise. But the PRC leadership has become increasingly insistent, now in the security realm as well as regarding economic issues, on defending China's national interests even in the face of Western opposition.

CHINA-U.S. RELATIONS

In 1989, President George H.W. Bush took office with the goal of integrating China, both politically and economically, into existing international institutions. His administration believed that China would eventually evolve into a more moderate political system. During the Reagan administration, members of Congress viewed China as a useful geopolitical ally against Soviet expansionism, and Bush, who had dealt extensively with China as head of the CIA and as

Reagan's Vice President, hoped to sustain that partnership. But the fall of the Berlin Wall, the collapse of the Soviet Union, and the June 1989 Tiananmen Square massacre of hundreds of peaceful democratic protestors prompted Congress to reevaluate its China policy. Bush resisted congressional pressure for many sanctions, arguing that an overtly harsh response would ruin bilateral relations with an important country and ultimately do more harm than good for the Chinese people. Iraq's invasion of Kuwait in August 1990 forced Western governments to engage with PRC leaders to prevent China's vetoing UN Security Council actions against Iraq. Even so, throughout his four-year term, Bush found it difficult to balance dealing with Beijing and Congress. Sino-American relations became strained by disputes over human rights, China's exports of missile and nuclear technologies, and U.S. military sales to Taiwan.

Through his "constructive engagement" policy, President Bill Clinton emphasized bilateral dialogue on China's domestic liberalization, global economic integration, and adherence to international norms. Clinton attempted to make China's Most Favored Nation (MFN) trade status contingent on the PRC's improving its human rights record, but Beijing denounced the effort as an unwarrantable intrusion into its internal affairs. Faced also with protests from U.S. business groups, Clinton eventually abandoned his efforts to make the renewals dependant on significant human rights progress. During Clinton's first term, from 1993 to 1996, domestic policy took center stage, while China-related issues received less attention. This loose White House supervision allowed individual U.S. government agencies to prioritize their own agendas, while Clinton rarely convened formal meetings of the National Security Council to coordinate these policies. Overall, the administration lacked a coherent official strategy for improving Sino-American relations. During Clinton's second term, congressional gridlock, the Lewinsky sex scandal, and other developments led Clinton to focus more attention on foreign policy. The administration made an effort to reinvigorate bilateral dialogue on regional security interests, especially in light of the 1995–1996 missile crises off the coast of Taiwan. But strained relations continued over China's World Trade Organization (WTO) status, as well as congressional allegations concerning Chinese commercial policies, human rights policy, and allegations of forced abortions and slave labor in China. The accidental U.S. bombing of China's Belgrade Embassy in May 1999, during the Kosovo air war, triggered one of the most serious modern Sino-American crises and resulted in the suspension of many official bilateral dialogues.

During his campaign for the presidency, George W. Bush described the Clinton administration's approach to China as "soft"—just as earlier presidential candidate Clinton described the prior administration's policy toward Beijing. Governor Bush characterized China as a strategic competitor, rather than a partner, and stated that he would do "whatever it takes" to defend Taiwan. PRC officials protested the Bush administration's unyielding position toward Taiwan.

Bush committed to strengthen U.S. nuclear forces and missile defenses. In office, he increased U.S. military surveillance flights near Chinese territory. Bilateral relations were further strained when a U.S. Navy surveillance plane collided with a Chinese fighter jet inside China's self-declared 200-nautical mile Exclusive Economic Zone in April 2001. However, the September 11 terrorist attacks later that year prompted Chinese and U.S. policymakers to devote more attention to their common interests, such as preventing regional terrorism and countering nuclear proliferation in East Asia. PRC leaders did not make a major effort to prevent the U.S. military invasions of Afghanistan and Iraq, and China then benefitted from the U.S. suppression of the anti-Beijing Uighur terrorists in Afghanistan and the new natural resource opportunities in both countries. The Bush administration's 2002 U.S. National Security Strategy called for better relations with China and saw PRC and U.S. diplomats join forces to restrain Taiwanese independence gestures. Through their many meetings at bilateral and multilateral events, Presidents Bush and Jiang developed good personal relations, which helped stabilize official ties.

The Barack Obama administration currently accepts China's rise as inevitable and not necessarily adverse to U.S. interests if Beijing can be persuaded to support U.S.-backed security and economic goals. These include the peaceful resolution of territorial disputes, freedom of maritime navigation, military transparency, respect for intellectual property, and fair commercial practices. In terms of tactics, the Obama administration relies heavily on making declarations of benign intent, strengthening international norms and institutions, increasing U.S. diplomacy and military engagement in the Asia-Pacific region, and deepening the interaction between PRC and U.S. civilian and military agencies. Perhaps the most original Obama administration strategy is attempting to build a regional economic and security multilateral architecture, consisting of diverse bilateral alignments, international organizations, formal rules, and informal norms that shape Chinese behavior in ways desired by the United States. U.S. officials note that—if successful—this constraining architecture could potentially reduce the need for active U.S. management and compensate for the anticipated decline of U.S. resources relative to those of China in the long run. The administration is committed to building a regional economic and security architecture that not only will engage ASEAN members through bilateral trade and security agreements, but also will constrain China's potentially disruptive behavior. Nonetheless, the Obama administration has also modified how it addresses Chinese concerns regarding its decisions. During Obama's first two years in office, the administration strived to avoid offending Beijing by not—for example—meeting with the Dalai Lama or selling the Taiwanese all the arms they desired. Even so, the PRC government still protested U.S. policies and—in some cases—elevated their demands in the face of the softer U.S. policies. In addition, the PRC confronted the United States over its naval presence in the

South China Sea. Since 2010, the Obama administration has tended to pay less attention to anticipated Chinese objections on the presumption that Beijing will still cooperate with the United States whenever it is in the PRC's interest to do so.

The Obama administration benefited from Chinese overreaching in 2009 and 2010, which alarmed many Asian leaders previously lulled by Beijing's earlier nonconfrontational policies in most of Asia. The Chinese provocations prompted newly anxious Asian countries to seek greater U.S. involvement in the region. PRC policymakers have since tempered their approach, which over time could weaken regional demands for a larger and more visible U.S. security presence in Asia. U.S. initiatives are widely seen—partly because of U.S. rhetoric—as aiming to counter China, which could limit support for some U.S. policies in some Asian countries. A deliberate U.S.-PRC military clash is extremely unlikely given the mutual economic interests of both countries and the obvious incentive for Beijing to bide its time while China—which recently became the second largest national economy in the world after the United States—continues its peaceful rise to global power. But the possibility of a military conflict through miscalculation always exists, so it is beneficial that both parties make clear their areas of security concern. In particular, the problem of Taiwan could also loom large in future relations. Yet, Sino-American tensions over Taiwan, U.S. military patrols near China, and mutual military buildups are downplayed rather than resolved. The long-term economic, ideological, and military sources of Sino-American tension persist and could easily manifest themselves in further confrontations over Iran, the Korean Peninsula, the South China Sea, or Taiwan.

EUROPE

The European Union's approach toward China in recent years has had a different dynamic than that of the United States. Even when operating collectively within the EU, Europeans do not exert the same level of influence over PRC policies that Americans often do. In the case of some of the most important security issues facing China, such as Taiwan and North Korea, PRC policymakers do not consider Europe a major player.[1] Meanwhile, Europeans are less influenced by the "China threat" than Americans. Because the EU's post-colonial governments no longer have a direct security concern in East Asia, the EU's China policy is economically focused on promoting the growth of Chinese imports from the EU, attract PRC investment, and protect the interests of European investors in China. Europeans simply do not perceive the PRC as a potential military adversary and have therefore been more open to transferring "dual-use" technology to the PRC, which can have military as well as civilian applications. From the European perspective, the "threats" that exist are mainly related to "soft areas," such as economic competition, environmental issues, illegal immigration, and transnational crime—these are issues where having Chinese cooperation is often helpful and sometimes vital.

Like the United States, Europe desires a well-integrated China that is a "responsible stakeholder" in the international system. Although the PRC may value the United States and the European Union on different strategic terms, both the United States and the European Union are attempting to engage Beijing while hedging against the emergence of a troublesome China. In the past few decades, China has become the EU's second-largest trading partner—behind the United States—and has purchased considerable European debt. EU firms engage in profitable joint investment, technology transfers, and coproduction with PRC firms. The agenda of EU-China relations includes political dialogue, security cooperation, regional security issues such as Iran and Africa as well as cultural and educational exchanges. Fundamental divergences exist regarding human rights, currency valuation, economic competition, arms sales, illegal immigration, transnational crime, intellectual property rights, and carbon emissions. However, through engagement in multiple areas, the European Union seeks to "socialize" the PRC by securing constructive Chinese participation in multilateral institutions and shaping Chinese actions to conform to international law and existing norms.

China-EU trade has grown 100-fold since the establishment of formal relations in 1975, making the PRC the EU's second largest trading partner after the United States. Meanwhile, the EU has become China's largest trading partner. The European Union was an earlier supporter of China joining the WTO; the entry did dramatically improve EU access to the Chinese market. However, the EU has also employed the regular Trade Policy Review of China in the WTO to address a number of issues it has with the PRC, including intellectual property rights, barriers to certain industries, and China's raw material trading practices. The EU-China High-Level Economic and Trade Dialogue, launched in Beijing in April 2008, has allowed the European Commission and the State Council of China to address these issues directly.[2] Although trade is the most notable indicator of strengthened Sino-European connections, ties have increased in other areas. Since 2003, the EU and China have acknowledged each other as "strategic partners."[3] The 2008 "Joint Statement of the 10th EU-China Annual Summit" indicated the comprehensive nature of EU-China relations, stressing political dialogue, multilateralism and the role of the UN, counterterrorism, acute regional issues such as Iran and Darfur, as well as business, cultural and educational exchanges. However, human rights disputes continue to disrupt relations between Europe and China. Beijing's actions in Tibet and Xinjiang have prompted prominent European criticism of China's human rights record.[4] Another source of tension is that, while the EU and China remain large trading partners, the deficit between the two countries is becoming an increasing concern for the EU.

The EU arms embargo, based on a 1989 European Commission declaration, is now seen by both Chinese and Europeans more as a symbolic act of protest than as a tool for actually changing Beijing's behavior. Technically, EU members are not legally forbidden from selling military items to China, though the declaration is widely seen as a political commitment. The constraints on arms exports do not aim to inflict economic punishment, but rather are designed to send a strong message about European values. There is no universal understanding of what the EU arms embargo entails in practice. Each EU member interprets the embargo in terms of its national laws, decision making processes, and regulations. Because the European Union lacks strong foreign policy institutions, the arms embargo against China is best seen as a collection of national EU arms embargoes. As a result, the EU's collective stance lacks coherence or a means of enforcement.

Proponents of repealing the arms embargo have offered a variety of arguments for removing it. First, they note that the embargo complicates the EU's relations with China and partially negates EU efforts to develop a strategic partnership with Beijing regarding key international issues. For example, in April 2012, Klaus Ebermann, a former EU ambassador to China, called for removing the arms embargo because it continued to "poison" EU-PRC ties.[5] It is publicly difficult for EU members to refuse to engage in defense industrial cooperation with Beijing when their leaders are describing China as a strategic partner. Some see ending the embargo as a step toward normalizing relations with China and helping it integrate in the modern liberal world as a responsible player. For many Europeans, China's rise has transformed the embargo from a symbolic gesture into a genuine trade impediment that decreases Beijing's willingness to do business with Europeans. PRC representatives acknowledge that the arms embargo has had little impact on their country's military capacity and has simply, in the words of China's ambassador to the European Union, denied European defense companies "a chunk of business."[6] PRC officials have pressed to obtain more advanced dual-use technologies from EU companies as well as a comprehensive repeal of the embargo. Chinese representatives have consistently described the embargo as an affront and have been lobbying the European Union to repeal it.[7] In January 2010, for instance, the PRC Foreign Ministry said that, "the [embargo's] discrimination does not go along with the current world trend and the development of a comprehensive strategic partnership between China and the EU."[8] Furthermore, the Chinese media belittles the EU's subordination to Washington: "if the EU repeatedly resorts to excuses of external factors . . . it will make people more convinced that the EU is still a political dwarf."[9] Yet, they complain about the embarrassment of EU governments placing China in the same category as other EU-sanctioned countries such as Sudan, Zimbabwe, and Myanmar. For example, in November 2011, Hua Chunying, counselor of the MFA's Department of European Affairs, said that the "Arms embargo against China, along with the [EU's denial of] market economy status issue, in essence, are symbols of political prejudice and inequality."[10] Similarly, Meng Xiangqing, deputy director of Strategic Research Institute at the PLA's National Defense University, said Beijing wanted to remove the embargo not to buy weapons but because "the arms ban is a purely political problem which embodies political discrimination and inequality." Despite its political nature, Meng explained that this issue was still important "because behind the political discrimination and inequality is whether there is strategic mutual trust between China and the EU."[11] Europeans obviously do not want to antagonize such an important trading partner, especially as they have become increasingly reliant on China's help for their economic recovery. But Beijing has taken self-defeating actions at key moments when it looked like the European Union might lift the embargo. For example, China enacted an "Anti-Secession Law" in March 2005 that legitimized its right to use force should Taiwan make moves toward independence. And in 2010, Chinese diplomats irritated many EU governments by urging EU embassies in Norway to not send representatives to the Nobel Prize awards ceremony for dissident Liu Xiaobo.[12]

Second, advocates of repeal note that the ban is poorly enforced, resulting in it being merely an annoyance for China without having much impact because of the embargo's porousness. According to the British Institute for Public Policy Research, despite the embargo, the United Kingdom has still been able to engage in the trade of weapons components and technologies with China, granting licenses to companies to sell £500 million worth of military technologies and parts to China between 1997 and 2006. In addition, the Chengdu Aircraft Corporation used French aircraft design software to develop its J-10 fighter.[13] There are many other examples of such sales.

Opponents of the arms embargo further believe it encourages China to develop its own domestic military research, development, and production capabilities, thus reducing the strategic comparative advantage of Western countries in these sectors and making it harder for Western analysts to follow developments regarding Chinese weapons capabilities. Increased dependence engendered by China-EU arms sales works both ways. EU governments could become more reluctant to challenge the PRC on disputed issues for fear of Beijing's curtailing its purchases of Western weapons. At the same time, expanding the EU's defense sales to the PRC could make the Chinese government hesitate to pursue policies Western governments oppose, for fear that the EU will retaliate by curtailing these sales. Some commercial considerations may also be at work in the effort to repeal the embargo. In light of the current global economic crisis and the low growth and elevated unemployment rates in many European countries, EU governments and companies are eager to remove barriers to their exports. Even if they do not sell arms to China, EU leaders might hope that China would reward a repeal of the embargo with increased purchases of EU goods. In addition, China is the largest creditor in the world; its foreign exchange reserves reached almost $3.2 trillion. Europe wants Beijing to use some of these vast reserves to help stabilize the euro and support the EU's economic recovery. The recent defense spending cuts imposed in many European countries as part of their austerity programs, which have followed years of reductions since at least the end of the Cold War, have decreased domestic sales opportunities for many EU defense companies. Meanwhile, the United States remains a reluctant purchaser of European military products. Sales to China could help European defense firms sustain their work forces, achieve economies of scale, and recoup R&D expenditures through larger production runs.

Perhaps more importantly, the embargo has had little effect in impeding China's military modernization. During the past decades, China has been able to buy entire weapons platforms—sophisticated warships, warplanes, and air defense missiles—from Russia, whose government and defense firms were eager to sell off excess Soviet weapons. Russia has also sold the PLA key defense components such as high-performance fighter aircraft engines and ship-to-ship missiles. Nevertheless, in recent years China's own defense industry has been able to make major weapons systems that are on par with late Soviet-era conventional weapons. In fact, China has ceased buying many Russian weapons because they no longer need the Soviet-era systems Moscow is eager to offer. Instead, the Chinese want Russia to sell its most sophisticated weapons systems, which Moscow refuses to do for fear that China would copy the technology or that the sales might disrupt regional military balances.

It is important to note that most advocates of lifting the embargo do not expect that the European Union would sell major weapons systems to China even if the EU lifts the ban. The intent is to normalize relations by eliminating an ineffective and offensive embargo. But China might be able to use the opening to acquire more dual-use technologies that could be used for military purposes. Proposals to relax the embargo have therefore always encountered strong U.S. opposition because the Pentagon could easily find itself fighting Chinese-armed countries if not the PLA itself.[14] The United States has potentially more to lose from China's military modernization compared to Europe. Unlike the Soviet Union, the PRC is not an existential threat to the EU's territorial integrity, political independence, or economic system. In contrast, the United States is concerned about China's military power because it potentially threatens U.S. forces and allies in Asia. For example, Beijing could plausibly interpret the embargo's lifting as signifying that Europe is less concerned about China's human rights practices, its growing and opaque military potential, Beijing's expansive territorial claims in the South China Sea, or China's position that it has the right to employ military force to recover Taiwan. Regarding the latter, there is a particular apprehension that EU action could precipitate an end to the recent warming of cross-Strait relations. The United States is also worried that strengthening economic and political ties between the European Union and China could risk neutralizing European support for U.S. efforts to deter Chinese aggression and direct China's rise in nonthreatening ways. U.S. officials occasionally encountered this problem in the past when Russia-EU ties were close. In addition, some U.S. policy makers fear that EU companies might transfer U.S. military technologies to China because of the extensive EU-U.S. defense industrial cooperation.[15] Members of Congress regularly threaten to limit such cooperation should the European Union lift the arms embargo on China. The U.S. retaliation would be even greater if China were ever to use European defense technology of even partial U.S. origin against the U.S. armed forces or those of U.S. allies. Lifting the ban on defense-related technology transfers to China could increase the PLA's access to useful military technologies that Beijing might incorporate in its own weapons. Most of these would go toward augmenting China's own military potential, but others could help the PRC raise its presence on the international arms market. However, China is not yet a major arms producer and exporter. It has supplied numerous governments (often with poor human rights records themselves) and militant groups with arms for decades, but with the exception of Iran and Pakistan and a few other countries, these sales have generally involved unsophisticated weapons. But helping develop the PRC's military-industrial complex could make the country a more formidable arms dealer. China's becoming a major arms seller could complicate international measures to influence the behavior of rogue states. For example, the United States and Israel led a successful campaign to induce Russia to cancel a lucrative contract with Tehran for S-300 surface-to-air missiles. The cancellation helped decrease pressure on Israel to launch an urgent air strike on Iran before the systems had become operational, which would have made any air strike against Iran much more difficult. At the time, Tehran approached China for such a system, but China's domestic equivalents to the S-300 were much less sophisticated. If the PRC could acquire more advanced defense-related technologies from the EU, Beijing might have been able to undercut the Western diplomatic victory and precipitate a Middle East war. Finally, China-EU mutual trade and investment have flourished despite the embargo, with Europe as the largest importer of PRC goods and China's second largest two-way trading partner.

Europeans generally agree that the arms embargo on China should be repealed at some point, but that now is a bad time to provoke another transatlantic crisis over the issue. The United States is currently pivoting its military capacity to Asia to better deal with China's rise. The Europeans could accelerate this trend if they offered to sell arms to China, which has already alarmed some Europeans who dread not having a major U.S. military presence in Europe. Not only could such sales increase U.S. fears about China's growing military capabilities, they might also stimulate American perceptions that ungrateful Europeans were free-riding on U.S. defense efforts in Asia and sacrificing common transatlantic security interests in the pursuit of commercial opportunities in Beijing. Japan and (more quietly) other East Asian allies of the United States have also cited these and other reasons as to why the European Union should not rush to repeal the embargo. "Economic pressures make it attractive to lift the embargo," a senior Japanese official told *The Daily Telegraph* in November 2010. "But we believe such an action will be short-sighted and dangerous."[16] The Japanese government subsequently lobbied hard against a December 2011 proposal by EU high representative Catherine Ashton to end the embargo, asserting that, "An end to the arms embargo would be a mistake, it would destabilize the situation in the region."[17] One proposal is to replace the embargo with a stronger EU "Code of Conduct" on arms exports that would better control weapons sales to China. The current 1998 EU Code of Conduct does not cover dual-use technologies, is not legally binding, and is subject to diverging interpretations by the various EU member governments.[18]

Another option—and a good one for many reasons in addition to the arms sales issue—would be to deepen the EU-U.S. dialogue regarding Asian security developments. That would ensure that Europeans appreciate the depth of current American concern about maintaining military balances in Asia and also allow Europeans an opportunity to explain their positions and perspectives. Arms sales by either party, including periodic efforts in the United States to grant waivers to U.S. companies for defense-related sales to China, should be discussed within this framework. At a minimum, the United States and European countries should notify all the participants in advance of any planned sales to China of weapons or dual-use technologies, which would allow for peer review of (and ideally peer pressure against) controversial exports. The parties could review the old multilateral Coordinating Committee on Export Controls (COCOM) system and the current Wassenaar Arrangement for guidance regarding what dual-use technologies should be subject to advanced notification. It would also be helpful if the parties routinely informed one another of the defense-relevant items that the Chinese express interest in acquiring, which would help apprise other Western governments of what capabilities the PRC is interested in and may soon be acquiring.

MIDDLE EAST

China has generally adopted a largely passive approach to many Middle Eastern developments during the past few decades. For example, it has allowed Russia, Europe, the United Nations, and especially the United States to play the lead role in the Israel-Palestine peace negotiations. However, China's growing Persian Gulf oil imports have made Beijing assume a more active role in the politics of the region. Ideally, the PRC does not want to alienate either the Middle Eastern regimes with whom Beijing enjoys significant energy partnerships or Western countries, which are its leading international economic partners. As of 2011, about half of China's crude oil imports came from the Middle East and

North Africa, with some 3 percent shipped from Libya.[19] Due in part to its growing oil imports and its expanding consumer goods exports, China surpassed the United States in 2009 to become the leading national trading partner of the Middle East. Before the recent crisis, about 75 Chinese companies engaged in $18.8 billion worth of business in Libya.[20]

The PRC government opposed the U.S. intervention in Iraq in 2003 and maintained that U.S. actions violated international law because of the lack of a supporting UN Security Council resolution authorizing military action. The PRC strongly supports traditional interpretations of national sovereignty that severely restrict the right of foreign powers or international organizations to intervene in a country's internal affairs. For example, they have regularly objected not only to U.S. and NATO military operations in the Middle East, but also to Russia's efforts to secure international recognition of the separatist governments of Abkhazia and South Ossetia, which successfully broke away from Georgia with the help of the Russian military intervention in 2008. Yet, strategic and economic concerns involving oil and construction contracts played a significant role in determining China's low-key response to the Iraq War as well. Since the 2003 invasion, the PRC has sought to restore commercial ties with Iraq by forgiving part of its debt to Beijing. In return, the PRC wishes to secure access to Iraq's oil reserves—as evidenced by a major oil deal involving the China National Petroleum Corporation in August 2008.

The PRC government defends Iran's right to pursue nuclear activities for peaceful purposes, such as civilian energy production.[21] PRC representatives also warn against holding Tehran to unjustly higher standards than other countries. The PRC's recent defense white paper, *China's National Defense in 2008*, published in early 2009, calls for an integrated approach that addresses "both the symptoms and root causes of proliferation." The paper insists that realizing this objective requires that "double standards must be abandoned" and that nonproliferation disputes must be resolved through "dialogue and negotiation."[22] In the case of Iran, the paper affirms that, "China maintains that the Iranian nuclear issue should be resolved peacefully by political and diplomatic means."[23] Unlike Western countries, PRC policy makers do not oppose Iran's nonproliferation program because they believe that Iran would not threaten to use nuclear weapons against China. Their main fear is that Iran's nuclear program will increase the risk of war in the Middle East, the source of about half of China's imported oil. With PRC-Iranian economic ties soaring in recent years, China has become the leading investor and trade partner of Iran, surpassing European countries and staying ahead of Russian and Indian business enterprises. PRC firms have helped modernize Iran's energy industry and transportation infrastructure (including highways and railroads and even Tehran's Metro system) as well as extract natural resources such as coal, copper, and aluminum. In addition, Chinese companies such as the NORINCO defense conglomerate have sold Iran important industrial and military technologies, especially suitable for cruise missiles. The 2003 U.S. invasion of Iraq and subsequent occupation has driven Beijing and Tehran closer, with China eager to secure additional Middle Eastern oil supplies and Iran seeking diplomatic allies to counterbalance Western military threats and economic sanctions. From 2005 through 2009, Iran has emerged as the second-largest purchaser of PRC weapons. One path to war would see Israel or the United States try to attack Iran preemptively. Another would be Iran, emboldened by its nuclear shield, acting more aggressively against its oil-rich neighbors in the Gulf. Perhaps the worst scenario would see Iran's acquisition of nuclear weapons prompting its neighbors to acquire their own nuclear deterrent, leading to a nuclear arms race and, through spiraling fears or miscalculation, escalation to a nuclear war. All these scenarios could disrupt oil deliveries to China and considerably raise the costs of China's energy imports. The 2011 Libyan War gave the Chinese a foreboding of all the complications that could arise from a war in one of their minor oil suppliers.

The PRC has invested heavily in developing these strategic and economic ties with Iran. Chinese officials may want the Iranian regime to change its behavior regarding its suspicious nuclear activities, but they fear regime change in Tehran more. They are well aware from the 2009 public protests that, should the opposition ever come to power in Tehran, China could lose all these investments. The new Iranian leaders would not view past Chinese backing for Iran's authoritarian clerical regime that kindly. Chinese interests would suffer even if the new government eschewed a punitive policy and simply reconciled Iran with the West by agreeing to make its nuclear programs more transparent and more constrained. Some Iranian businesses would naturally gravitate toward Western partners, undermining China's monopoly position, while the end of active confrontation between Iran and the West would allow U.S. diplomacy and military power to refocus elsewhere, probably including the Asia Pacific region. Beijing may also be unable to play its Iran card because Washington would no longer need China's help to constrain Iran. This would deprive Beijing of the implicit threat of supporting an anti-American government in Tehran if the United States sold more arms to Taiwan.

With regard to the war in Libya, the PRC juggled the interests of many involved actors: the Arab League and the African Union supported foreign military intervention; whereas Gaddafi's ample oil and gas reserves were attractive to Chinese leaders. Though Gaddafi did not respect China and often criticized the PRC government, the economic cooperation between the two parties kept relations positive and profitable. The Libyan situation proved to be a true balancing act for China, which criticized the NATO airstrikes that it tacitly allowed. With Gaddafi out of power, the Chinese have accepted the new regime and have pursued access to Libya's oil and gas reserves. The PRC leaders never considered Libya or Syria to be vital interests to Beijing—unlike Taiwan, Tibet, Xinjiang, and the South China Sea. The PRC's share of trade with Syria comprises only a marginal share of its overall trade. Furthermore, China does not conduct arms sales with Syria or have access to a Syrian naval facility.[24]

Beijing could have made stronger moves to ensure that Western powers limited their use of force, but China did not want to alienate Middle Eastern regimes and Western countries with whom Beijing had cultivated valuable energy and other economic ties. Western countries pointed out that in 2005, China supported a UN resolution endorsing the "responsibility to protect" policy whereby the international community should protect populations from genocide, war crimes, ethnic cleansing and crimes against humanity if a government is unwilling or unable to protect its people. Beijing's most noteworthy measure regarding the Libyan War was how the PLA conducted its most complex military operation in the Mediterranean to date by undertaking a major air and sea evacuation of the approximately 36,000 Chinese nationals from the region in the days before the no-fly zone took effect.[25] They were employed mainly in the country's energy sector, but also were assisting with the construction of railway lines, irrigation systems, and communications infrastructure.[26] Although most Chinese workers left on ferries leased from Greece—a recent beneficiary of a large Chinese loan—the PLA Navy diverted the *Xuzhou* frigate from its anti-piracy patrol duties in the Gulf of Aden while Chinese transport planes arrived from Xinjiang.[27] Smaller numbers of Chinese nationals were evacuated from Tunisia, Egypt, and other Middle Eastern countries during this wave of civil strife.

In contrast, the PRC government has taken an atypically strong stand in joining with Russia in opposing the efforts of most Arab countries—supported by Western governments—to change the Syrian government of President Bashar al-Assad. Both governments have rejected several draft UNSC resolutions condemning Assad. The one blocked on February 4, 2012 would have supported an Arab League peace plan that would have required Assad to transfer power to a deputy, who would then have negotiated with the opposition to form a unity government within two months. Interestingly, China, unlike Russia, seems motivated primarily by ideological principles rather than concrete strategic and economic interests in Syria, of which Beijing has few compared with Moscow. In the case of Syria, "China maintains that any attempt by the international community to help Syria solve its crisis must respect the sovereignty, independence and territorial integrity of the country."[28] PRC officials have sought a peaceful solution to the conflict through negotiations within the framework of international consensus; they claimed that the resolution's backers were trying to interfere in the internal affairs of a UN member country by seeking to change its regime in pursuit of their larger goals of controlling the region. "Western powers hoped to further exert pressure on Syrian President Bashar al-Assad to step down," opined a commentary published in *China Daily* after the February 2012 UN vote, "thus paving the way for the removal of a regime that is an obstacle to their policies in the Middle East."[29] They argue that the Syrian people should be able to choose their leaders without outside interference. Furthermore, PRC analysts do not think that Assad's resignation alone would end the fighting in Syria. Rather than pacify Assad's opponents, Chinese officials fear that Assad's removal would simply encourage them to escalate their demands. Regime collapse would result in fighting among the elements of the winning coalition over their division of the spoils, with the most ruthless factions—often Islamist extremists—having the best shot at power. A *China Daily* editorial noted that the Libyan example showed how Qaddafi's overthrow did not bring "democracy and freedom" to the Libyans, but instead led to the country "falling into a sectarian civil war."[30] That Western governments had explicitly ruled out military intervention against Syria might have emboldened Chinese resistance because Beijing could plausibly interpret Syria as being of less importance to the West than Libya or Iran. In these cases, China has most likely consented to sanctions because Western governments have refused to exclude the use of force against them. A more-credible Western threat to intervene in Syria might have induced Beijing to agree to sanctions or other measures to avert it. But making threats to invade Syria, or actually doing so, might further increase tensions with Beijing and make it even more difficult to secure Beijing's help in future engagements.

SUB-SAHARAN AFRICA

In the past decade, Sino-African relations have increased in importance. Recent trends point to Chinese involvement in three areas of interest: economic policy, diplomacy, and military cooperation. Beijing's policies with reference to sub-Saharan Africa reflect clear goals: expanding export markets (to Africa's growing middle class), gaining access to the continent's mineral riches (oil, gas, rare earth minerals), and increasing China's international influence. China overtook France as sub-Saharan Africa's number two trading partner in 2006 and three years later overtook the United States to become sub-Saharan Africa's main trading partner. By 2011, direct trade between China and Africa had increased to $166 billion, with China running a $20-billion deficit.[31] In the past few years, China's Export-Import Bank, the Chinese Development Bank, and other Chinese financial institutions have provided more loans to African countries than the World Bank.[32] The PRC has soft power in Africa based on its diplomatic relations, cultural exchanges, multilateral summits, its policy of noninterference, and its large personnel training program. Between 2006 and 2009, the PRC trained 15,000 African personnel, a number that was supposed to increase from 2010 to 2012.[33]

Finally, the PRC's military presence in Africa has grown in the past decade, marked by an increase in Chinese involvement in UN peacekeeping operations and military-to-military relations. In November 2011, China had sixteen attaché offices in Africa, as well as 1,600 personnel assigned to six UN peacekeeping operations.[34] The PLA's role in Africa likely will increase if current trends continue. As China's economic presence in the region grows, maintaining a capable security presence is crucial in protecting Chinese nationals in Africa and in promoting regional stability. Beijing has demonstrated a growing willingness to pursue its economic and diplomatic goals in Africa through peacekeeping and military-to-military relations. Africa functions as a place where the PLA can test its capabilities during UN peacekeeping missions and other multilateral security operations. PRC involvement in Africa, often portrayed as a "mad scramble" for natural resources, has been viewed as a threat to U.S. interests, as well as to the stability and democratization on the continent. Others suggest that cooperation between Africa, China, and the West is possible since Africa is large enough to accommodate trade among all parties. Another debate concentrates on the reality of a coherent Chinese strategy in Africa with Beijing facing many policy challenges in Africa because of China's noninterference policy, its controversial arms sales, the recent increase of Chinese immigration to Africa, and private-sector business practices.

Sino-African relations date back to the early fifteenth century, when Fleet Admiral Zheng He sailed to East Africa. PRC officials cite the history of China's peaceful involvement in Africa as evidence of mutual trade and friendly relations.[35] Since colonialism ended in Africa, China has maintained a subtle presence on the continent by offering aid and support to protect its interests, but claims to have never intervened in the internal affairs of African states. The PRC's early involvement in Africa had a strong ideological nature, with their foreign policy aiming to "export revolution" during the 1960s and 1970s. In 1962, China sent advisers to train rebel forces opposing Cyrille Adoula in the Congo.[36] They also provided weapons and propaganda pamphlets to dissident underground groups in Cameroon.[37] In 1964, China assisted the National Front for the Liberation of Angola (FNLA), sending small arms and light weapons. Chinese arms that had been stockpiled in Mobutu's Zaire were used to supplement the FNLA forces' inventory when shipments in Tanzania were not allowed to pass through Zambia.[38] Two years later, after President Kwame Nkrumah of Ghana was overthrown in a February 1966 coup, China sent thirteen guerrilla warfare instructors to assist the new military regime.[39] A year later, 500 Chinese automatic rifles were sent to Eritrea and 25 revolutionaries were allowed to train in the PRC.[40] The PRC's military presence in Africa after the Cold War is best characterized by support for status quo regimes and regional stability through military-military relations, peacekeeping missions, and arms sales. During the late 1960s and 1970s, competing with Moscow for leadership within the world communist movement became more important. In the 1980s, Chinese policy shifted toward an economic focus, with the idea of "common development" through PRC investment projects that benefited China as well as Africa. PRC policy makers also tried to use pledges of official development assistance to induce African governments to transfer their recognition from Taiwan to the PRC.[41] Military support for revolutionary insurgencies decreased while that for established governments grew. The trend toward greater Chinese emphasis on economic goals increased during the 1990s.

The year 2000 marked a significant milestone in Sino-African relations: the establishment of the Forum on China-Africa Cooperation (FOCAC). The "going out" (*zou chuqu*) strategy that was then incorporated in the 2001–2006 five-year plan, which established favorable policies, regulations, and support for overseas investment, represented a significant policy shift and an important evolution in Chinese strategic thought.[42] The PRC demonstrated further commitment in 2006 by publishing "China's Africa Policy," a white paper that outlined Beijing's position on politics, economics, security, education, science, culture, and health regarding the continent. PRC officials use the regular FOCAC meetings not only to demonstrate commitment to Africa but also to announce future initiatives. The 2006 Forum launched a $5 billion China-Africa Development Fund, whereas in 2009 Beijing pledged an additional $10 billion in concessional loans to show its commitment to mutual economic growth. Under the FOCAC's auspices, China has launched initiatives in education, work training, health, agriculture, clean energy, drinking water, medical care, disease prevention, and food production as features of the "eight-point plans" that extend beyond traditional economic and trade cooperation.[43] The PRC also supports the African Union (AU), both financially and publicly. A recent example of China's support was the unveiling of the new Chinese-funded $200 million AU headquarters in Addis Ababa in January 2012.[44] China has funded a variety of infrastructure projects across Africa, including dams, sports stadiums, and even mosques.[45] In accordance with its noninterference policy, China defers to the AU on all human rights cases claiming that, "[The African Union is most] qualified to make judgments on the domestic affairs of African countries."[46]

Despite not having military bases in Africa, China has increased its military presence in the region over the past decade—primarily through peacekeeping missions, security assistance, arms sales, and military exchanges. As previously stated, the PRC was militarily involved in Congo, Cameroon, Ghana, Eritrea, and Angola during the 1960s and 1970s. Because of China's current economic and diplomatic goals, "exporting revolution" is no longer the motivation for maintaining a military presence in Africa. Instead, ensuring that valuable resources continue to flow to China has emerged as a major priority, best pursued through maintaining some degree of stability and order in Africa and the international waters around it. The PLA is beginning to develop capabilities to protect sea lanes as well as Chinese citizens in times of political instability.

China sells weapons to African governments and contributes to regional peace-keeping forces. Furthermore, the PRC increasingly promotes meetings between PRC and African officers, technological exchanges, and joint military co-operation. These efforts are relatively small, but Africa offers a training ground for the PRC's extended military deployment capabilities. At present, China mostly deploys forces in Africa under the auspices of multilateral organizations, which decreases concerns about the PLA's presence in Africa. The PLA Navy counterpiracy contributions in the Gulf of Aden have also increased international acceptance of the PLA's expanding military reach.

In the past decade, the PLA has increasingly participated in multilateral secu-rity arrangements in response to Africa's fragile security situation. Since 2000—when China deployed fewer than 100 peacekeepers—there has been nearly a twenty-fold increase in troops-on-the-ground. In recent years, China has pro-vided more troops, police, and observer teams to UN peacekeeping missions than Great Britain, Russia, and the United States.[47] The United States pays a higher proportion of UN peacekeeping costs in Africa than does China, but has fewer personnel assigned to Africa.[48] As of March 2012, China contributed 1,904 troops, military police and civilians to UN operations, while the United States deployed only 131 personnel.[49] Nearly 75 percent of China's peacekeeping forces are concentrated in Africa, while only 7 of the 16 UN operations are cur-rently deployed in Africa.[50] Skeptics of China's intentions in Africa frequently point to Chinese presence in resource-rich countries and claim that gaining access to resources is the primary motivation for Chinese involvement in UN peacekeeping efforts. In response, the PRC cites its peacekeeping role in Western Sahara, where China has little interest in trade.[51] As of April 2012, missions with some PRC presence include Western Sahara (MINURSO), the Democratic Republic of Congo (MONUC), Darfur (UNAMID), Sudan (UNISFA), South Sudan (UNMISS), Cote d'Ivoire (UNOCI), and Liberia (UNMIL).[52]

One benefit of the continued deployment and redeployment of Chinese peace-keeping troops in Africa is the accumulation of operational knowledge through experience-based training: China's increasing interaction with other militaries has helped teach the PLA about its own strengths and weaknesses in deploying ground forces operationally.[53] According to a U.S. Army report, "Lectures and case studies cannot substitute for experience because experience-based training is the most effective method for acquiring action-based skills."[54] Serving in regional peacekeeping operations (PKO) is one of the few opportunities PLA personnel have to serve in the field. The PLA is able to cycle more than 2,000 officers and troops through Africa annually since their tours of duty on PKOs are typically six to twelve months long.[55] Because these forces are drawn from select units, many Chinese officers are deployed to Africa several times during their careers. As a result, these officers often obtain a high level of tactical and operational knowledge. Peacekeeping consists of more than blue-helmeted soldiers—behind these soldiers are peacekeepers known as "blue-berets."[56] They are responsible for nation-building and act as an intermediary for the military elements and civilian law and order. In recent years, the PLA has increased its number of "blue-berets" on UN peacekeeping missions. These officers have been involved in reforming political, judicial and penal processes, training police, providing electoral assistance, and disarming and rehabilitating former combatants.[57] By placing PLA officers in highly visible assistance positions, China adds an important diplomatic aspect to its military presence in Africa and also encourages citizen-to-citizen exchanges. PRC participation in UN peacekeeping operations not only lends credibility to its economic and diplomatic efforts on the continent, but also helps it secure a reputation as a responsible stakeholder among African populations and within the international community. Furthermore, participation in PKOs downplays international perceptions of China as a military threat. At the same time, the PRC benefits from responding to African countries that request that the PLA take a more active role. China recognizes that political stability in Africa complements its economic interests, and thus trumps ideological commitments to noninterference in particular situations.

High-level military visits are an important part of China's security relationship with Africa. More than two dozen African countries have defense attachés in Beijing whereas China has almost as many defense attaché offices in Africa.[58] Although the PRC's military presence is relatively small compared to that of the United States—which, by contrast, has an entire African Command (AFRICOM) for Africa—the PRC is rapidly increasing its military presence.[59] The PRC has strengthened its military-to-military cooperation with African states—notably with its assistance in counterpiracy operations, antidrug smuggling training, and peacekeeping operations. These long-term military commitments—coupled with Chinese loans and aid for Africa—give the PRC significant influence on the continent. High-level visits between Chinese and African military officers foster open and meaningful relations between the respective militaries. Between 2001 and 2006, senior PLA officers visited Africa more than 30 times.[60] At a press briefing in October 2011, a Ministry of Defense spokesman stated that China attaches great importance to cooperation with developing countries and this is abundantly clear in Africa.[61] The PLA Navy has been engaged in antipiracy operations and involved in the protection of Chinese merchant vessels off the coast of Somalia—in the Gulf of Aden—for quite some time. This operation accounts for the largest Chinese military presence in Africa and is China's most visible military activity associated with the continent; the Chinese supplied three ships in 2009 to contribute to the operation. Pirates routinely threaten Sino-African trade by hampering shipments of goods in the region. In response, China has invested in maritime security and has invited the South African Navy to assist China.[62] As Sino-African trade continues to grow, more Chinese ships may engage in international maritime security operations. In December 2011 the

Republic of Seychelles invited China to set up a military base to enhance antipiracy measures along the eastern coast of Africa—an indicator of growing Chinese military influence. The Seychelles government cited Chinese interests in the region and the PLAN's experience in antipiracy operations as reasons to engage with the Chinese; moreover, a 2004 military cooperation agreement between the two countries enabled about 50 Seychelles soldiers to train in China.[63] A naval base in the Seychelles would not only boost China's prestige, but would also provide a platform for the PLAN to train and conduct operations, and augment the PLA's presence in the Indian Ocean.

The PRC has sold military technologies in Africa and has improved the security capabilities of African militaries for some time. Between 1955 and 1977, China sold $142 million worth of military equipment to Africa. From 1996 to 2003, China was responsible for about 10 percent of the conventional arms trade in Africa.[64] The Sino-African arms trade has continued to grow, with 17 percent of China's $2.1 billion arms sales going to African countries in 2005.[65] From 2006 to 2010, the PRC was the largest supplier of major conventional arms to sub-Saharan Africa (excluding South Africa), accounting for 25 percent of arms exports to the region.[66] As of August 2011, the PRC government has sold armaments and military equipment to 23 out of 57 African countries.[67] The PRC also sends military advisers to many of Africa's resource-rich countries, such as Nigeria and Angola—both of which are major oil producers. Chinese infrastructure projects supervised by the Chinese Ministry of Defense have included the construction of arms factories in Uganda and Sudan.[68] Chinese military relations with Zimbabwe have also spanned several decades.[69]

However, the PRC's noninterference policy affects Chinese military strategy. Beijing rarely holds African governments accountable for any misuse of weapons or technologies and frequently draws criticism from the international community for its indiscriminant sale of arms on the continent. Article Five of the amended set of *Regulations on Export Control of Military Items* that China follows states: "military-products export should proceed under the following principles: being useful to the self-defense capabilities of the recipient country; being not harmful to the peace, security, and stability of the relevant region or the world; and staying hands off the recipient country's internal affairs."[70] The first principle does not limit China, because dictators, warlords, and juntas wish to increase their self-defense capabilities as much as anyone else; thus, regimes with poor human rights records have access to weapons under this criterion. The last two principles are somewhat contradictory; the internal stability of Sudan is a perfect example. In this instance, circumventing a UN arms embargo on Darfur by supplying Khartoum with weapons directly arguably harms regional and global "peace, security, and stability."

In addition to Sudan, other countries such as Angola, Burundi, Equatorial Guinea, Eritrea, Ethiopia, Nigeria, Tanzania, and Zimbabwe have purchased weapons from Chinese companies, many of which are state-controlled. Arms sales have helped the PRC gain important African allies in the United Nations. PRC arms sales have also been coupled with oil and other raw resource deals. Recently, the PRC sold $100 million worth of fighter jets to Sudan, including a dozen supersonic F-7s.[71] In 2008 and 2009, the PRC sold Sudan $23 million worth of artillery and nearly $11 million worth of tanks and other armored vehicles to complement the $1.8 million worth of firearms they had already sold.[72] The PRC profited from arms deals during the 1998–2000 Ethiopia-Eritrea border conflict, selling $1 billion worth of arms to both sides during the conflict.[73] The PRC is a long-standing supporter of Zimbabwe. China has sold jet fighters, military vehicles, and weapons as well as radio-jamming devices to Robert Mugabe's regime. Reports indicate that jamming devices are used to "prevent independent [radio] stations from contradicting the state-controlled media."[74] In 2004, Zimbabwe paid $200 million for twelve fighter jets and 100 military vehicles and, in 2005, it spent $245 million on a dozen K-8 light attack aircraft from China.[75] Furthermore, Zimbabwe purchased six training aircraft for $120 million from the China Nanchang Aircraft Manufacturing Corporation, which has very close ties to both the People's Liberation Army (PLA) and Chinese Communist Party (CCP).[76] The Chinese have provided military training in Equatorial Guinea for equipment that the host country does not yet possess—presumably in anticipation of a future agreement.[77] Furthermore, PLA heavy artillery specialists were sent to Equatorial Guinea to help conduct training exercises.

Though China's involvement in the African arms trade is relatively small at present, the transfer of armaments and military technologies has grown, along with the frequency of peacekeeping operations and the increase in military-to-military relations. By combining these elements, China secures access to African resources and voting partners in international institutions like the UN. The PLA's role in Africa will also likely grow. Considering that the number of Chinese nationals in Africa is increasing because of Sino-African infrastructure deals, there may be around one million PRC citizens in Africa at any one time.[78] In January 2012, the MFA confirmed that militants in the South Kordofan region abducted 29 Chinese nationals after an attack on a Chinese energy company.[79] Sudanese forces rescued the workers who escaped the attack; however, the International Red Cross ultimately brokered the deal for the release of the captured Chinese workers.[80] Providing adequate ground security for Chinese citizens remains a significant challenge to the PLA. When events in Libya endangered Chinese nationals in the country, the PLA conducted a successful noncombatant evacuation operation of 35,000 PRC citizens in February 2011, setting a precedent as the first time that China sent military assets to a distant part of the world to protect its citizens.[81] During the Libya operation, four PLA Air Force (PLAAF) IL-76s heavy transport planes used Khartoum, Sudan as a waypoint for refueling on the inbound and outbound legs of the flight—a signal that the Sudanese government is comfortable with complying with Chinese requests.[82] African countries that may have future security issues that threaten PRC economic and diplomatic interests could well see the PLA intervene to rescue Chinese citizens, protect PRC investments, and otherwise assume the gendarmerie functions commonly pursued by other great powers in Africa.

SOUTH AMERICA

Starting from a level of low engagement in all areas, China's involvement in South America has increased rapidly in the past decade. Trade in both directions has flourished and Chinese investment is playing a substantial role in shaping South America's socioeconomic development. Beijing's South America policy focuses overwhelmingly on pursuing policies that will help fuel the PRC's continued growth, while maintaining a low profile in the more incendiary areas of political and military ties. Beijing has deliberately limited its military involvement in South America to avoid adding yet another source of tension with the United States. The PRC's regional security activities comprise mainly limited exchanges, arms sales, and modest participation in regional humanitarian missions. However, China's involvement in these areas continues to grow, both to serve economic objectives and to lay the foundation for possible increased ties in the future.

The PRC's most substantial involvement in the security realm is military exchanges with South American countries, though these occur less frequently than those with China and Asian, Western, and African countries. This activity comprises both visits by high-ranking officers and officials as well educational exchanges through military educational programs.[83] Although the most frequent participants in these programs come from Brazil, Chile, Colombia, and Venezuela, PRC military schools and institutions have hosted personnel from many other South American countries.[84] These visits are important for developing relationships and enabling the Chinese military to gain intelligence concerning South American militaries and the regional security environment.[85] The high-level visits also allow arms sales to be discussed, an important element of China's security ties with some South American countries such as those that adhere to an anti-American, populist line or whose cash-strapped militaries cannot afford the more advanced weapons sold by Russia, Europe, or the United States. Given the recent paucity of interstate wars in South America, these countries can logically accept less sophisticated Chinese weapons that are still useful for internal security purposes, such as combating threats from nonstate actors and thwarting international organized crime, such as drug trafficking. Major Chinese sales to South America in recent years have included aircraft, radar systems, and small arms and light weapons. Important customers have included Argentina, Bolivia, Ecuador, Peru, and Venezuela.

Nonetheless, certain barriers have limited Chinese arms sales to South America. These impediments have resulted in only 6 percent of China's total arms sales going to South America during the 2007–2011 period.[86] Some militaries still consider PRC-made weapons as inferior to Russian or Western-made ones. They are willing to pay a price premium for the perceived higher quality or for prestige and status considerations. In addition, many South American countries are reluctant to switch to new arms suppliers, which would present compatibility challenges as well as the need for retraining, and new maintenance and logistics procedures.[87] One additional negative factor associated with PRC arms is that they often end up in the hands of regional paramilitary groups such as Columbia's FARC guerrillas or with Mexican drug cartels. Although China does not sell them the arms directly, its reputation suffers when third-party dealers transfer PRC-made small arms and light weapons without Beijing's approval.

China has kept its military presence in South America limited, fearing that a larger presence would alarm the United States. The PRC's participation in military operations has therefore been restricted to the area of humanitarian assistance. The largest mission thus far has been in the United Nations Stabilization Mission in Haiti (MINUSTAH), which Beijing has supported since the UN Security Council first authorized the mission in 2004. Even here, China's contribution has been in the form of 100 or more riot police rather than military personnel. In 2010 China conducted its first bilateral military exercises in the region during the Peace Angel mission in Peru, which was a humanitarian exercise simulating the provision of medical services in a disaster scenario.[88] China also sent its "Peace Ark" hospital ship to the Caribbean. The ship traveled to Cuba, Trinidad and Tobago, Jamaica, and Costa Rica, where it provided medical services to citizens and military personnel. While part of the motivation for sending the ship may have been genuine humanitarian concern, the deployment also raises China's "soft power" by increasing goodwill toward China in the region. The cruise could also give the PLA Navy experience in sending a ship on a long-term mission across the world. More generally, these humanitarian deployments emphasize Beijing's attempts to make positive contributions to international security and can benefit the PLA at home because the humanitarian missions proudly display its growing global role and could help it win some budget battles and prestige in China.[89]

Nonetheless, the PLA's small military presence in South America seems intended primarily to support the main nondefense foreign-policy goals of the Chinese government, namely facilitating China's economic growth while eschewing unnecessary confrontations with the United States and other countries. The limited number of military exchanges, arms sales, and humanitarian missions generate goodwill between China and South American countries, helping to foster economic cooperation without provoking a seriously negative response in Washington. Even this limited range of activities in South America yields useful on-site intelligence regarding the regional security environment and provides a foundation that could prove strategically useful if China chose to raise its regional defense profile in the future.[90]

It is important to keep China's economic presence in Latin America in perspective. Though growing quickly, South America still lags behind other regions in terms of economic importance for China. Although the PRC is the top trade partner for several key Latin American countries, it is far from being the only international actor in the region. The United States, European countries, Russia, Iran, and India are all important players in the region that complicate and compete with the PRC. Furthermore, "China" is far from being a unitary actor, and analyzing Beijing's foreign policies is really examining a diverse array of government, state-owned companies, and private sector policies. Even so, as China's economic ties with South America continue to develop, political links could become closer. PRC leaders will remain wary of antagonizing the United States, but if South American countries calculate that political and even military ties with Beijing are a valuable complement to those with Washington and other powers in the region, the PRC could see its role both increase and diversify.

NOTES

1. Andrew Rettman, "EU-China Diplomacy Fails to Convince Sceptics," *EUobserver.com*, April 30, 2010, http://euobserver.com/884/29981; and John Lee, "EU Not on China's Chessboard," *The Diplomat*, May 13, 2010, http://the-diplomat.com/2010/05/13/eu-not-on-china%E2%80%99s-chessboard.

2. Europe China Research and Advice Network, "The High-Level Economic and Trade Dialogue," ECRAN, accessed February 3, 2013, http://www.euecran.eu/high-level-economic-and-trade-dialogue.

3. Nicola Casarini, "The Evolution of the EU-China Relationship: From Constructive Engagement to Strategic Partnership," *EU Institute for Security Studies Occasional Paper*, no. 64, October 2006, 23, http://www.iss.europa.eu/uploads/media/occ64.pdf.

4. U.K. Foreign and Commonwealth Office, "Unrest in Xinjiang Province China," British Embassy in Washington, DC, June 8, 2009, http://ukinusa.fco.gov.uk/en/newsroom/?view=News&id=20541202.

5. Martin Banks, "EU Urged to Scrap Arms Embargo against China," *TheParliament.com*, April 2, 2012, http://www.theparliament.com/latest-news/article/newsarticle/eu-urged-to-scrap-arms-embargo-against-china/.

6. Martin Banks, "EU Arms Embargo Against China Dismissed as 'Unimportant,'" *TheParliament.com*, August 2, 2011, http://www.theparliament.com/latest-news/article/newsarticle/eu-arms-embargo-against-china-dismissed-as-unimportant/.

7. Leo Cendrowicz, "Should Europe Lift Its Arms Embargo on China?," *Time Magazine*, February 10, 2010, http://www.time.com/time/world/article/0,8599,1961947,00.html.

8. China Daily, "EU Arms Ban a 'Prejudice Against China,'" *China Daily*, January 29, 2010, www.chinadaily.com.cn/china/2010-01/29/content_9396856.htm.

9. Fang Lexian, "Arms Ban Tarnishes EU Image," *China Daily*, February 9, 2010, http://www.china.org.cn/opinion/2010-02/09/content_19393030_2.htm.

10. Xinhua, "EU Arms Embargo against China Is Political Prejudice," *China Radio International*, November 29, 2011, http://english.cri.cn/6909/2011/11/29/2743s669477.htm.

11. Ibid.

12. Andrew Rettman, "EU to Keep China Arms Embargo Despite Massive Investments," *EU Observer*, May 1, 2011, http://euobserver.com/884/31592.

13. Richard Fisher, "China's Aviation Sector: Building toward World Class Capability," *International Strategy and Assessment Center*, May 20, 2010, http://www.strategycenter.net/research/pubID.226/pub_detail.asp.

14. Anton La Guardia, "US Fury Over EU Weapons for China," *The Telegraph*, January 15, 2005, http://www.telegraph.co.uk/news/worldnews/1481253/US-fury-over-EU-weapons-for-China.html.

15. Kristin Archick, Richard F. Grimmett, and Shirley Kan, "European Union's Arms Embargo on China: Implications and Options for U.S. Policy," U.S. Congressional Research Service, April 15, 2005, 3, http://fpc.state.gov/documents/organization/45458.pdf.

16. Praveen Swami and Malcolm Moore, "Japan Warns West against Lifting China Arms Embargo," *The Telegraph*, November 18, 2010, http://www.telegraph.co.uk/news/worldnews/asia/china/8144383/Japans-warns-West-against-lifting-China-arms-embargo.html.

17. Andrew Willis, "Japan: Ashton Was Wrong on China Arms Ban," *EU Observer*, May 9, 2011, http://euobserver.com/9/32360.

18. David Shambaugh, "Don't Lift the Arms Embargo on China," *New York Times*, February 23, 2005, http://www.nytimes.com/2005/02/22/opinion/22iht-edshambaugh.html?_r=0.

19. Keith B. Richburg, "China, After Abstaining in U.N. Vote, Criticizes Airstrikes on Gaddafi Forces," *Washington Post*, March 21, 2011, http://www.washingtonpost.com/world/china_after_abstaining_in_un_vote_criticizes_airstrikes_on_gaddafi_forces/2011/03/21/ABwL4M7_story.html?wprss=rss_homepage.

20. Ibid.

21. John Calabrese, "China and Iran: Mismatched Partners," Occasional Paper, Jamestown Foundation, August 2006, http://www.jamestown.org/programs/recentreports/single/?tx_ttnews%5Btt_news%5D=41&tx_ttnews%5BbackPid%5D=63&cHash=40f244bff8.

22. State Council Information Office (PRC), China's National Defense in 2008 (Beijing: State Council Information Office (PRC), 2009), chap. 14, http://english.gov.cn/official/2009-01/20/content_1210227.htm.

23. Ibid.

24. Xinhua, "China Denies Arm Sales to Syria," *China Radio International English Service*, Feb. 11, 2012, http://english.cri.cn/6909/2012/02/11/53s680485.htm.

25. Mu Chunshan, "China's Nimble Libya Pullout," *The Diplomat*, March 22, 201, http://the-diplomat.com/china-power/2011/03/22/china%e2%80%99s-nimble-libya-pullout/.

26. David Pierson, "Libyan Strife Exposes China's Risks in Global Quest for Oil," *Los Angeles Times*, http://www.latimes.com/business/la-fi-china-oil-20110310,0,6747704.story.

27. Jonas Parello-Plesner, "Civis Sinicus Sum: China's Great Power Burdens in Libya," *World Politics Review*, March 3, 2011, http://www.worldpoliticsreview.com/articles/8072/civis-sinicus-sum-chinas-great-power-burdens-in-libya; see also Gabe Collins and Andrew S. Erickson, "Implications of China's Military Evacuation of Citizens from Libya," *China Brief*, March 10, 2011.

28. China Daily, "Avoiding Civil War in Syria," *China Daily*, February 6, 2012, http://www.chinadaily.com.cn/cndy/2012-02/06/content_14540573.htm.

29. Ibid.

30. Ibid.

31. Xinhua, "New Features Highlight Sino-African Relations," *Sina.com*, July 18, 2012, http://english.sina.com/china/2012/0718/487414.html.

32. Rachael Akidi, "Ask Not What China Wants from Africa, But What Africa Wants from China," *Huffington Post*, June 11, 2012, http://www.huffingtonpost.co.uk/rachael-akidi/africa-china-ask-not-what-china-wants-_b_1578719.html.

33. Xinhua, "New Features Highlight Sino-African Relations."

34. David Shinn, "China's Growing Role in Africa: Implications for U.S. Policy," *Senate Committee on Foreign Relations Subcommittee on African Affairs Hearing*, November 1, 2011, http://www.foreign.senate.gov/imo/media/doc/David_Shinn_Testimony.pdf.

35. Jennifer G. Cooke, "China's Soft Power in Africa," in *Chinese Soft Power and Its Implications for the United States: Competition and Cooperation in the Developing World*, ed. Carola McGiffert (Center for Strategic and International Studies, 2009), 31, http://csis.org/files/media/csis/pubs/090403_mcgiffert_chinesesoftpower_web.pdf.

36. Emmanuel John Hevi, *The Dragon's Embrace: The Chinese Communists and Africa* (New York: Fredrick A. Praeger, 1966), 99.

37. Ibid., 111.

38. Raymond L. Garthoff, *Détente and Confrontation: American-Soviet Relations from Nixon to Reagan* (Washington, DC: The Brookings Institute, 1994), 565–569.

39. Alaba Ogunsanwo, *China's Policy in Africa, 1958–1971* (Cambridge: Cambridge University Press, 1974), 187.

40. Dan Connell and Tom Killion, *Historical Dictionary of Eritrea* (Lanham, MD: Scarecrow Press, 2011), 145.

41. Li Anshan, "China and Africa: Policy and Challenges," *China Security* 3, no. 3 (2007): 71, http://www.chinasecurity.us/index.php?option=com_content&view=article&id=105.

42. Cooke, "China's Soft Power in Africa."

43. Xinhua, "Cooperation Framework Key to Further Promote China-Africa Relations," *Forum on China-Africa Cooperation*, December 24, 2010, http://www.focac.org/eng/zt/10th/t781406.htm.

44. BBC, "African Union Opens Chinese-funded HQ in Ethiopia," *BBC*, January 28, 2012, http://www.bbc.co.uk/news/world-africa-16770932.

45. Foreign Policy, "The Chinese-African Union," *Foreignpolicy.com*, March 19, 2012, http://www.foreignpolicy.com/articles/2012/03/19/african_union_addis_ababa#0.

46. Anshan, "China and Africa," 76.

47. Bates Gill and Chin-hao Huang, "China's Expanding Peacekeeping Role: It's Significance and the Policy Implications," *Stockholm International Peace Research Institute Policy Brief*, February 2009, http://books.sipri.org/files/misc/SIPRIPB0902.pdf.

48. David Shinn, "China's Growing Role in Africa: Implications for U.S. Policy," Senate Committee on Foreign Relations Subcommittee on African Affairs Hearing, November 1, 2011, 3, http://www.foreign.senate.gov/imo/media/doc/David_Shinn_Testimony.pdf.

49. United Nations, "Monthly Summary of Contributions (Police, UN Military Experts on Mission and Troops)," United Nations, March 31, 2012, http://www.un.org/en/peacekeeping/contributors/2012/March12_1.pdf.

50. United Nations, "Peacekeeping Fact Sheet," United Nations, March 31, 2012, http://www.un.org/en/peacekeeping/resources/statistics/factsheet.shtml.

51. Global Times, "Respecting Africa's Decisions Will Benefit China," *Global Times*, November 3, 2011. http://www.globaltimes.cn/NEWS/tabid/99/ID/682394/Respecting-Africas-decisions-will-benefit-China.aspx.

52. Gill and Huang, "China's Expanding Peacekeeping Role"; and *Global Times*, "Respecting Africa's decisions will benefit China."

53. Ibid.

54. Peter, J. Varljen, "Leadership: More than Mission Accomplished," *Military Review*, March/ April 2003, http://usacac.leavenworth.army.mil/cac/milreview/download/English/MarApr03/varljen.pdf.

55. J. Peter Pham, "Pandas in the Heart of Darkness: Chinese Peacekeepers in Africa," *World Defense Review*, October 25, 2007, http://worlddefensereview.com/pham102507.shtml.

56. Bonny Ling, "China's Peacekeeping Diplomacy," *International Relations and Institutions*, November 1, 2007, http://hrichina.org/sites/default/files/oldsite/PDFs/CRF.1.2007/CRF-2007-1_Peacekeeping.pdf.

57. Ibid.

58. David Shinn, "China's Growing Role in Africa: Implications for U.S. Policy," Senate Committee on Foreign Relations Subcommittee on African Affairs Hearing, November 1, 2011, 3, http://www.foreign.senate.gov/imo/media/doc/David_Shinn_Testimony.pdf.

59. USAFRICOM has a base in Djibouti with about 3,000 military and civilian personnel used for countering terrorism, piracy, and illicit trafficking; improving peacekeeping, assisting with disaster response, and promoting maritime security; see Donna Miles, "Priorities Set U.S. Africa Command's Agenda," *American Forces Press Service*, June 12, 2012, http://www.africom.mil/getArticle.asp?art=7978.

60. Susan Pushka, "Military Backs China's Africa Adventure," *Asia Times Online*, June 8, 2007, http://www.atimes.com/atimes/China/IF08Ad03.html.

61. Ministry of Foreign Affairs (PRC), "Foreign Ministry Spokesperson Jiang Yu's Regular Press Conference on May 26, 2011," *Ministry of Foreign Affairs (PRC)*, May 27, 2011, http://www.fmprc.gov.cn/eng/xwfw/s2510/t826007.htm.

62. Augustus Vogel, "Navies versus Coast Guards: Defining the Roles of African Maritime Security Forces," *Africa Security Brief*, December 2009, http://www.ndu.edu/press/lib/pdf/Africa-Security-Brief/ASB-2.pdf.

63. Agence France-Presse, "Seychelles Invites China to Set Up Anti-Piracy Base," *Defense News*, Dec. 2, 2011, http://www.defensenews.com/article/20111202/DEFSECT03/112020302/Seychelles-Invites-China-Set-Up-Anti-Piracy-Bases.

64. Sanou Mbaye, "Matching China's Activities with Africa's Needs," in Axel Harneit-Sievers, Stephen Marks, and Sanusha Naidu, eds., *Chinese and African Perspectives on China in Africa* (Cape Town: Pambazuka Press, 2010), 43.

65. Ian Taylor, *China's New Role in Africa* (Boulder, CO: Lynne Rienner Publishers, 2009), 119.

66. Stockholm International Peace Research Institute, "SIPRI Arms Transfers Database," *Stockholm International Peace Research Institute*, accessed May 7, 2012, http://www.sipri.org/databases/armstransfers.

67. Central Intelligence Agency, "Africa," *The World Factbook*, August 5, 2011, https://www.cia.gov/library/publications/the-world-factbook/wfbExt/region_afr.html.

68. Robert I. Rotberg, *China into Africa: Trade, Aid, and Influence* (Cambridge, MA: World Peace Foundation, 2008), 9.

69. Kent Hughes Butts and Brent Bankus, "China's Pursuit of Africa's Natural Resources," in Amy Richmond Krakowka and Laurel J. Hummel, eds., *Understanding Africa: A Geographical Perspective* (U.S. Army War College Center for Strategic Leadership, 2009), 5, http://www.csl.army.mil/usacsl/publications/understanding_africa.pdf.

70. Taylor, *China's New Role in Africa,* 117.

71. J. Peter Pham, "Hu's Selling Guns to Africa," *World Defense Review,* June 28, 2007, http://worlddefensereview.com/pham062807.shtml.

72. Amnesty International, "Arms Trade Fuels Violations in Sudan Conflict," *Amnesty International,* July 8, 2011, http://www.amnesty.org/en/news-and-updates/arms-trade-fuels -violations-sudan-conflict-2011-07-08.

73. Joshua Eisenman and Joshua Kurlantzick, "China's Africa Strategy," *Current History* (May 2006), 222, http://www.carnegieendowment.org/files/Africa.pdf.

74. David Beresford, "Chinese Ship Carries Arms Cargo to Mugabe Regime," *The Guardian,* April 17, 2008, http://www.guardian.co.uk/world/2008/apr/18/china.armstrade.

75. Associated Press, "Zimbabwe Buys Six Fighter Jets," *The Guardian,* April 14, 2005, http://www.guardian.co.uk/world/2005/apr/14/zimbabwe.

76. Pham, "Hu's Selling Guns to Africa."

77. Christopher Alessi and Stephanie Hanson, "Expanding China-Africa Oil Ties," Council on Foreign Relations, February 8, 2012, http://www.cfr.org/china/expanding-china-africa -oil-ties/p9557.

78. David Shinn, "China's Growing Role in Africa: Implications for U.S. Policy, Hearing Held by Senate Committee on Foreign Relations Subcommittee on African Affairs," November 1, 2011, 2 http://www.foreign.senate.gov/imo/media/doc/David_Shinn_Testimony.pdf.

79. Hao Zhou, "29 Chinese Abducted by Sudan Rebels," *Global Times,* January 30, 2012, http://www.globaltimes.cn/NEWS/tabid/99/ID/693721/29-Chinese-abducted-by-Sudan -rebels.aspx.

80. International Committee of the Red Cross, "Sudan: ICRC Organizes Transfer of Released Chinese Citizens," *International Committee of the Red Cross,* February 7, 2012, http:// www.icrc.org/eng/resources/documents/news-release/2012/sudan-news-2012-02-07.htm.

81. Gabe Collins and Andrew S. Erickson, "Implications of China's Military Evacuation of Citizens from Libya," *China Brief* 11, no. 4 (March 10, 2011), http://www.jamestown.org/ programs/chinabrief/single/?tx_ttnews[tt_news]=37633&tx_ttnews[backPid]=25&cHash=c13 02a9ecaddfc23450fb6ec13a98136.

82. Ibid.

83. From 2005 to 2011 senior Chinese military leaders visited Argentina (twice), Cuba (three times), Uruguay, Chile (three times), Brazil (twice), Colombia (twice), Mexico, Bolivia, Peru and in 2010–2011 senior military officials from Bolivia, Cuba, Guyana, and Peru visited China. This list excludes visits that were parts of exercises or involved lower-level officials; this information is from "Annual Report to Congress: Military and Security Developments Involving the People's Republic of China 2011," United States Department of Defense Office of the Secretary of Defense, 2011, 82–83, http://www.defense.gov/pubs/pdfs/2011_cmpr_final.pdf and "Military and Security Developments Involving the People's Republic of China 2012," United States Department of Defense Office of the Secretary of Defense, May 2012, 35–36, http://www.defense.gov/pubs/pdfs/2012_CMPR_Final.pdf.

84. R. Evan Ellis, *China-Latin America Military Engagement: Good Will, Good Business, and Strategic Position* (Carlisle, PA: U.S. Army War College, August 2011), 14–15, http://www .strategicstudiesinstitute.army.mil/pubs/display.cfm?pubid=1077.

85. Ibid., 17.

86. Paul Holtom, Mark Bromley, Pieter D. Wezeman, and Siemon T. Wezeman, "Trends in International Arms Transfers, 2011," Stockholm International Peace Research Institute Fact Sheet, March 2012, 5, http://books.sipri.org/product_info?c_product_id=443.

87. Alex Sanchez, "Arms Sales, Especially By Russia And China, Continue To Penetrate Latin America," *Eurasia Review,* February 22, 2011, http://www.eurasiareview.com/analysis/arm-sales-especially-by-russia-and-china-continue-to-penetrate-latin-america-22022011/.

88. Ellis, *China-Latin America Military Engagement,* 20.

89. Guy Taylor, "China's Caribbean Mission Shows Growing Naval Capability," *World Politics Review,* November 7, 2011 http://www.worldpoliticsreview.com/trend-lines/10586/chinas-carribbean-mission-shows-growing-naval-capability.

90. Ellis, *China-Latin America Military Engagement,* 8–9.

CHAPTER 5

Global Security Issues

Since the early 1990s, China has launched a sustained campaign to enter other important international institutions. The country has obtained full membership in the IMF, the World Trade Organization (WTO), and developed strong relations with the African Union (AU) and the Association of Southeast Asian Nations (ASEAN). China also plays a dominant role in some multilateral institutions, such as the Shanghai Cooperation Organization (SCO) and the Six-Party Talks. During the past decade, China has emerged as a leading force contributor to UN peacekeeping missions, building on the PRC's traditional influence as one of the five permanent members of the United Nations Security Council (UNSC). In addition to general status considerations, concerns about terrorism and energy security have also been driving Beijing's growing international outreach.

INTERNATIONAL INSTITUTIONS

As in many areas, the dual goals of defending concrete Chinese national interests, while burnishing Beijing's image as a responsible global stakeholder that supports international norms, drive China's changing role in the UN and other major international security institutions. For years after the PRC assumed the Chinese seat in the UN in 1971, the Chinese government declined to participate in international peacekeeping operations or support other coercive measures adopted by the UNSC under Chapter VII, finding them hard to reconcile with Beijing's strong support for noninterference in another country's internal affairs, a guiding principle of Chinese foreign policy that is repeatedly emphasized in government documents: "China respects the right of the people of other countries to independently choose their own social system and path of development, and does not interfere in other countries' internal affairs" and "China never uses foreign aid as a means to interfere in recipient countries' internal affairs or seek political privileges for itself."[1] Noninterference is one of the Five Principles of Peaceful Coexistence—first established in 1954 between China and India—which have since become a cornerstone of the PRC's foreign relations. These principles include mutual respect for territorial integrity and sovereignty, mutual nonaggression, mutual noninterference in internal affairs, equality and mutual benefit, and peaceful coexistence.[2] The PRC government cites its noninterference policy to justify its close relationships with internationally unpopular regimes. Governments alienated from the West value China's noninterference policy, as the investment and aid provided help these regimes maintain legitimacy and stability. Furthermore, noninterference also reinforces their view of China as a business partner, as opposed to the West, which they perceive as meddlesome and imperialistic.

Beijing's attitude changed, at least with respect to UN peacekeeping, after the Cold War. Since 1990, China has contributed more than 11,000 military or police personnel to 18 UN peacekeeping operations.[3] After 2001, China emerged as a leading force contributor to such missions. Several factors might explain the transition in the PRC's UN peacekeeping policies.[4] First, China has become a wealthier country, more able to contribute to such international public goods. Second, China's rising economic, diplomatic, and military power has made Beijing more eager to assume its proffered role as a responsible global stakeholder. Third, Chinese foreign-policy doctrine now considers peacekeeping operations legitimate if they are supported by the host governments and approved by the UNSC.

Although Chinese officials have become more comfortable authorizing and contributing to peacekeeping operations, they still regularly oppose employing force or coercive sanctions to induce other governments to change their behavior. PRC diplomatic statements constantly affirm a commitment to upholding traditional interpretations of national sovereignty, which severely limit the right of external actors to challenge a national government's domestic policies. Chinese leaders defend their noninterference doctrine by appealing to international law, though they make a major exception in forcing security partners and aid recipients to eschew close ties with Taiwan. PRC officials also do not want Western countries to criticize Beijing's human rights and civil liberties practices or to seek to depose authoritarian governments friendly to China by citing humanitarian considerations in justifying their intervention. Furthermore, unlike the United States, which has over a century of experience in sending military forces into foreign nations to reconstruct their political and economic systems, the PRC has never used the PLA for nation-building purposes outside of Chinese territory.[5]

Chinese leaders frequently express a desire to strengthen the role of transnational security organizations to which Beijing belongs—especially the United Nations. Because of the PRC's status as a permanent member of the UNSC,

Chinese officials can use their right to veto actions to prevent the United States and its allies from obtaining formal UN endorsement of any military operations they oppose. For this reason, the U.S. decision to lead military interventions in the former Yugoslavia in 1998 and in Iraq in 2003 without explicit UNSC approval evoked dismay. In recent years, Chinese officials have joined with their Russian counterparts to prevent the imposition of rigorous sanctions against Iran, Sudan, North Korea, and other countries that have pursued policies that Western governments consider violations of international laws and norms. In January 2007, Beijing and Moscow cast their first parallel vetoes in the UNSC against a U.S.-sponsored resolution censuring Myanmar's authoritarian government. Chinese Ambassador Wang Guangya simply observed that, "No country is perfect . . . Similar problems exist in other countries as well."[6] The repeated sanctioning of Chinese government agencies and private defense trading companies by the United States and its allies has likely contributed to Beijing's distaste for such measures.

PRC policymakers have readily supported other transnational institutions that are seen as constraining Washington's ability to pursue unilateral actions that might harm Beijing's security interests. After the United States invaded Iraq, the Chinese government took the lead in organizing a regional forum, the Six-Party Talks, which helped avert a similar unilateral U.S. strike against North Korea by providing all parties with multilateral diplomatic options. Through the Six-Party Talks, Beijing has worked closely with Washington to persuade North Korea to abandon its nuclear weapons program. The value of a regional forum of the Six-Party Talks, from Beijing's perspective, is that it allows Beijing to exercise a degree of control over Washington's decisions, providing a marked contrast to the lack of cooperation between the United States and China prior to the invasion of Iraq.

Chinese diplomacy has used a similar strategy, involving the Shanghai Co-operation Organization (SCO), to constrain Russian influence in Central Asia while Beijing and Moscow pursue their overlapping security interests in Eurasia. Since its founding in 2001, the SCO has essentially functioned as a Chinese-Russian condominium, providing Beijing and Moscow with a convenient trans-national institution to manage their interests in the newly independent countries of Central Asia. The SCO helps China compensate for certain asymmetries that tend to enhance Moscow's influence in the region. Unlike Russia, China lacks permanent bases in Central Asia outside neighboring Chinese territory; in addi-tion, the other main transnational security institutions active in the region, NATO and the Moscow-led Collective Security Treaty Organization, exclude China from membership. By working through the SCO, China can enjoy equal status with Moscow, which must adopt policies acceptable to Beijing to secure the SCO's endorsement.

The one exception in China's membership roster is its absence from the Group of Eight (G8). The PRC has the world's largest population and one of the globe's most influential governments in many areas of concern to the G8, especially those dealing with energy, economics, and peacekeeping. Since 1999, Chinese representatives have participated in many G8-sponsored meetings. The PRC also belongs to a larger and separate organization known as the G20 finance ministers and central bank governors. The Chinese government also gained entry into the World Bank, the IMF, and the World Trade Organization (WTO), abandoning its earlier antipathy toward these institutions. Although the PRC's share of global GDP in 1990 was 5.7 percent, it reached 15.4 percent in 2005 and, according to IMF forecasts, could exceed Europe's share of the global GDP by 2015, making the PRC an increasingly relevant actor in the global economy. Beijing's support is also essential for addressing climate change, Africa's development, and other issues of concern to the G8. In many other areas, the PRC has the potential to be a major spoiler to effective collective action.

After years of debate over how to deal with China's rising economic power and diplomatic weight, President Hu Jintao was invited to participate in portions of the discussions at Évian les Bains in 2003. Following this step, it became difficult to "disinvite" China's leader from future meetings without making it seem as a gratuitous insult in the absence of any particular egregious Chinese behavior.[7] At the July 2005 summit at Gleneagles, Prime Minister Tony Blair said the G8 should grow to include India and China, but acknowledged other members' opposition to the proposal. The following year, the new French president, Nicholas Sarkozy, said that China, India, Brazil, South Africa, and Mexico should gradually become G8 members.[8] Sarkozy later explained that, "I think it is not reasonable to continue to meet as eight to solve the big questions of the world, forgetting China—one billion 300 million people—and not inviting India— one billion people."[9] Sarkozy warned that the continued exclusion of these two powers could weaken the G8's legitimacy by increasing concerns about the Group's unrepresentativeness. Yet, the Chinese have never been formally offered full G8 membership, nor have they shown any official interest in receiving it.

The main obstacle to China's transition to full membership status has been its authoritarian political system. Allowing Beijing to enter would challenge the institution's commitment to the shared values of democracy and respect for human rights. Critics have already cited Russia's entry as having a deleterious effect given its government's deviation from certain liberal democratic principles. But Russian citizens still exercise more civil rights than Chinese nationals. The PRC is a one-party state that imposes tight control over media access and its people's civil rights. In addition, as shown with the case of Russia and the G8, it is easier to deny a country membership in an international organization than to expel it after that state has joined. Indeed, one reason why the Chinese government might not be eager to join the G8 is that its membership would provide critics with additional opportunities to attack the regime for failing to adhere to the Group's core principles of democracy and human rights. At the 1989 "Summit of the Arch" in Paris, the leaders of the then G7 announced collective sanctions against China after the Tiananmen Square incident, when the People's Liberation Army (PLA) forcefully repressed nonviolent students and workers who had demanded political liberalization and other changes.[10] In addition, the Chinese leadership may not wish to enhance the status of an institution that could potentially compete with the United Nations, where the PRC enjoys elite status as one of five permanent members of the Security Council—and the only one from East Asia. In a "G9," China would have to share that status with Japan, and given Tokyo's closer ties with most of the other G8 members, Japan could well enjoy superior influence to China. In fact, Tokyo would likely not support full membership for Beijing without receiving reciprocal PRC support for Japan's aspirations to become a permanent UN Security Council member. At present, Tokyo receives enhanced international status as the G8's only Asian member. Japanese leaders have consciously sought to defend Asian values and interests at G8 summits. Japanese officials have also arranged formal pre- and post-summit briefings for other Asian governments.[11] Given all of this, it is fair to assume that Tokyo would not want to share its special diplomatic position with Beijing. The reactions of developing nations to China's becoming a G8 member might also be deterring Beijing from membership. PRC officials might characterize their entry as helping them to better promote the interests of developing countries within an important global forum. But joining the G8 as its sole ninth member, without a similar opportunity for the other four regular outreach partners, could also lead to criticism that Beijing was abandoning its commitment to the developing world to join a "rich man's club."

It is possible that the PRC might be given a status similar to that of Russia in the 1990s, where the Chinese president would be allowed to participate in some sessions as a formal member but not others. Although Yeltsin attended the political sessions during this period, Russia's global economic capacity was minimal at the time, so Yeltsin was excluded from the economic sessions. Obviously, Beijing's growing economic clout would suggest that the PRC president has more of a place at these sessions than did Russia's leader two decades ago. For this reason, President Hu was regularly invited to attend the four 8+5 outreach sessions that took place at the summits, which allowed him to represent China's views to the other world leaders. Yet, while Beijing exerts tremendous political influence in many world regions, its political system does not respect the liberal democratic principles formally shared by the other G8 adherents. The PRC media has expressed satisfaction with the degree of China's engagement in the 2007 summit, at a time when the issue of Beijing's possible G8 membership was under most intense discussion: "At the outreach session, President Hu had in-depth discussions with 12 foreign leaders on a broad range of issues. They agreed to enhance political dialogue, strengthen mutually beneficial economic co-operation, cultural exchanges and coordination on international affairs. Applauding China's positive role on the international scene, the foreign leaders agreed to boost coordination with China to jointly safeguard world peace and security and promote common development."[12] Although the relationship between the PRC and the G8 has generally been cooperative, tensions have arisen over Beijing's policy of providing generous loans to African nations with minimal conditions. G8 finance ministers worry that the lax terms of these agreements will lead to excessive borrowing by African countries, to which G8 lenders had recently written off billions of dollars of unpaid debts. For now, the rise of the G20, which does include China as a full member, has removed attention from the G8 issue, but the question could soon return.

TERRORISM

Like many countries, the PRC faces security problems from its alienated Muslim minority. For at least two decades, Islamic groups have been advocating independence for China's Xinjiang Uighur Autonomous Region, an area comprising one-sixth of China that borders Pakistan, Afghanistan, and several Central Asian countries. Of the region's twenty million inhabitants, approximately half are non-Han Chinese Muslims with ethnic and religious links to neighboring Turkic populations in Central Asia, though this percentage has been steadily falling because of Beijing's policy of encouraging Han migration into Xinjiang to strengthen its integration with the rest of China.[13] During the early 1990s, Xinjiang experienced assassinations, bombings, and other endemic violence from some Uighur nationalists who sought to establish an "East Turkestan Islamic Republic" by attacking PRC government targets and Han Chinese civilians. The Beijing government accused them of constituting a Uighur-based East Turkestan Independence Movement (ETIM) that received training and support from the Taliban.[14]

Beijing faces another challenge in the Tibetan struggle for autonomy—though only PRC officials classify the threat as terrorism. As the spiritual home of the exiled Buddhist leader, the Dalai Lama, Tibet presents Beijing with a uniquely difficult set of circumstances. Tibet constitutes one of the two provinces in the PRC in which Han Chinese do not represent the overwhelming ethnic majority of the province's residents—Xinjiang is the other. Though Tibet has effectively been under Chinese rule for centuries, there has been a renewed push in recent decades to establish Tibetan independence. Although Beijing has tried to grant a certain degree of autonomy to Tibet, discontent among Tibetans persists because the PRC strives to maintain authoritative control and encourages the migration of ethnic Han Chinese into the territory.[15] Complicating the issue even further for the PRC is the amount of international attention and sympathy devoted to Tibet, manifested in the widespread global protests during the international torch relay for the 2008 Olympic Games set in Beijing. The Tibetan struggle for autonomy recently attracted further international attention after Tibetan monks initiated mass protests against what they described as oppression by the PRC turned violent. When dozens of Tibetan monks and other civilians were killed by the PRC's military, it sparked international outcry and condemnation. In addition, Tibetan monks continue a high-profile campaign of self-immolation and other public protests. Beijing's policy of opposing meetings between the Dalai Lama and foreign leaders is another recurring source of tension.

Despite decades of repressive Chinese countermeasures, Xinjiang and nearby Tibet have experienced major resurgences of nationalist and ethnic unrest. Starting in early 2008, Chinese officials accused groups linked with al-Qaeda and the Dalai Lama of various plots to disrupt the August Summer Olympics.[16] The number of publicly announced arrests in Xinjiang for "endangering state security" also soared in 2008.[17] Nonetheless, the July 2009 ethnic riots in Xinjiang, in which some 200 people died and more than 1,600 were injured when Uighurs and Hans engaged in vicious street battles, have made clear that Beijing has yet to solve its Muslim minority problem.

In terms of the PRC's regional security concerns, *China's National Defense in 2008* warned that "terrorist, separatist and extremist forces are running rampant" in the Asia-Pacific region.[18] Their alleged activities within China are weakening the government's ability to counter foreign threats, because "China is faced with . . . strategic maneuvers and containment from the outside while having to face disruptions and sabotage by separatist and hostile forces from the inside."[19] The defense white paper describes how the government has been strengthening the ability of the People's Armed Police Force (PAPF) to counter what Chinese officials commonly refer to as the "three evil forces" of separatism, terrorism, and religious extremism. The PAPF, under the dual leadership of the State Council and the CMC, encountered surprising difficulty in suppressing the 2008 anti-Beijing riots in Tibet, and the Chinese authorities have apparently made enhancing its internal control capacities a priority—though without much success in averting the ethnic riots in Xinjiang in July 2009.[20] The PAPF also has an important role in countering domestic terrorism.

But PRC analysts also perceive terrorism as a global threat. With the rise of the country's export-driven economy, the Chinese government now considers the safety and security of international shipping of vital importance. PRC and foreign authorities now regularly collaborate to enhance the security of shipping containers to and from Chinese ports and have intensified cooperation with the International Maritime Organization (IMO), whose programs extend from piracy prevention to environmental protection.[21] In the wake of the highly publicized scandals of lethal pet food and lead paint–tainted toys sold by China on international markets, imports from the PRC have received elevated scrutiny in many countries. Through participation in the U.S. Container Security Initiative (CSI), the Department of Energy's Megaports Initiative, and similar programs, the PRC presumably hopes to burnish its antiterrorist credentials, improve its image as a responsible international stakeholder, and avert the commercial disaster that would befall Chinese trade if a container carrying a weapon of mass destruction enters a major port.

The expansion of Beijing's diplomatic and especially commercial presence throughout the globe has increased the vulnerability of Chinese citizens and corporations to overseas terrorism. For example, terrorists have attacked Chinese nationals in Pakistan, Sudan, and other countries. These acts have weakened Chinese perceptions that their country's history of anticolonialism and efforts to cultivate good relations with all foreign governments would shield them from global clashes between civilizations. The 9/11 shocks and the subsequent war in Iraq catalyzed concerns about Islamic terrorism in China; PRC officials were quick to express solidarity with Americans after the September 2001 terrorist attacks and even acquiesced in the U.S.-led invasion of Afghanistan, despite their unease about American military operations on the Chinese periphery.[22] China has signed a number of international conventions against terrorism, such as those against nuclear terrorism and money laundering. The PRC's decision to host a China-Arab Cooperation Forum not only sent a strong political signal of greater Chinese receptivity to strong ties with the Arab world, but also reached out to Islamic groups that may view Beijing's policies as anti-Muslim.[23] Furthermore, China is extending development assistance to Muslim-dominated regions, such as Xinjiang within China and Indonesia in Southeast Asia, in hopes of "winning the hearts and minds" of their citizens.[24]

Many human rights activists consider Beijing's claims of terrorist plots in Xinjiang, Tibet, and other Chinese minority regions as exaggerated. They fear the PRC authorities are citing fictitious terrorist threats to justify repressing nonviolent domestic opponents among China's ethnic minorities.[25] These activists have pressed the Obama administration to adopt a harder line regarding PRC human rights violations.[26] In turn, Chinese commentators criticize Western counterterrorist policies as overly militarized and for employing an alleged "double standard" by seeking cooperation against terrorists that threaten the United States and its allies while downplaying terrorist threats to China.

ENERGY SECURITY

China is no longer able to sustain its rapidly growing economy without importing energy. Beijing's energy security strategy includes three major elements: reforming the domestic energy sector to maximize production and attract foreign direct investment; diversifying the energy mix to reduce the nation's dependency on fossil fuels and contain pollution; and diversifying sources of foreign energy to limit dependence on any single country or energy-producing region. China's ambitious "energy diplomacy," which has kept Chinese diplomats engaged throughout the globe, has thus far proven successful in achieving these three pillars; however, the PRC has alarmed other countries in the process. These countries worry that the Beijing's vision of a zero-sum world energy game could threaten their own energy security. In addition, for a PRC government that has always sought to limit its dependence on foreigners, the country's growing reliance on external energy sources presents a major economic, political, and diplomatic challenge. Because energy policy, environmental policy, economic policy, national security policy, and foreign policy are all inextricably linked with one another, PRC policymakers remain alert to developments that could compromise their diverse goals in these areas.[27] They have enforced principles and safeguards such as insisting on noninterference in Chinese domestic policies, tight control over information on government decisions and actions in the energy market, and treating international pressure to change its policies as an affront to China's sovereignty. As in other areas, the central government has experienced difficulty in recent years in controlling the large number of newly independent actors in China's energy sector—which range from energy companies to military and intelligence agencies—especially when these operations extend to China's provinces or to foreign countries.[28] Past bureaucratic restructuring has failed to assure the development and implementation of an integrated Chinese national energy policy under Beijing's direction.

Additional Chinese vulnerabilities result from conditions in important foreign energy regions. Because China obtains more than half of its energy imports from the Persian Gulf, PRC policymakers remain concerned that these flows are vulnerable to local political instability—whether in Iraq, Iran, or elsewhere—as well as interception by potentially hostile military powers, especially the U.S. Navy, or predations by pirates. China's energy trade with neighboring Russia and certain Central Asian countries has increased in recent years and can be expected to grow further. Because oil and gas from Russia and Central Asia can reach the PRC via land, these supplies—though more expensive to transport—are less vulnerable to Western interdiction efforts. Despite this proximity, however, various problems have resulted in Russian and Central Asian energy supplies currently accounting for less than 10 percent of China's total supplies. The PRC has also fostered energy supply relationships with African and South American nations. Beijing's ties with several of these countries is diplomatically contentious because of the ripple effects of dealing with the United States and Europe while also conducting business with governments hostile to Western powers. Similarly, although China cooperates with India, Japan, and the United States on many energy issues, the PRC's expanding energy ambitions and exclusionary practices have already brought Beijing into conflict with these other major energy-importing countries.

Since the early 1980s, China's economy has grown at an unprecedented rate, with a concomitant increase in energy consumption. Combined with a population of more than a billion people and limited domestic supplies of fossil fuels, these transformations have led the PRC to become a net importer of oil in 1993, following years of exporting oil. By 2006, China had become the world's third-largest net importer of oil and second-largest consumer of energy. The gap between China's stagnant domestic energy production and rapidly increasing consumption is projected to expand even further in the next two decades as more Chinese consumers become sufficiently wealthy to buy more energy consuming devices, especially automobiles. China surpassed the United States in 2009 as the world's largest auto market, when it grew by almost 50 percent, making it attractive to industry leaders hit hard by the economic recession. The rise of the Chinese middle class will continue making tidal waves in the energy market, as more cars means more oil consumption.[29]

China's energy resources will not cover the PRC's growing demand, particularly for oil and natural gas. Although China has substantial coal reserves—with 33 percent of global supply, the third-largest reserve in the world—its oil (2 to 3 percent) and gas (1 percent) reserves are extraordinarily small compared with China's relative share of the world's population or geographic area.[30] Despite Beijing's continued hopes regarding the domestic exploration and production of oil, the mature oil fields that currently produce the majority of the PRC's crude oil—including Daqing, Shengli, and Liaohe—are depleting rapidly. Although gains in offshore production help offset declines in onshore production, China's crude output is projected to remain relatively flat during the next two decades. Natural gas consumption as a proportion of China's total energy consumption was only 4 percent in 2008, but is expected to rise over time. In contrast, China is the world's largest producer and consumer of coal.[31]

PRC policymakers have increasingly placed their hopes on developing nuclear, hydroelectric, and other renewable energy sources. Although China's electricity will continue to be overwhelmingly supplied by burning conventional coal supplies, the PRC plans to substantially increase its use of nuclear power. In 2007, China's nuclear reactors produced 2.3 percent of the country's electricity, compared with over 25 percent in Japan and approximately 75 percent in France. The Chinese government has set official targets that amount to a ten-fold increase in nuclear capacity from its current capacity of 8.6 gigawatt electrical (GWe)—80 GWe by 2020, 200 GWe by 2030, and 400 GWe by 2050. Nuclear power production is projected to grow at an average of 8.4 percent every year from 2007 to 2035, second only to India in magnitude.[32] In 2009, 43 percent of the world's active nuclear construction projects were located in China. At this rate, the EIA anticipates that the PRC will have 66 GWe of net generation capacity by 2035.[33] The 2011 nuclear accident in Japan does not appear to have disrupted these plans.

Despite the PRC government's best efforts, China's domestic uranium supplies meet less than half of the requirements of the PRC's expanding nuclear energy program, whereas China's efforts to create alternative nuclear fuel cycles has not yet made substantial progress. As a result, China has been forced to seek foreign supplies of uranium to fuel its nuclear energy programs. Two large State-Owned Enterprises—the CNNC subsidiary China Nuclear International Uranium Corporation (CNIUC) and China Guangdong Nuclear Power Company (CGNPC)—and their subsidiaries hold primary responsibility in overseas exploration and trade negotiations. They have negotiated long-term contracts with several uranium-exporting countries. Many of these are unstable or have other unfavorable attributes from Beijing's point of view.

China's total uranium imports in 2010 amounted to 17,136 tons, a threefold increase from the previous year. The fall in uranium prices on the spot market by two-thirds during the global recession in 2008 gave China a great opportunity to stockpile uranium, but the PRC's ambitious plans to expand its nuclear program beyond 2020 will soon exhaust even this horde. Central Asia provides China with many valuable raw materials, including natural uranium. Kazakhstan, the world's largest producer of natural uranium, sells more uranium to China than to any other country. The CNNC and CGNPC both hold stakes and contracts for uranium mines in that country. In November 2008, the Chinese and Kazakhstani prime ministers signed a uranium and nuclear cooperation agreement between the two countries. The state-owned KazAtomProm signed deals for joint development and exploration of uranium resources, production of fuel, long-term trade, and construction of power plants with the CGNPC. CNNC has signed long-term nuclear projects, while KazAtomProm invests directly in China's nuclear power, and both countries have created a joint venture in uranium production. On June 18, 2010, PRC President Hu and Kazakhstani President Nursultan Nazarbayev signed an additional deal on the construction of a gas line. KazAtomProm and CGNPC also reached a deal on increasing uranium sales to China. Under its term, China is importing 24,000 tons of uranium during the 2008–2012 period. The first results of the above agreements were the Semizbay-U joint venture in Irkol, Kazakhstan, created in April 2009 and capable of producing 750 tons of uranium per year. In 2011, China and Kazakhstan signed a deal to deliver 55,000 tons of uranium during the following decade. Chinese companies have also displayed interest in acquiring uranium from other Central Asian countries. In June 2010, the CGNPC signed a contract with Uzbekistan's state-owned Navoi Mining & Metallurgy Combine for a significant amount of uranium imports. In August 2010, China and Uzbekistan also created a joint venture company—Uz-China Uran LLC—to research viable sources of the mineral in the Navoi region of southwest Uzbekistan. China's uranium quest in Central Asia has met some obstacles. The region's underdeveloped energy infrastructure has necessitated additional Chinese investment. China also faces heavy competition for Central Asian uranium. Corporations from Russia and Japan are eagerly seeking the uranium, which creates volatile world prices. Kazakhstan and the other Central Asian countries pursue a balanced strategy of seeking lucrative relationships with all foreign buyers except Iran. Russia in particular has provided an attractive alternative by offering to enrich Kazakhstani uranium and help Kazakhstan construct nuclear reactors.

Mongolia has likewise been torn between China and Russia in deciding where to sell its uranium, generating another source of global price and supply shocks. In 2007, the China Nuclear Energy Industry Corp came to an agreement with Century City International to help discover and utilize uranium in eastern Mongolia. In 2008, China and Russia signed a $1 billion deal on building an enrichment facility in China, which will supply the People's Republic with low-enriched uranium. Several African countries also sell uranium to China. The French company Areva agreed to sell the CGNPC and Chinese sovereign wealth funds a 49 percent stake in its Areva Resources Southern Africa, which will give the CGNPC access to more than half (the precise amount was undisclosed) of that organization's output, most of which will initially come from the Namibian Trekkopje mine. The CNNC recently started probationary mining at its first overseas mine in Azelik, Niger. SinoU has a 37 percent share of the mine. Beijing has begun seeking out uranium in Tanzania, Zambia, and Zimbabwe as well. China holds a joint-venture agreement to mine uranium in Zimbabwe, which may have as much as 455,000 tons of uranium. Niger received a loan for $99 million from the Export-Import Bank of China to help support the mine. Unlike Western corporations, the PRC government can "encourage" other state-run institutions, such as its development banks and government agencies, to support the overseas acquisition efforts of Chinese corporations. This bundling is seen most often in Africa. Compared with Western aid, few strings are attached to this Chinese money, allowing authoritarian governments to use the funds to entrench their power. Meanwhile, African workers complain about their atrocious working conditions and lack of adequate labor rights. Chinese public relations attempt to justify the situation by pointing out that Beijing-backed economic cooperation has benefited Africa by building hospitals, schools, and other public infrastructure.

Beijing's uranium quest reaches other continents as well. China signed two important agreements with Australia in 2006. The Nuclear Transfer Agreement lets China use Australian uranium in specified installations, while the Nuclear Cooperation Agreement lets the Chinese search Australia for uranium. Altogether, China imports around 500 tons of uranium from Australia each year. The only independent entity from the Chinese nuclear industry (but still state-owned) is Sinosteel, a corporation that holds stock in an Australian uranium company and a joint-venture in a mine there. In the future, Sinosteel plans to sell its uranium to either CGNPC or CNNC. In 2008, the Chinese company

Sinosteel and an Australian company, Monaro Mining NL, came to an agreement where Sinosteel would take charge of all Monaro's uranium mining operations in Kyrgyzstan. Moreover, Hebai Mining, a PRC company, possesses almost 11 percent of Raisama Ltd., a company that engages in uranium-mining activities in Kyrgyzstan. In addition, Chinese companies have been investing heavily in uranium-mining operations in Australia. On February 7, 2007, China's Sinosteel and Australia's PepinNini Minerals signed a joint venture agreement to explore uranium deposits in Australia's heartland. However, relations have not always developed smoothly. The Rio Tinto mining scandal was a blow to relations between the Australian and Chinese governments as well as their business communities, with the PRC authorities seemingly retaliating for a failed investment deal by arresting the firm's PRC-based representatives.

On June 24, 2010, CNNC's China Nuclear Energy Corporation signed a long-term contract with Canada's Cameco Corp. for importing 10,000 tons of uranium over a 10-year period. That November, Cameco signed an agreement with China Guangdong Nuclear Power Holding to import 13,000 tons of the mineral through 2025. Also in November 2010, during China's President Hu's visit to France, the French nuclear giant AREVA signed deals with CNNC and CGNPC to construct reactors and export uranium. CGNPC and AREVA signed a $3.5 billion contract to export uranium to China, as much as 20,000 tons over a 10-year period.

Although Japan's uranium requirements have fallen dramatically following the 2011 accident and subsequent closure of all Japan's nuclear power plants, the PRC still faces stiff international competition for uranium from Russia and India. Russia has contracted with some of the same countries as China in a multitude of uranium deals. Russian companies have aimed to develop the Semizbai and Kosachinoye deposits in northern Kazakhstan, and there are already three uranium-mining joint ventures in the area. In 2007, Russia signed an agreement with Mongolia regarding uranium exploration, mining, and processing. The Russians are also interested in helping develop Mongolia's Erdes uranium deposit. AtomRedMetZoloto has also made a bid to take over Australian uranium-mining company Mantra Resources Ltd. India too is a major competitor for uranium. Indian corporations have signed contracts to purchase uranium from Niger, Kazakhstan, Namibia, and Mongolia. Most recently, India has begun to explore the availability of uranium in markets elsewhere in Central Asia and sub-Saharan Africa.

An even more important renewable energy source than nuclear power, at least in the near term, is hydropower. Total hydroelectric output in China in 2009 was 615.64-billion kilowatt hours (kWh), constituting 16.6 percent of all electricity generated, which was the highest total in the world. Completed in July 2012, the Three Gorges Dams project is the largest hydroelectric power station in the world, with a total capacity of 22.5 GWe. China is also looking to import hydropower from Russia. An October 2010 agreement signed between Euro-SibEnergo PLC and China Yangtze Power Co should see hydropower produced in Siberia powering parts of Northwest China.[34] The PRC has been investing heavily in its renewable energy sector since the adoption of the 2005 Renewable Energy Law. Between 2005 and 2009, China invested $34.6 billion in renewable energy technologies—almost twice as much as the United States for that period.[35] The PRC has become the largest manufacturer of wind turbines and solar panels in the world. Renewable energy consumption accounted for 9 percent of total energy use in 2009, with a target of 15 percent in 2020. Wind power capacity alone grew 30-fold, from 0.8 gigawatts (GW) at the end of 2004 to 26 GW by the end of 2009.[36] The PRC also leads the world in coal-to-liquids production, and will account for more than half of the world's total production of these sources by 2035.[37] Even here, however, China's domination of renewable energy technologies has created tensions between Beijing and foreign countries. In September 2010, the United Steelworkers union joined with the U.S. Trade Representative in charging that PRC authorities have provided hundreds of billions of dollars in subsidies and other support to China's renewable energy sector in violation of WTO provisions.

As in other areas, the Chinese government has had difficulty ensuring effective top-down direction within the energy sector now that so many more independent actors are involved because of the partial transition to a market economy. Beginning in the 1980s, the Chinese government has slowly modernized its bureaucratic infrastructure to manage energy resources more efficiently. To move from a command economy to one more dependent on market forces, Beijing converted its energy ministries into state-owned enterprises (SOEs). However, this shift was less dramatic than implied because bureaucrats continued to control the energy companies.[38] When the PRC finally created a National Energy Commission in January 2010 to produce a better-integrated domestic energy policy, Premier Wen Jiabao designated himself as its head instead of appointing a civil servant. Still, it remains unclear whether this latest restructuring will prove more effective than previous attempts at establishing cabinet-level energy management mechanisms. In any case, the energy regulatory apparatus in China is understaffed and underfunded.[39] The human and other resources of many PRC energy enterprises are often greater/larger than the government bodies mandated to supervise them—the end result is a regulatory body that must rely on the regulated for information and policy recommendations.[40]

PRC policymakers recognize their need to draw on the best global energy technologies and practices in developing their own energy sector. Despite remarkable success in promoting foreign direct investment in general, continued loyalty to state-owned petroleum firms by PRC regulators, inadequate economic transparency, and persistent price distortions because of subsidies for petroleum products have worried foreign companies doing business in China's energy sector.

Currently, the majority of imported, refined, and processed oil flows through four state trading companies: the China National Petroleum Corporation (CNPC), the China Petroleum and Chemical Corporation (Sinopec), the China National Offshore Oil Corporation (CNOOC), and Shaanxi Yanchang Petroleum Corporation. The government grants only limited quota volumes to nonstate trading partners.[41] The two primary state petroleum firms, Sinopec and CNPC, are protected against the newly licensed nonstate trading partners by regulations limiting the latter's crude oil sales solely for refinement and precluding their investing in highly regulated petroleum product markets such as gasoline and diesel, which remain within the jurisdiction of the four state trading entities.[42] In most cases, foreign companies cannot own or produce natural energy resources, and must establish joint ventures to participate in energy refining and retailing within China.[43]

ARMS SALES

Although the PRC's arms exports are still considerably less than those of Russia or the United States, China will probably become a leading arms exporter in coming years because of its ability to sell increasingly sophisticated weapons at affordable prices—often as part of a package deal with economic, trade, and R&D cooperation—to almost any regime regardless of its domestic policies. During the Cold War, Beijing provided revolutionary movements, Maoist guerrilla forces, and friendly governments other unsophisticated weapons at heavily subsidized rates or for free. During the 1980s and 1990s, Chinese exporters began to sell more advanced weapons systems, especially ballistic missile systems and related technologies, to Middle Eastern countries. The PRC can today offer prospective buyers two fourth-generation fighters (the FC 1 and the J 10), MA60 transport aircraft, the L 15 trainer jet, Project F 22P frigates, Z 9 and Z-11 helicopters, Type 90 tanks, light armored vehicles, self-propelled and towed artillery, many types of trucks, and a variety of antiship, antitank, and antiair missile systems. The Middle East remains China's largest arms market in terms of value.[44] Through sales of conventional weapons to Iran and other states, Chinese officials may hope to profit from the sales directly to these energy-rich states but also by strengthening ties with major sources of China's foreign oil. Iran and Saudi Arabia regularly rank as two of China's most important oil exporters.[45] At the same time, China has become the second-largest supplier of conventional weapons to sub-Saharan Africa. Although such exports probably do not yield much revenue in the context of China's overall foreign commerce, PRC policymakers probably consider them useful means for improving diplomatic ties and securing access to certain untapped energy reserves and other raw materials in African countries. The sales also help defray the costs to China of developing some new systems. The PRC recently produced its first Mine Resistant Ambush Protected (MRAP) carriers, which it is selling to the Ugandan police force but which will enter service with the PLA as well.[46]

Chinese arms sales to Latin America also have been growing. PRC officials may have hoped the arms sales would enhance their influence in this important region, but financial considerations also appear to have motivated many of these deals. The PLA, which at the time was able to run its own businesses, often profited directly from these transactions.[47] Today, developing countries that need inexpensive weapons and that cannot purchase Western weapons for political reasons (such as Iran, Sudan, Syria, or Venezuela) often find Chinese systems attractive. In addition, some countries buy PRC-made arms in an effort to strengthen their diplomatic ties with China.

In this sense, China's arms sales result in a variety of "win-win" situations. Selling major weapons generates foreign currency for China while supplying uniforms and small arms for free or at a subsidized price generates good will for Beijing at low cost. In addition, arms transfers to friendly regimes help fortify them against military coups, popular uprisings, and foreign adversaries. On the one hand, the recipient leaders can bribe their defense establishments with Chinese armaments; on the other hand, they can use PRC-provided weapons to repress popular uprisings and deter or defeat threats from potential foreign adversaries. In coming years, China could become Africa's leading arms supplier. PRC leaders continue to cultivate defense ties with Africa's political and military leaders—many of whom are interchangeable. China typically charges less for its weapons than do competing Western and Russian defense companies; in addition, China's ongoing military modernization should result in the PLA's discarding large numbers of older weapons that can be sold on international arms markets. Although incompatible with China's plans to wage high-tech information warfare against potential regional adversaries, these earlier models could still prove quite deadly in Africa's myriad regional and internal conflicts.

The Chinese government insists that it adheres to rigorous arms export principles that conform to international law and UN Security Council resolutions. These standards include selling only defensive weapons that do not destabilize regional force balances or violate international weapons bans adopted by the Security Council. Chinese officials also maintain that—pursuant to Beijing's policy of noninterference in recipients' internal affairs—the PRC only provides arms to sovereign countries and not to nonstate actors such as terrorist groups.[48] Even so, some of China's recent conventional arms sales have embarrassed the Chinese government, caused tensions with other countries, or both. In June 2008, for instance, Beijing suffered the "Ship of Shame" incident when dockworkers in South Africa and other African countries refused to unload a delivery of ammunition, small arms, and light weapons from a Chinese ship intended for the Zimbabwean government. The electoral tensions in the country made evident that the government of Robert Mugabe would likely use these

Chinese-manufactured weapons to repress his domestic opponents. The ship eventually returned to China, though the PRC continues to deliver arms to the Mugabe regime despite its pariah status.[49]

Beijing's relations with Washington and London became strained after U.S. officials determined that insurgents in Iraq and Afghanistan were using Chinese-made weapons. Although some of these arms may have left China before September 2001, others appear to have been weapons the PRC more recently sold to Iran. Experts disagree over the extent to which Chinese officials were involved or even aware of these transfers. The Bush administration, depending on Beijing's assistance regarding North Korea, downplayed the issue of culpability and—at least in public—simply called on the Chinese government to "do a better job of policing these sales."[50] The Foreign Ministry issued a statement insisting that the Chinese government never sold arms to "non-country entities or people" because it "takes a scrupulous and responsible attitude to the export of its arms," a formulation that conveniently ignored the issue of retransfers from Iran or by nongovernmental Chinese entities.[51] Hamas has launched Chinese-made Grad-model Katyusha rockets at Ashkelon, Ashdod, and Beersheba. Israeli intelligence believes that Hamas had smuggled the rockets into Gaza after insurgents breached the Sinai border wall the previous January. The Chinese version of the Grad is more advanced than those manufactured in Iran; in addition to its 40-kilometer range, each weapon contains metal balls that can tear through people and material up to 100 meters from the point of impact. Israeli analysts believe that the Chinese-made Grads had been purchased by Iran and then transferred to Hamas—perhaps with Hezbollah's assistance. An Israeli official spoke of "a complicated smuggling system that involves many different people around the world."[52] Even so, Chinese policymakers might worry that these incidents could jeopardize their ability to purchase additional foreign military technology. Members of NATO and the EU continue to ban the sale of arms to the Beijing government since the 1989 Tiananmen crackdown, when the Chinese military killed hundreds of unarmed protesters. Israel sells only a limited range of weapons to keep China from aligning too closely with Iran, Syria, or other potential adversaries of Israel.

NOTES

1. State Council Information Office (PRC), *China's Peaceful Development* (Beijing: State Council Information Office (PRC), 2011), http://english.gov.cn/official/2011-09/06/content_1941354.htm.

2. People's Daily Online, "The Five Principles of Peaceful Co-existence," *People's Daily Online*, June 28, 2004, http://english.peopledaily.com.cn/200406/28/eng20040628_147763.html.

3. State Council Information Office (PRC), *China's National Defense in 2008* (Beijing: State Council Information Office (PRC), 2009), http://english.gov.cn/official/2009-01/20/content_1210227.htm.

4. For a broader discussion of this issue see for example: International Crisis Group, *China's Growing Role in UN Peacekeeping* (International Crisis Group, April 17, 2009), http://www.crisisgroup.org/~/media/Files/asia/north-east-asia/166_chinas_growing_role_in _un_peacekeeping.pdf.

5. Banning Garrett and Jonathan Adams, *U.S.-China Cooperation on the Problem of Failing States and Transnational Threats*, Special Report (United States Institute of Peace, September 2004), http://www.usip.org/publications/us-china-cooperation-problem-failing -states-and-transnational-threats.

6. Colum Lynch, "Russia, China Veto Resolution on Burma," *Washington Post*, January 13, 2007, http://www.washingtonpost.com/wp-dyn/content/article/2007/01/12/AR2007 011201115.html.

7. Risto E.J. Penttilä, *The Role of the G8 in International Peace and Security* (New York: Oxford University Press, 2003), 88.

8. Times Of India, "French Prez Wants India in G8," *Times Of India*, August 31, 2007, http://articles.timesofindia.indiatimes.com/2007-08-31/india/27989683_1_french-president -nicolas-sarkozy-g13-nicholas-sarkozy.

9. Reuters, "France's Sarkozy Says Not Reasonable to Meet as G8," *Reuters* (Paris, July 5, 2009), http://www.reuters.com/article/2008/07/05/us-g8-france-sarkozy-idUSPAC0096322 0080705.

10. G-7, "Declaration on China," *University of Toronto*, July 15, 1989, http://www.g7 .utoronto.ca/summit/1989paris/china.html.

11. Hugo Dobson, *Japan and the G7/8: 1975–2002* (London: Routledge, 2004), 188.

12. Ding Ying, "The Sum of all Summits," *Beijing Review*, no. 25 (June 21, 2007), http:// www.bjreview.com/world/txt/2007-06/18/content_66532.htm.

13. Preeti Bhattacharji, "Uighurs and China's Xinjiang Region," *Council on Foreign Relations*, July 6, 2009, http://www.cfr.org/publication/16870/#5.

14. Philip P. Pan and John Pomfret, "Bin Laden Network's China Connection: Beijing Estimates 1,000 Muslims Have Received Training in Al Qaeda Camps," *Washington Post*, November 11, 2001; BBC, "Anger over Guantanamo Bay Ruling." BBC, October 7, 2008, sec. Americas. http://news.bbc.co.uk/2/hi/americas/7658045.stm.

15. Maureen Fan, "China Moves to Tighten Control Over Religion in Tibet," *Washington Post*, March 26, 2008, http://www.washingtonpost.com/wp-dyn/content/article/2008/03/25/ AR2008032501665.html.

16. Chris Buckley, "Chinese Anger and Terror Warnings Cloud Olympics," *Reuters*, April 12, 2008, http://uk.reuters.com/article/topNews/idUKPEK20364920080411 ?feedType=RSS&feedName=topNews.

17. Edward Wong, "Arrests Increased in Muslim Region of China," *New York Times*, January 5, 2009, http://www.nytimes.com/2009/01/05/world/asia/05iht-06china.19097680 .html.

18. State Council Information Office (PRC), *China's National Defense in 2008*.

19. Ibid.

20. Ibid.

21. International Maritime Organization, "IMO Adopts Comprehensive Maritime Security Measures" (International Maritime Organization, December 13, 2002), http://www.imo .org/blast/mainframe.asp?topic_id=583&doc_id=2689.

22. Denny Roy, "China and the War on Terrorism," *Orbis* 46:3 (Summer 2002), 511–521.

23. Chris Zambelis and Brandon Gentry, "China Through Arab Eyes," *Parameters* (Spring 2008).

24. Joshua Kurlantzick, *Charm Offensive* (New Haven: A New Republic Book, 2007), 36–60; and Xinhua, "China-Indonesia Relations Moving toward Maturity," *Xinhuanet*, October 30, 2006, http://news.xinhuanet.com/english/2006-10/30/content_5268705.htm.

25. Amnesty International, "China—Amnesty International Report 2008," *Amnesty International*, 2008, http://www.amnesty.org/en/region/china/report-2008#.

26. Agence-France Presse, "Obama Urged to Pressure China on Human Rights," *Sino Daily*, January 27, 2009, http://www.sinodaily.com/reports/Obama_urged_to _pressure_China_on_human_rights_999.html.

27. David Rothkopf, "New Energy Paradigm, New Foreign Policy Paradigm," *The Global Politics of Energy*, eds., Kurt M. Campbell and Jonathan Price (Washington, DC: The Aspen Institute, 2008), 186.

28. Linda Jakobson and Dean Knox, *New Foreign Policy Actors in China*, Policy Paper (Stockholm International Peace Research Institute, September 2010), http://books.sipri.org/ files/PP/SIPRIPP26.pdf.

29. Norihiko Shirouzo, "China's Auto Sale Run Hot," *Wall Street Journal*, October 23, 2010.

30. World Energy Council, "2010 Survey of Energy Resources," *World Energy Council*, http://www.worldenergy.org/documents/ser_2010_report_1.pdf.

31. World Coal Association, "Coal Statistics," *World Coal Association*, August 2012, http:// www.worldcoal.org/resources/coal-statistics/.

32. U.S. Energy Information Administration, "International Energy Outlook 2010— Highlights," *U.S. Energy Information Administration*, May 2010, http://www.eia.gov/ forecasts/archive/ieo10/highlights.html.

33. U.S. Energy Information Administration, *International Energy Outlook 2010*, chap. 5.

34. What's On Xiamen, "China Yangtze Power Signs with EuroSibEnergo to Invest in Russia," *What's On Xiamen*, October 14, 2010, http://www.whatsonxiamen.com/invest326.html.

35. Pew Charitable Trust, *Who's Winning the Clean Energy Race?* (Pew Charitable Trust, 2010), http://www.pewtrusts.org/uploadedFiles/wwwpewtrustsorg/Reports/Global_warming/ G-20%20Report.pdf.

36. Eric Martinot, "Renewable Power for China: Past, Present, and Future," *Frontiers of Energy and Power Engineering in China* (2010), http://www.martinot.info/Martinot_FEP4 _prepub.pdf.

37. U.S. Energy Information Administration, *International Energy Outlook 2010*, chap. 2.

38. Jeffrey Bader, "Rising China and Rising Oil Demand: Real and Imagined Problems for the International System," *The Global Politics of Energy*, ed. Kurt M. Campbell and Jonathan Price (Washington, DC: The Aspen Institute, 2008), 101.

39. National Development and Reform Commission, "Brief Introduction of the NDRC," *National Development and Reform Commission*, accessed February 3, 2013, http://en.ndrc.gov .cn/brief/default.htm.

40. Daniel H. Rosen and Trevor Houser, *China Energy: A Guide for the Perplexed*, *The Peterson Institute for International Economics*, May 2007, http://www.petersoninstitute.org/ publications/papers/rosen0507.pdf.

41. Julie Walton, "China Must Push Through Reforms in Its Energy Sector—Especially Price Reform," *China Business Review* (September-October 2005), 10.

42. Ibid., 14.

43. Keith Bradsher, "Security Tops the Environment in China's Energy Plan," *New York Times*, June 17, 2010, http://www.nytimes.com/2010/06/18/business/global/18yuan.html.

44. Peter S. Goodman, "Big Shift in China's Oil Policy," *Washington Post*, July 13, 2005, http://www.washingtonpost.com/wp-dyn/content/article/2005/07/12/AR2005071201546 .html.

45. C. Fred Bergsten, Charles Freeman, Nichlas R. Lardy, and Derek J. Mitchell, *China's Rise: Challenges and Opportunities* (Washington, DC: Peterson Institute for International Economics and the Center for Strategic and International Studies, 2008), 222.

46. China Defense Blog, "Rebranded in China, Exported to Africa." China Defense Blog, December 16, 2011, http://china-defense.blogspot.com/2011/12/rebranded-in-china -exported-to-africa.html; and Chinese Military Review, "New Ambush Protected Vehicles For Peoples Liberation Army (PLA)," *Chinese Military Review*, February 25, 2012, http:// chinesemilitaryreview.blogspot.com/2012/02/new-ambush-protected-vehicles-for.html.

47. Kristen Gunness, "China's Military Diplomacy in an Era of Change," National Defense University Symposium on China's Global Activism: Implications for U.S. Security Interests, *National Defense University*, June 20, 2006, www.ndu.edu/inss/symposia/ pacific2006/Gunnesspaper.pdf.

48. State Council Information Office (PRC), *China's National Defense in 2008*, chap. 11.

49. Levi Tillemann, "Blowback from Zimbabwe: China's Faltering Strategy and Arms Exports," *China Brief* 8, no. 13 (June 18, 2008), http://www.jamestown.org/single/?no _cache=1&tx_ttnews%5Btt_news%5D=5000.

50. Demetri Sevastopulo, "U.S. Concerns over China Weapons in Iraq," *Financial Times*, July 6, 2007, http://www.ft.com/cms/s/0/82ce0740-2c03-11dc-b498-000b5df10621.html.

51. Agence-France Presse, "China Takes Aim At US Over Claims Chinese Missiles Are In Iraq," *Sino Daily*, July 26, 2007, http://www.spacewar.com/reports/China_Takes_Aim_At _US_Over_Claims_Chinese_Missiles_Are_In_Iraq_999.html.

52. Yaakov Katz, "Latest Rockets Manufactured in China," *Jerusalem Post*, January 1, 2009, http://www.jpost.com/servlet/Satellite?cid=1230733119975&pagename=JPost%2FJPArticle %2FShowFull.

Biographies

MAO ZEDONG

Mao Zedong was the first chairman of the Communist Party of China (CPC), founder of what later became the People's Liberation Army, and China's first and most important paramount leader. He established the People's Republic of China (PRC), developed a doctrine of revolutionary guerrilla war that still influences insurgents today, and helped lay the foundations of China's reemergence as a unified great power after centuries of decline. But Mao was also responsible for inflicting great harm on China and its people through his callousness to human suffering, cult of personality, lust for political power, and his policy errors, especially in applying inappropriate socialist principles on China.

Mao was born December 26, 1893, in Shaoshan, Hunan Province, to a land-owning peasant family. He had a strict father but kind mother. Mao quickly lost interest in his father's farm and rejected the bride selected for him when he was a young teenager. In 1911, Mao, then a student in the provincial capital in Changsha, briefly served in Sun Yat-Sen's new Republican Army, which was established after the overthrow of the Qing Dynasty. After graduating from the First Provincial Normal School, Mao traveled to Peking (now Beijing) to work as a library assistant, where he was exposed to Marxist literature. He returned to Changsha in 1920 and in 1921 became secretary of the Hunan branch of the CPC after traveling to Shanghai and leading the Hunan delegation at the Party's first national congress. Following Moscow's advice, the CPC initially allied with the Kuomintang (KMT), led by Sun Yat-Sen, but Chiang Kai-Shek, who took control of the KMT in 1927, soon turned against the Communists. Mao fled to the mountains of Jiangxi after leading a failed Communist uprising against the KMT in Hunan. With Communist militant Zhu De, Mao formed the Red Army as a peasant-based guerilla force, breaking with the Marxist tradition of disdain toward the backward peasantry in favor of glorification of the urban proletariat, which was then weak in China. With this military force, whose strategy and tactics Mao developed in his writings on guerrilla war, the Communists built their presence in the region and established the Jiangxi Soviet. Mao served as chairman of the Soviet and demonstrated strong organizational and leadership skills, but his leadership was often challenged. By 1934, KMT forces surrounded the Jiangxi Soviet and, facing almost certain defeat, Mao led the besieged Red Army on a Long March to freedom in which he emerged as the undisputed CPC leader. Under his command, more than 80,000 soldiers carried out a heroic strategic retreat that saw them trek through mountains and blizzards for a distance of more than 6,000 miles to the remote northern city of Yan'an in the Shaanxi Province. He gradually rebuilt the Red Army and attracted recruits from throughout China. During this time, Mao developed his political thinking and crafted the fundamentals of Maoist thought. He also engaged in various extramarital affairs and remarried for the third time. The Communists, under Mao's leadership, exploited the Japanese attack on the KMT in the late 1930s to secure a truce as well as some U.S. and Soviet military assistance, The Red Army subsequently gradually expand its control over the rest of China against the increasingly ineffective and corrupt KMT government, which eventually had to flee the mainland and establish a government in exile on the island of Formosa (Taiwan).

On October 1, 1949, Mao proclaimed the PRC's establishment and became its first president as well as the CPC chairman. He then made his first trip abroad to Moscow but failed to secure much support or respect from the suspicious Stalin, who was concerned about not exercising total control over the CCP, as the Soviet Union did over its East European satellites. Even so, Mao committed the Red Army to fight against the United States and its Western allies in the Korean War. Although the Red Army suffered massive casualties, and received minimal aid from the Soviet Union, it did succeed in keeping the U.S. Army away from the Korean-China border. The PRC soon began supporting revolutionary movements in Asia, Africa, and Latin America. However, views concerning the path that Communism should take after Nikita Khrushchev came to power in Moscow in the late 1950s led to the Sino-Soviet split in the 1960s, which had a momentous impact on the global communist movement. Mao felt that he rather than Khrushchev, who sought to break with Stalinism and moderate the Soviet Union's revolutionary ideology, represented the true heir to Marxist-Leninism. Under its doctrine of Maoism, the PRC continued to support world revolution and confrontational policies with the West regardless of the risk of nuclear war. The Soviet government refused to support this adventurism, ended its nuclear and other aid to China, and engaged in a major military buildup along the Sino-Soviet frontier, the scene of bloody border clashes as the Chinese denounced the unequal treaties by which the Russian Empire had forced a weak China in the nineteenth century to surrender enormous swathes of territory.

At home, the CPC suppressed freedoms and promoted a personality cult around Mao. Former KMT officials, landowners, and intellectuals were deprived of their property through land reform, suffered public humiliation, and sometimes lost their lives. Furthermore, Mao began to overhaul China's economic structure by introducing the first Five-Year Plan in 1953—a program that, with assistance from the Soviet Union, sought to transform China into an industrial country like the USSR. During this time, the Party attempted to increase literacy by introducing a simplified system of Chinese characters. In 1956, Mao introduced a short-lived Hundred Flowers Campaign to allow what he thought would be a few intellectuals and malcontents a chance to let off steam. Surprised by the widespread attacks on his policies in publicly displayed posters, in 1958 he cracked down on public opponents of his government in an Anti-Rightist Movement. Hundreds of thousands of "Rightists" lost their jobs while tens of thousands were sent to prison camps. Mao never again experimented with political democracy and, along with a sense of paranoia that infected PRC politics for decades, his economic and other views became increasingly radical.

Fearing that the Revolution was stagnating and eager to exploit what he saw as China's great comparative advantage in human labor, Mao introduced a second Five-Year Plan in 1958—known as the Great Leap Forward—that had much more ambitious goals for accelerating China's agricultural and industrial growth. Against Soviet advice, the Great Leap Forward called for massive collectivization of hundreds of thousands of people and private plots, the construction of hundreds of thousands of small steel mills, and increasingly high production quotas. Although the campaign succeeded in mobilizing more people than ever before in history, most of the steel proved useless while the preoccupation with making so much steel led people to neglect the harvest, which ultimately caused the worst man-made famine in history that killed up to forty million people prematurely between 1959 and 1961. Many others survived only through cannibalism. When the scale of the disaster became evident to the Party elite, they forced Mao to accept responsibility for the failures of the Great Leap Forward and quietly resign as PRC president.

Mao remained CPC chairman, and watched with increasing unease as the PRC's new leadership moderated his revolutionary policies and, in his eyes, reintroduced capitalism. In 1966, at the age of 73, Mao made a well-publicized swim in the Yangtze River to highlight his return to the political scene. Mao then organized mass rallies of young people in Beijing who venerated him as a demigod. He soon launched the so-called Great Proletariat Cultural Revolution that enlisted the support of radical young soldiers known as Red Guards to spearhead a revolution against "reactionaries" who Mao argued had become a new privileged class of exploiters. Motivated by Mao's personality cult and brandishing his compilation of selected quotes in the *Little Red Book*, the Red Guards caused mass social upheaval throughout China. Many CPC members were purged, works of history and art were destroyed, while perhaps one million students, scholars, and technocrats were either killed or forced to engage in manual labor in rural areas. Current CCP General Secretary Xi Jinping is one of these "sent-down youth." By 1969, Mao had regained dominant influence as the "Great Helmsman" of the Chinese ship of state. He declared an end to the Cultural Revolution and disbanded the Red Guards, but the PRC has yet to recover from the trauma inflicted by that revolutionary period.

During the 1970s, Mao revolutionized Chinese foreign policy by deciding it made tactical sense to side with the United States against what looked to be ascending Soviet military power. The Vietnam War catalyzed this process because the new Nixon administration wanted China's help in extricating the United States from its losing war effort in Indochina as well as additional leverage against Moscow. After decades of enmity, Mao drew encouragement from informal communications passed through Pakistan and other intermediaries and invited Nixon to visit China in 1972. The two governments then set about reconciling their competing views to align against Moscow. At home, Mao tried to support the radical Gang of Four—which included his wife, Jiang Qing—against more moderate political leaders. After Mao died on September 9, 1976, China's new leaders gradually repudiated his economic policies while trying to pay respect to his early revolutionary triumphs.

ZHOU ENLAI

Zhou Enlai was born March 5, 1898 into an affluent and well-educated family, and lived most of his early life in the Jiangsu Province. After mastering the Chinese Classics at the well-regarded Tianjin Nankai High School, he studied at both Meiji and Kyoto Universities in Japan. While working in exploitative conditions in France in the 1920, Zhou joined the international Communist Movement and became a major recruiter for the Socialist Youth League in France—a position that awarded him numerous travel opportunities and made him the natural leader of the many young Chinese Communists then in that country, such as Deng Xiaoping, six years his junior. In 1924, Zhou returned to China as a well-practiced party organizer and joined the CCP. Although Sun Yat Sen, leader of the Kuomintang (Nationalists), proclaimed an alliance with the Communists against the Chinese warlords, Zhou was acutely aware that many right-wing members of Sun's party considered the CCP the real enemy. Such a difference is important to note, as Zhou was an early advocate of the CCP maintaining its own army. After Sun Yat Sen's death in 1925, Chiang Kai Shek, the new leader of the Kuomintang, turned against the Communists. Zhou became a central figure in the CCP's Red Army. Following Japan's invasion of China in 1937, Zhou served as the CCP's representative to the Kuomintang when the two renewed their alliance to fight the Japanese occupiers. When fighting resumed between them, Zhou helped the Communists achieve victory over the Kuomintang. He then became China's premier in 1949 and served in that capacity until his death in 1976. Zhou married Deng Yingchao in 1925. They did not have any natural children, but adopted several, including future premier Li Peng.

Zhou also served as foreign minister from 1949 until 1958. From 1953 to 1955, he developed the Five Principles of Peaceful Coexistence—one of his primary contributions to Chinese foreign policy. First applied in China's relations with India, these principles were included in a number of communiques and agreements that China signed with various countries and became a staple of PRC speeches and declarations at international conferences. They were written into the PRC Constitution in 1982. The Five Principles included mutual respect for sovereignty and territorial integrity, mutual nonaggression, noninterference in internal affairs, equality and mutual benefit, and peaceful coexistence. Following growing tensions with the Soviet Union, which included armed clashes along the Sino-Soviet border in the late 1960s and early 1970s, Zhou set aside his animosity toward the United States for preventing the Red Army from attacking Taiwan and supporting other anti-Communist forces in the Third World and became a key of the Sino-U.S. reconciliation. Zhou participated in the renewal of diplomatic relations with the United States through dialogues with Henry Kissinger and Richard Nixon, and met Nixon on his historic 1972 trip to China.

As a result of Zhou's duty to carry out the policies developed by Mao Zedong, he bore much of the responsibility in the public eye for their disastrous failures. However, under Mao's more moderate successor, Deng Xiaoping, Zhou later sought to reverse the damage caused by Mao's more radical policies. In January 1976, Zhou lost a two-year battle with bladder cancer just eight months before Mao's death. Much of the country erupted in spontaneous and genuine mourning when he died, reflecting Zhou's status then as a moderate reformer.

DENG XIAOPING

Deng Xiaoping built on Mao's legacy but sought to overcome its weaknesses. He moderated China's economic policies and helped set the stage for China's economic rise. When he came to power, the country was torn apart by the Cultural Revolution and living in poverty, with an average per capita income of $100 per year. More a skilled manager with an openness to experimentation and a long-term vision of China's bright future than an original or creative reformer, Deng helped heal China's Mao-era national divisions and raise national incomes to unimagined levels, allowing hundreds of millions of Chinese to escape poverty. Nonetheless, he was also responsible for authorizing the Tiananmen Square massacre, denying China the potential opportunity of joining most of the rest of the Communist world at the end of the Cold War in rejecting Marxist-Leninism as a ruling ideology.

Deng was born to a landowning family on August 22, 1904, in Xiexing, Sichuan Province. In 1920, Deng traveled to France on a work-study program, where he was exposed to Marxism and subsequently joined the Chinese Communist Youth League in 1921 and CPC in 1924. He did not return to China until 1926, after studying Marxist-Leninism for one year in Moscow, the capital of the new Soviet Union, which was fortuitously then experimenting with economic reform under its New Economic Policy. Upon his return, Deng joined the Communist guerrilla war against the KMT and, like Mao, secured a significant CPC leadership role during the Long March. In the 1930s, when he was a provincial leader, he was criticized for leading the Mao faction within the Party, an attack that endeared him to Mao. The two men then bonded. Unlike Mao and the other Party leaders who were in the relatively safe region of Yan'an and focusing on developing Communist theory and how it might apply to China, from 1937 to 1949, Deng served as a political commissar with frontline troops during the war against Japan and the renewed post-World War II assault against the KMT.

Following the PRC's establishment, Deng quickly rose through the ranks. From 1949 to 1952 he was in charge of the Southwest Bureau, six provinces in southwest China, with more than a hundred million residents. Deng became CPC general secretary and a member of the Politburo Standing Committee in 1956—one of the highest posts in the CPC. He served to 1966, managing party affairs while Mao was making high-level policy as president. Mao's resignation from presidency after the failure of the 1959 Great Leap Forward allowed Deng to achieve even more power, and with new president Liu Shaoqi, Deng began to push for more pragmatic economic policies. Deng became a target of Mao's counterattack a few years later when, at the beginning of the Cultural Revolution, Mao accused Deng of taking the "capitalist road." Mao thought he could be taught a lesson so, in 1969, Deng was exiled to Jiangxi Province and underwent punishment and "re-education" rather than being tortured to death. He was reinstated into the CPC in 1973, becoming vice premier and eventually regaining a position in the Politburo. During his final years, Mao attempted to plant Hua Guofeng as his successor and Deng was briefly purged from the Party again by Mao in 1975, when Mao feared he would not continue the revolutionary struggle after his death. However, Deng was able to outmaneuver Hua after Mao's death in 1976 and consolidate power as PRC leader by 1978. Though Deng never became CPC chairman, he used his position as chairman of its Central Military Commission (CMC) and his state positions to supplement his still considerable influence in the Party apparatus to achieve preeminence. As leader, Deng condemned the excesses of the Cultural Revolution, deemphasized the class struggle, and moderated the country's domestic and foreign economic policies. Although he was careful to avoid excessive criticism of Mao, Deng held a show trial of the Gang of Four and purged others who remained committed to radical Maoism.

Deng's most significant impact came through his economic reforms, known as the "Four Modernizations" of agriculture, industry, military, and technology. They sought to expand rural income and incentives, encourage experiments in enterprise autonomy, reduce central planning, and attract foreign direct investment to the PRC. Deng also decentralized the economy, encouraged the decollectivization of agriculture, allowed people to migrate within China, and permitted more private enterprise. Breaking with Mao's isolationist economic policies, Deng created four Special Economic Zones in coastal cities that featured incentives for foreign investment and trade. However, he did follow Mao in further moderating Chinese foreign policy. In 1978, China entered into a Treaty of Peace and Friendship with Japan. Under Deng's rule, relations between the PRC and the United States also warmed, and the United States recognized the PRC and broke ties with the Republic of China on Taiwan in 1978. Deng became the first Chinese head of state to visit the United States. Following his lead, tourism and educational exchanges between the two countries became increasingly common. Deng successfully concluded a Sino-British Joint Declaration that returned Hong Kong to Chinese sovereignty in 1997. Deng made a similar deal with Portugal to regain control of Macao. He implemented a "one country, two systems" policy in the returned territories that gave them some political and economic autonomy.

Despite abandoning economic socialism, Deng was unwilling to allow similar political reforms. By calling his reformed economy "socialism with Chinese characteristics," Deng implied that he wanted to improve the economic condition of China without fundamentally changing the ideology behind the ruling CPC. In 1978, activist Wei Jingsheng demanded true democracy as a Fifth Modernization, but was quickly imprisoned. Throughout the 1980s, Deng suppressed prodemocracy organizations and demonstrations, which were inspired in part by his economic reforms. The prodemocracy movement reached a climax in 1989, when thousands of peaceful student demonstrators established a massive makeshift democracy camp in Tiananmen Square. Denounced by many of the protest leaders, who accuse Deng of being corrupt and politically intolerant, Deng accuses the students of seeking to overthrow the CCP government. As head of the CMC, he declares martial law and orders a military crackdown that kills hundreds of students in Beijing and results in massive arrests, with some deaths, throughout the country. Following the Tiananmen protests, Deng removed himself from China's political scene. He stepped down as chairman of the CMC in 1989 and then from all political positions in 1992 as Jiang Zemin took over as paramount leader. Despite his retirement, Deng continued to push for his economic policy and made a famous tour of the large cities of southern China promoting economic reforms. Throughout the 1990s, his influence in China declined steadily. At the age of 92, Deng died on February 19, 1997, in Beijing.

JIANG ZEMIN

Handpicked as Deng Xiaoping's successor, Jiang Zemin furthered economic reforms in China and improved foreign relations, which continued Deng's policy of rejecting major political reforms and maintained suppression of political dissent.

Jiang was born in 1926 and raised in Yangzhou, Jiangsu Province, into a Communist family. Jiang graduated from Shanghai Jiao Tong University in 1947 with a degree in electrical engineering. During the 1950s, he traveled to Moscow to work in an automobile factory and entered government service after returning to China. Jiang quickly rose through the CPC ranks and, in 1985, became mayor and party chief in Shanghai, China's largest and most prosperous city. As mayor, he was known for his support of Deng's economic reforms and his peaceful suppression of prodemocracy protests. Many people of Shanghai, however, thought of Jiang as more of a figurehead and credited the economic growth of Shanghai to his subordinate and future mayor, Zhu Rongji. As party chief in Shanghai, Jiang was elevated to a seat on the CPC Politburo in 1987. As the national leadership scrambled to handle the crisis over the Tiananmen Square protests, Party leaders publicized Jiang's successes in handling protestors in Shanghai. Deng soon designated Jiang as his successor, replacing Zhao Ziyang, who, as CPC general secretary, was sympathetic to the protestors. Later in 1989, Jiang also took over as chairman of the Central Military Commission after Deng stepped down.

Although Jiang lacked a strong base of support within the Party, Deng's strong support assured Jiang's ascent. He surrounded himself with Shanghai's aides and became the PRC president and paramount in 1993. He continued Deng's economic policies. The PRC experienced increased economic growth, but also saw a widening of the class gap between rich and poor and a rise in organized crime and political corruption. To handle increasing crime, Jiang led a crackdown known as the "Strike Hard" campaign, which led to many arrests and executions. Jiang added a new layer of theory to the Party line before transferring power to the next generation of leadership. At the 16th Party Congress in 2002, Jiang introduced his "Three Represents" ideology, which was then adopted by the Party. This ideology emphasized that the CPC should represent the advanced and socially productive forces in China, which was seen as constituting a majority of the people. Jiang sought to transform the Party ideology from that of a revolutionary body to that of a representative ruling party. Although some believe that Jiang introduced the Three Represents to bolster his image and political legacy, others praise his efforts in adapting the Party ideology to fit a modern and realistic standard.

Shortly after introducing his Three Represents, Jiang began to remove himself from positions of power within the Party to make way for the fourth generation of leadership. He stepped down from the Politburo in 2002, from the presidency in early 2003, and finally as the CMC chairman in September 2004. He was replaced in all capacities by Hu Jintao, who became the next PRC leader on September 19, 2004. Ultimately, Jiang's impact on the direction of the PRC was not revolutionary; rather, he continued Deng's economic reforms and political authoritarianism. His policies led to significant economic growth, but at the expense of the increasing gap between the rich and poor and continued indifference toward environmental and human rights issues. Since resigning from the Central Military Commission, Jiang has largely stayed out of the political scene, although he has made several public appearances at high-profile events.

HU JINTAO

As leader of China until late 2012, Hu Jintao has focused on increasing China's influence in the international community while maintaining domestic political stability despite socioeconomic and ethnic tensions. Hu was born on December 21, 1942, in Taizhou, Jiangsu Province, to a relatively poor family. Hu attended Qinghua University in Beijing and graduated in 1965 with a degree in hydraulic engineering. During this time he joined the CPC and, after graduating, moved to the Gansu Province to work as an engineer. While in Gansu, Hu became active in the CPC grassroots work. He rose through the local Party ranks and was promoted to a prominent position in Gansu after Deng introduced his Four Modernizations. In 1981, Hu went to Beijing to receive political training at the Central Party School, where he befriended Deng's daughter. With connections to the Deng family and the well-known Gansu Party Secretary Song Ping, Hu became secretary of the Guizhou Provincial Party Committee in 1985.

In 1988, Hu became the Party chief of the Tibet Autonomous Region. Some have connected him to the 1989 death of the tenth Panchen Lama—Tibetan Buddhism's second most important lama. That same year, Hu declared martial law in the capital Lhasa several times to curb separatist protests. Although Party leaders in Beijing were delighted by Hu's efforts, many Tibetans criticized his rule. Hu struggled with altitude sickness and spent much of his time in Beijing. The lack of attention to Tibet drew additional criticism from locals and ultimately his rule alienated many in the Tibet Autonomous Region, which saw increasingly public protests in subsequent years.

The fourteenth National Congress of the CPC in 1992 saw the elevation of the third generation of leadership to the Politburo Standing Committee. Looking to add an additional, younger member as an anchor for the future fourth general, Song recommended Hu. With Deng's approval, Hu became the youngest member of the Politburo Standing Committee. A year later, Hu was selected as the heir apparent to third generation leader Jiang Zemin, taking over the leadership of the Secretariat of the CPC Central Committee, in addition to the Central Party School. Throughout the 1990s, Hu actively backed Jiang's policies and slowly began receiving more leadership authority. He became PRC vice president in 1998 and, at the 16th National Congress in 2002, took over the presidency—although Jiang retained some power by choosing to remain as CMC chairman for another two years.

In 2004, Hu became the paramount leader of the PRC. He emphasized his goal of creating a "Harmonious Society" driven by the "Scientific Development Concept." Hu's ideology stressed social welfare and economic development, while also proclaiming a desire to decrease the growing gap between the rich and the poor and between the rapidly developing coastal cities and China's interior regions. Hu also pledged to create new jobs for the estimated 100 million migrant workers, who had abandoned the countryside and moved to eastern China, becoming known as the "floating population." Hu's government has sought to curb the antiauthoritarian effects of the Internet through strict regulation of online activities and the banning of social networking sites that may encourage political opposition. In 2007, Hu did curtail use of the death penalty, but several thousand people are still executed every year. Human rights groups have also criticized Hu's government for abuses against China's Tibetan and Uighur minority groups.

Hu has characterized his foreign policy as promoting "Peaceful Development." Under Hu, the PRC has become increasingly active in international activities and has shifted away from its previous U.S.-centered foreign policy. Because of China's growing demand for imported energy, Hu has cultivated ties with Venezuela, Iran, Sudan, and other states alienated from the West. He has also devoted efforts to gaining influence in Africa through official development aid, foreign direct investment, resource-for-infrastructure loans, and participation in UN peacekeeping operations. To assuage concerns about China's growing economic and military capabilities, Hu promoted the concept of China's "peaceful rise" to greater international responsibility. China's relations with Taiwan remained strained until the Kuomintang (KMT) returned to power in 2008. After that, Hu sought to improve cross-Strait economic and cultural ties. In 2008, at the 11th National People's Congress, Hu was reelected president as well as chairman of the Central Military Commission. He was recently succeeded by his vice president, Xi Jinping.

YANG JIECHI

Yang Jiechi currently serves as China's foreign minister and chief diplomat. He has spent extensive time in Washington, D.C., serving in various diplomatic posts and has therefore had a major impact in representing China to its most important partner, the United States.

Yang was born in Shanghai in 1950. Yang began preparing for higher education abroad by presumably learning English at a middle school in Shanghai that was attached to the Shanghai Foreign Language Institute. At the age of 21, Yang joined the Communist Party. In 1973, he traveled to the United Kingdom to attend the University of Bath and then the London School of Economics, from which he graduated in 1975 with a Ph.D. in History. Yang came of age at a time when it was still unusual for young Chinese to enroll in foreign universities. Upon returning to China, Yang took a job at the Ministry of Foreign Affairs, where he worked as a staff member in the Translation and Interpretation Department, undoubtedly benefitting from his fluency in English. He was soon promoted to second secretary in the same department. After eight years in the ministry, Yang was sent abroad. From 1983 to 1987, he served in the Chinese embassy in Washington, D.C., where he worked his way up from a councilor to second secretary. In 1987, Yang returned to the foreign ministry's Translation and Interpretation Department in Beijing and became the division director in 1990. Then, he was transferred to the ministry's North American and Oceania Affairs Department and worked his way up to division director, ultimately reaching deputy director-general. In 1993, Yang returned to the United States for his second of three assignments at the Chinese Embassy, where he worked as a minister and then deputy chief for two years. In 1995, Yang was called back to Beijing to serve as assistant and then vice minister of Foreign Affairs. In 2001, he was awarded the prestigious position of ambassador to the United States.

Yang's successful career was because of his perfect English and media savvy, which many older Chinese officials lacked, including his predecessor as Chinese ambassador to Washington, Li Zhaoxing. Originally from rural Shandong, Li studied English and French literature in Beijing. His English was never as good as Yang's and he did not have many friends in the United States because of his hard-line mentality and his propensity to lecture others. Conversely, Yang had good ties with many Americans, including George H.W. Bush, whom he befriended when Bush served in China. Despite Yang's polite manners and personal ties, his tenure as ambassador was, at times, tumultuous. Soon after Yang took his post, a collision of a U.S. surveillance aircraft and a Chinese jet fighter near China created an international incident. The Chinese pilot was killed and the American crew held hostage by the Chinese for several days. Yang used his position to present the Chinese view of the incident in the American media. He appeared on several news programs and—in his perfect English—asked the American public to consider how they would react if the situation were reversed and a Chinese aircraft had been spying off their coast. Yang later protested the Dalai Lama's meeting with senior U.S. officials and the decision to grant Taiwanese President Chen Shui-bian transit through the United States.

Returning to Beijing in 2005, Yang served as vice minister of Foreign Affairs for two years. During this time, he was also an alternate member of the 16th

Party Central committee. These positions prepared him for his final promotion, in 2007, to the post of foreign minister. Yang replaced Li Zhaoxing, who had reached the retirement age for ministry positions. During his tenure as foreign minister, China's international presence and prestige continued to grow. In 2008, China hosted the Beijing Olympics and managed to continue growing despite the global economic downturn. At the same time, China has become ever more confident and assertive on the international stage, seen in Yang's statements defending Beijing's expansive claims in the South China Sea and criticizing U.S. efforts to intervene in the dispute. Yang will not reach the mandatory retirement age of 65 until 2015.

LIANG GUANGLIE

Until recently, General Liang Guanglie was China's minister of defense and a member of the CMC. In terms of military seniority, he was second only to the CMC's vice chairman and its head, both of whom traditionally have been the PRC president. Liang was previously military chief of staff and an expert on amphibious operations and strategy. His tenure as defense minister was noteworthy for helping raise the profile of what until recently had been largely a ceremonial position with little real power over defense policy.

Liang Guanglie was born in Santai, Sichuan province, in 1940. He joined the People's Liberation Army (PLA) at the age of 18 and the following year became a CCP member. He worked his way up the ranks from a common foot soldier into the headquarters' staff. From 1963 to 1964, Liang trained at the Xinyang Infantry School in Henan Province. In 1970, he was sent to the Operations Department in the headquarters of the Wuhan Military Region where he remained for nine years. Liang helped command the PLA forces that fought a border war with Vietnam in 1979. This distinguishes him from most of the PLA's high command, as very few Chinese Generals have seen active combat.

Laing subsequently transferred to the 58th Division of the 20th Army, where he served as deputy division commander and then as division commander. During this time, he studied at the PLA's Military College. Between 1983 and 1990, Laing worked his way up the command structure of the 20th Group Army, eventually becoming an army commander. In 1990, he became commander of the 54th Group Army and, three years later, became chief of staff for the Beijing Military Region. Liang remained in Beijing for four years until he was dispatched to command the Shenyang Military Region in 1997.

In 1999, Taiwan's President Lee Teng-Hui began voicing proindependence sentiments, which precipitated a period of high tension across the Taiwan Strait. Because Liang was a battle-tested commander and an amphibious operations specialist, Beijing transferred him to the coastal Nanjing Military Region directly across from Taiwan to underscore PRC's resolve to resist Taiwanese independence.

Liang used his time commanding the Nanjing Military Region to further develop his strategic understanding of the cross-Strait situation. He launched several military exercises on Dongshan Island to test amphibious and naval military capacities and threaten Taiwan. In addition, Liang headed up a research team that produced a book concerning cross-Strait military strategy. Named *The Study of Sailing Across the Strait*, the book analyzed the Ming and Qing era conquests of the island and the lessons that were applicable to current strategy. Liang also studied U.S. amphibious actions in the Second World War.

After spending three years in the Nanjing Military Region, Liang was promoted to full general and made chief of the General Staff; he also received a seat on the CMC. Liang was in competition with another PLA general, Chen Bingde, for the chief of staff position. Both men were Taiwan specialists, illustrating the importance the PRC's military and government places on the island. Liang emerged victorious because of his ability to work with others and his calm demeanor; in contrast, Chen was reputedly self-centered and difficult to work with. Nevertheless, Chen eventually succeeded Liang in the post after Liang was promoted.

Liang served five years as PLA chief. In 2008, he was promoted to become minister of defense and state councilor. It was notable that, unlike his predecessor Cao Gangchuan, Liang was not made a vice chairman in the CMC. Hu Jintao, as head of the CMC, had decided to return the body to its former structure with two instead of three vice-chairs. Even though he did not possess the title of vice chairman, Liang had similar authority. Liang was both an important military leader in charge of PLA operations and an influential policy adviser to the senior PRC civilian leadership. Liang served as the PLA's senior representative to foreign militaries, attending high-profile international conferences and various official bilateral and multilateral meetings of the PRC government. At home, Liang stressed the PLA's role in preserving China's sovereignty from foreign powers and combating the "three forces" of separatism, terrorism, and extremism. He also oversaw the PLA's continued military buildup, including the launching of its first aircraft carrier.

XI JINPING

Xi Jinping is China's new president, CCP general secretary, and chairman of the Central Military Commission. He is known as a "princeling" because he is the son of Xi Zhongxun, a former CCP Politburo member, PRC vice premier, and economic reformer. Xi Jinping is also a protégé of former PRC President Jiang Zemin and Vice President Zeng Qinghong. Despite his prominence, Xi's public record is that of a hard worker, competent administrator, and elite consensus builder, without any strong substantive commitments or writings, which made a safe choice for China's next leader. He successfully managed a series of government posts of increasing responsibility as well as several recent large-scale events, including the Beijing Olympics. He has also cultivated a large network of influential contacts throughout China. Like other PRC leaders, he has endorsed further economic but not political reform. His main conceptual theme has been to raise ideological and moral purity of Party leaders to counter corruption and any erosion of Party discipline. The PRC media has strived to dispel the negative impression of Xi's being a "princeling"—that he rose to power through various elite connections because of birth rather than merit—by highlighting his personal hardships and talents.

A native of Fuping County, Shaanxi province, Xi was born in 1953. His father, Xi Zhongxun, was an important guerrilla commander during the Japanese occupation and became an influential CCP leader and vice premier. During the Cultural Revolution, Xi's father was accused of plotting against the Party and jailed. The young Jinping and his six siblings also faced persecution because of their father's fall from grace. Local party officials and zealous Red Guards forced him to attend daily "struggle" sessions where he had to prove his loyalties by denouncing his father. In the end, however, Xi decided to make the most out of his predicament and adopt a positive attitude toward his work. At the age of 16, Xi went to Liangjiahe village in northwest China's Shaanxi Province to labor at shepherding animals, gathering wheat, and cutting hay. Villagers of Liangjiahe who supposedly knew Xi said he left a positive impression because of his work ethic and physical prowess. Xi became CCP branch secretary for the village after joining the Communist Party in 1974. Xi describes his exile to the desert province as a "defining experience" in his life.

In 1975, the local government recommended Xi for admission to the prestigious Tsinghua University in Beijing and four years later he graduated with a degree in chemical engineering. By this time Mao had died, the Cultural Revolution was over, and Xi's father was rehabilitated and governor of Guangdong Province, where he played a major role in promoting the SEZ and other economic reforms Xi's family connections helped him find jobs in Beijing. From 1979 to 1982, for example, he worked at the General Office of the CMC as an aide to his father's former subordinate, Geng Biao, then a vice premier and CMC secretary-general. The post helped Xi develop ties to the PLA.

In 1982, Xi moved from Beijing to Zhengding County in north China's Hebei Province. Between 1982 and 1985, he held the positions of deputy secretary and later secretary of the local Party Committee. Xi reportedly said that he asked for the transfer to this low-profile province because he did not like the institutional culture in Beijing. Xi may have made the move to disarm fears that he had senior PRC political ambitions. The elders who had purged his father worried that the younger Xi might try to retaliate. In 1985, he made a short trip to the United States when he traveled to Muscatine, Iowa as the head of a delegation concerned with animal feed. While there, Xi studied ways to raise hogs and stayed with a local family. The individual who hosted Xi, Eleanor Dvorchak, said that, "He was a very polite and kind guy. I could see someone very devoted to his work," adding that, "He was serious. He was a man on a mission." The organizer of the trip, Sarah Lande, observed that, "You could tell he was in charge . . . he seemed relaxed and welcoming and able to handle things," and "He had the words he wanted to express himself easily."

That year, Xi became Party chief of Ningde Prefecture in Fujian Province, which is located in southeast China, across from Taiwan. He would spend the next 17 years in Fujian province, holding various government and leadership positions, until he finally attained the status of provincial governor in 2000. His successes enabled Xi to survive his father's third and final fall from power for advocating liberal views. The younger Xi made a name for himself in Fujian by rooting out local corruption. He also worked to attract overseas investment, tried to improve relations with Taiwan, promoted environmental conservation, and sought to improve public services. His slogan of "Do it now" aimed to convey the message to work efficiently and respond swiftly to issues. Xi's success in Fujian made him popular and helped his political ascension. The 15th Party Congress in 1997 elected Xi as an alternate member of the CCP Central Committee.

In 2002, Xi became a full CCP Central Committee member and moved to Zhejiang Province, where he stayed through 2007. He served as secretary of the CPC Zhejiang Provincial Committee, acting governor of the province, and chairman of the Standing Committee of Zhejiang's Provincial People's Congress. As he did in Fujian, he tried to lure foreign investment to the province. A U.S. diplomatic cable later released by WikiLeaks suggested that Xi helped U.S. businesses expand their presence in Zhejiang. Xi also attempted to restructure Zhejiang's industrial base, trying to reduce pollution and energy consumption and working more closely with Jiangsu Province and the municipality of Shanghai. He managed the successful evacuation of approximately one million people during an August 2006 typhoon.

In 2007, Xi became Secretary of the CPC Shanghai Municipal Committee following a corruption scandal. However, he would be in charge of Shanghai only for a short while, as he was promoted to the nine-member Political Bureau Standing Committee, the country's top governing body, at the 17th Party Congress six months later. He also became a member of the CCP Secretariat and president of the Central Party School, the Party's cadre-training and ideological education wing. On March 15, 2008, the 11th National People's Congress elected Xi PRC vice president. He was put in charge of preparing for the Beijing 2008 Summer Olympics and Paralympics, as well as the Hong Kong and Macao Affairs. From 2010 until 2012, he was the vice chairman of the CPC Central Military Commission. His October 2010 appointment is widely seen as a step toward Xi's succeeding President Hu Jintao.

During the past five years, Xi traveled to more than 40 countries to meet foreign leaders interested in China's new leader-in-waiting. During a five-day visit to the United States in February 2012, Xi said that the relationship between China and the United States was at a "new historical starting point." He has met frequently with Vice President Joseph Biden. When meeting former U.S President Jimmy Carter in Beijing in December 2012, he called for imparting more "positive energy" to the China-U.S. partnership. Xi has regularly defended his country's human rights record and economic policies and denounced "separatist activities" in Tibet that are associated with the Dalai Lama.

At the age of 59, Xi was elected at the 18th CCP Central Committee on November 15, 2012 as the first CCP leader born after the PRC's founding in 1949. Since becoming CCP general secretary, Xi has reaffirmed the Party's commitment to "socialism with Chinese characteristics." His promotion to CMC chair has allowed Xi to extend his fight against corruption, which he warned could destroy the Party, to the PLA, by limiting lavish entertainment budgets. Xi's economic policies have sought to sustain China's economic growth while moderating inflation and preventing a bursting property bubble. He reacted moderately to mass protests in Hong Kong calling for greater democracy and limits in Beijing's influence over Hong Kong's internal affairs. Xi has yet to make a major mark on Chinese foreign policy, an area that was not previously part of his portfolio.

In terms of his personal life, Xi's first wife was the daughter of the former PRC ambassador to the United Kingdom. Xi then remarried, Peng Liyuan, who until recently was more famous than Xi as the lead performer in a song and dance company attached to the PLA. Their only daughter, Xi Mingze, attends Harvard University under an assumed name, while Xi's sister, Xi An'an, may live in Canada.

LI KEQIANG

Under Hu Jintao's patronage, Li Keqiang rose through the Communist Youth League (CYL) and recently became PRC premier, a Politburo member, and the deputy secretary of the Leading Party Members' Group. He is widely considered China's number two leader, after Xi Jinping, and has publicly advocated strengthening China's economic reforms.

Li was born in 1955, in Dingyuan County, Anhui Province. Although his father was a local official, Li's roots in this impoverished inland region distinguish him from many of China's current leaders. Li came of age during the final years of the Cultural Revolution and followed Mao's instruction for youths to learn from the peasants by working in the countryside. In 1974, the 19-year-old Li was sent to Fengyang, an impoverished county in east China's Anhui Province, to perform farming and other manual labor. Two years later, he became a CCP member and, by 1978, he was the Party Secretary for his production brigade. He then entered the Law School of Peking University and in 1980 became head of the university's Student Federation. Upon graduation in 1982, he remained head of Peking University's CYL chapter.

After graduating with a bachelor's degree in law in 1982, Li continued to study part time and eventually obtained masters and doctorate degrees (1994) in economics. Li's doctoral dissertation, "On the Tri-structure of China's Economy," won the Sun Yefang Prize, the top honor for economics. At the same time, he continued his work with the CYL for the next 15 years, becoming an alternate member of the CYL Secretariat. Between 1983 and 1985, Li worked under Hu Jintao, then CYL First Secretary. In 1985, Li became a full member of the CYL Secretariat and was responsible for the national youth and children's associations. In 1993, Li became the CYL First Secretary. Though making sure the organization followed Hu's leadership, under Li's leadership, the CYL declined in popularity among young members.

In 1997, Li was made a full member of the CCP Central Committee. At the age of 43, Li became China's youngest governor with a doctoral degree when, in June 1998, he was appointed Governor of Henan, one of China's most populous provinces. Li drew insights, capital, and experts from China's east coast provinces to help bring more industry to what had until then been a largely agricultural province. He also encouraged enterprises to sell products to western provinces that had lagged behind the coastal provinces in development. As a result of this clever positioning, Henan rose in provincial GDP rankings during the seven years Li was in charge of the province, from 20th to 17th in the national per capita GDP rankings. It also emerged as the most developed of China's interior provinces. However, some blame him for a scandal in which tens of thousands of people were infected with HIV after donating blood in the 1990s.

Li was transferred to Liaoning Province in northeast China, where he was Party secretary from 2004 to 2007. He left his mark through ambitious projects to develop transportation infrastructure and remove slums in the province's once vibrant industrial cities. With government support, more than one million people moved from shantytowns to newly built apartment buildings. The project's success was because of Liaoning's access to lavish central government funding and loans through his close relationship with President Hu, who treated him as his protégé. Regardless, Li's slum-removal project marked his greatest success up to that point and likely secured his political future.

After three years in Liaoning, Li was appointed to the PRC's most powerful body, the Politburo Standing Committee, joining his contemporary, Xi Jinping, as the senior member of the CCP's fifth-generation leadership. This broke with tradition; in previous years, only one clear "core" leader was usually visible, though it soon became clear that Xi would receive the highest position and Li would succeed Wen Jiabao for the second-ranked premier position. At the 2008 National People's Congress, Li was elected first vice premier in charge of economic development and reform, fiscal affairs, urban-rural construction, environmental protection, land and resources, and public health and food safety for the State Council. Through his election, Li became China's youngest vice premier in nearly 20 years. In this capacity, Li led the formulation of China's 12th Five-Year Plan (2011–2015). Hu Jintao probably wanted Li to succeed him as CCP general secretary but, reflecting the trend toward consensus rule, Hu was unable to secure the appointment of his protégé to that post, which went to Xi.

At the 2010 World Economic Forum in Davos, Li briefed the audience on China's commitment to sustainable development, green energy, reduced income inequality, and modernization of key industries. In a February 2010 speech to ministerial and provincial-level leaders, Li stressed that China has come to a historical juncture when its economic structure must change for the country to continue growing. He emphasized the need to boost domestic consumption and address sprawling urbanization. In October 2011, Li led a delegation that visited both North and South Korea, suggesting he may play a role in China's Korean diplomacy in the future. He knows English well and his wife, Cheng Hong, is an English professor at the foreign language department of Capital University of Economics and Business.

In his speeches, Li has called reform "the biggest dividend for China." He has studied international reports assessing China's economic challenges and reform opportunities. He encouraged publication of "China 2030," prepared by the World Bank and China's state-backed Development Research Center, which advocates breaking apart China's powerful state sector monopolies. Li has declared support for increasing employment, offering more affordable housing, providing basic health care, balancing regional development, and promoting innovation in clean energy technology. Li reportedly also is skeptical of some of government's economic numbers, describing them as "for reference only." Yet, Li's influence in the new leadership is presently much less than that of Xi because only propaganda czar Liu Yunshan, another product of the Communist Youth League system, appears to share his left-wing populist views.

BO XILAI

Bo Xilai was born on July 3, 1949 in Dingxiang Country in Shanxi Province. He was the fourth child of Bo Yibo, who until 1965 had served as minister of finance. Bo Xilai enjoyed a privileged lifestyle throughout most of his princeling childhood. Together with his brothers and other party cadre children he attended Number 4 High School in Beijing, one of the most prestigious schools in the whole country. When in 1966 Mao unleashed the Cultural Revolution, the 17-year-old Bo, together with friends, formed a radical Red Guard faction known as the liandong ("United Action"), which on the one hand embraced far-reaching ideological purges, while on the other tried to protect their family and status as red nobility. Nonetheless, Bo Yibo was labeled as "rightist" and "counter-revolutionary" and sent to prison for 12 years, while his wife was either beaten to death or committed suicide after being abducted by the Red Guard in Guangzhou.

In 1972, after his release from labor camp, Bo Xilai started to work at a machine repair factory for the Beijing Second Light Industry Bureau. With Mao's death in 1976, things rapidly changed for the now 27-year-old Bo Xilai. Bo Yibo was politically rehabilitated by his wartime friend Deng Xiaoping, becoming vice premier in 1979 and becoming one of Deng's most trusted aides. Bo Xilai married Li Danyu; his first wife was a military doctor and daughter of Beijing party secretary Li Xuefeng. Bo's academic career also found traction in 1977 when he enrolled in Peking University, where he studied world history, a field that distinguished him from his many political peers with engineering degrees. In 1982, he graduated with a masters degree in International Journalism from the Chinese Academy of Social Sciences. Bo joined the Communist Party in 1980. About this time, he began an extramarital affair with Gu Kailai, a daughter of a politically influential family. Bo's father had to intervene to secure Bo's divorce from Li Danyu, who successfully resisted a divorce for several years. Bo Xilai and Gu Kailai married in 1986.

Beginning in 1984 Bo Xilai's political career was following an upward trajectory, starting from a low-ranking government official in the Dalian Economic and Technological Development Zone to becoming the mayor of Dalian between 1992 and 2000. In 2001 Bo was appointed permanent governor of the Liaoning province. He became famous for his success in attracting investment to city, major public works projects, and his hardline approach toward Falun Gong practitioners. In 2004 Bo secured himself a spot as commerce minister and CCP commerce secretary, his first high-ranking position within the party. Even so, it took several attempts by his family to secure Bo a seat on the CCP Central Committee, which occurred at the 17th Party Congress in 2007. Bo's hard-charging ways were not appreciated in the government, where Bo was seen as arrogant, self-aggrandizing, and disrespectful of other leaders' interests.

In 2007, Bo's influential father died, and he was forced to leave Beijing for a political backwater: to serve as Communist party secretary of the large (with some 30 million residents) but remote southwestern interior city of Chongqing. Bo sought to revive his political fortunes by promoting what became known as the "Chongqing model" of development. This campaign urged residents to sing "red songs" and display slogans from the Maoist era. He also supported lavish public spending on road building and other infrastructure as well as on social programs to improve the lives of the city's poor. Bo cultivated a casual and charismatic image in the media. He launched a high-profile aggressive anti-corruption campaign known as Dahei ("Striking Black") against criminal gangs that secured unjust convictions and ignored civil rights. Wang, a trusted ally, was instrumental in carrying out the fierce crackdown on organized crime that resulted in thousands of arrests, including of senior police officers, wealthy businessmen, and high-level Party officials accused of shielding criminal leaders. More than a dozen people were executed after speedy and seemingly unfair trials that critics claimed were aimed at eliminating political rivals and stealing their money.

Bo was notorious for his political ambitions. His self-promotion campaigns ran against the PRC political tradition of hiding one's ambitions. Bo's admirers included Jiang Zemin, other princelings, and those who admired his seeming ability to secure results. He also appealed to those alienated or excluded from China's socioeconomic benefits, put off by the rise of crime and corruption, or nostalgic for the Mao era and its sense of community and equality. Yet, Bo's style unnerved some legal professionals, liberal intellectuals, and many party and military leaders who feared his tactics and revolutionary rhetoric threatened to revive the destructive ways of China's leftist past. Conversely, some considered Bo a political opportunist who exploited neo-Maoism as a public relations tool. The high-profile escapades of his son, who was posting pictures on the Internet of his partying while studying at Oxford and Harvard, brought unwelcome attention to the practice of many Chinese political leaders of sending their children to elite schools abroad whose entry fees were far in excess of their parents' official salaries. Locals also criticized what they saw as Bo's ruthless and arrogant behavior. He reportedly extorted money from business leaders to fund high-profile public shows and displays. Employees described him as a demanding and unforgiving boss who physically assaulted those who failed to deliver what he wanted. Many economists consider Chongqing's massive public debt unsustainable and certainly no model for other parts of China.

Bo's plans to rise further became undone in February 6, 2012, when his former police chief, Wang Lijun, sought refuge in the U.S. Consulate in Chengdu after he feared that Bo was planning to make him take the fall for the central government's investigations into the abuses during the Dahei campaign, which Wang had led, gaining the reputation as one of the most ruthless police leaders in all of China. Wang brought along with him lurid evidence of the murder of Neil Heywood, a British businessman who tried to fix deals between Chinese and foreign people and institutions, by Bo's wife. Although U.S. authorities denied Wang asylum on human rights grounds, they helped him surrender to the central government in Beijing rather than Bo's men in Chongqing. In any case, the move triggered one of the most serious Chinese political scandals in recent years since his act attracted massive publicity to the corruption and abuse of power at the highest levels of China. Bo's last-ditch effort to accuse his rivals of jealousy and attempting to derail his Maoist revival failed as he was stripped of his position in March and his wife was arrested for murder. At the end of September 2012, Chinese leaders announced that Bo had been officially expelled from the Communist Party and would be brought up on criminal charges.

Chronology

1972 U.S. President Richard M. Nixon visits Beijing, Hangzhou, and Shanghai, meeting with the chairman of the Chinese Communist Party (CCP), Mao Zedong, and with Chinese Premier Zhou Enlai. The meeting ends 25 years of isolation between the United States and the People's Republic of China (PRC). At the end of the trip, the United States and the PRC issue the Shanghai Communiqué, which has remained the cornerstone of modern U.S.-Chinese relations. The communiqué pledges the normalization of relations, including increased contact and trade relations. China also signs a communiqué with Japan on September 29, establishing diplomatic ties between the PRC and Japan and severing relations between Japan and the Republic of China (ROC).

1974 China for the first times competes in the 1974 Asian Games, whereas the Asian Games Federation excludes the ROC.

1976 China's two legendary Communist leaders, Premier Zhou Enlai (on January 8) and Mao Zedong (September 9), die. Hua Guofeng, a moderate but loyal follower of Mao, succeeds to both positions, becoming the only person in PRC history to hold simultaneously the posts of premier, CCP chairman, and chair of the Central Military Commission (CMC). In October, Hua arrests the so-called Gang of Four, radical leaders committed to the Cultural Revolution.

1977 Hua introduces the Open Door policy, which allows China to engage in international trade. Deng Xiaoping reemerges in the public and assumes the offices of the CCP vice chairman, vice premier of the State Council, CMC vice chairman, and chief of the General Staff of the People's Liberation Army (PLA). Deng reopens the universities and reintroduces the national entrance exam, which consists of questions designed to assess students' merits rather than the political correctness of their views.

1978   Deng becomes the PRC's new "paramount leader" and begins experimenting with market socialism, such as establishing Special Economic Zones (SEZ) near Hong Kong in China's southeast. These experiments prove successful and begin to be imitated in other parts of China. In December, the Third Plenary Session of the Eleventh CCP Central Committee adopts the "Four Modernizations" (agriculture, industry, military, and science and technology). These reforms achieve their goals of expanding rural income and incentives, encouraging experiments in enterprise autonomy, reducing central planning, attracting foreign direct investment to the PRC, encouraging Chinese students to study abroad, and generally leading to China's growing engagement with the outside world. Deng identifies the Soviet Union as the PRC's main security threat and calls for improving ties with the United States. On December 15, the U.S. government announces it will establish diplomatic relations with the PRC on January 1, 1979.

1979   The PRC formally establishes diplomatic relations with the United States with the issuance of a second communiqué on January 1. The U.S. government severs official diplomatic relations with Taiwan and ends its bilateral defense agreement with Taipei. Deng becomes the first top PRC leader to visit the United States. He meets President Jimmy Carter, visits the headquarters of Coca-Cola and Boeing, and attends high-profile public events that make him a popular figure with some Americans. China and the United States sign various agreements in the science and technology, education, cultural, and other sectors that result in a surge of exchanges between the two countries, including tens of thousands of Chinese who visit the United States. From February 17 to March 6, China launches a limited incursion into Vietnam, following that country's invasion of Cambodia. The PLA performs poorly and Vietnam forces do not withdraw from Cambodia. The Soviet Union backs Vietnam and accuses the United States of having endorsed China's attack during Deng's visit to Washington. In March, the PRC and the United States opens embassies in each other's capitals. In April, the U.S. Congress enacts the Taiwan Relations Act (TRA), which reinstates unofficial economic and security ties between the United States and Taiwan. The TRA commits the United States to supply Taiwan the arms it needs to maintain a "sufficient self-defense capability." The PRC institutes a "One-Child" Policy in an attempt to reign in population growth. Critics complain it results in forced abortions and the infanticide of female fetuses.

1980 China establishes additional Special Economic Zones in Shenzhen, Zhuhai, Shantou (Guangdong), Xiamen (Fujian), and the entire province of Hainan. The PRC ends its above-ground nuclear test program in Xinjiang province.

1982 In July, President Reagan delivers six assurances on U.S. policy toward Taiwan. In August, China and the United States jointly issue the 817 Communiqué, which touches on the U.S. arms sales to Taiwan. From September 1 to 11, 1982, the CCP Twelfth National Congress sees Hua Guofeng lose formal power while reformer Hu Yaobang, an ally of Deng, gains influence, delivering the keynote speech and becoming CCP general secretary, after one year as party chairman. In December, the Fifth National People's Congress adopts a new constitution for China.

1983 A new "Household Responsibility System" allows individual farm families to sell on the free market whatever they could produce in excess of their plan quota at the official government price.

1984 President Ronald Reagan visits the PRC, signaling improved ties after several years of deterioration because of Reagan's outspoken anticommunism, granting of asylum to dissident Hu Na, the stationing of troops in South Korea, and his support for Taiwan. In December, Britain and China sign the Sino-UK Joint Declaration on Hong Kong, which stipulates that Beijing would govern the territory as a Special Administrative Region according to Deng's policy of "one country, two systems." Although Beijing would determine Hong Kong's foreign and defense policies, Hong Kong would retain its free press, rule of law, democratic politics, and capitalist economy for the next 50 years.

1987 In January, conservative CCP leaders, known as the "elders," force Hu Yaobang to step down as general secretary because of his tolerance of student protests demanding greater political freedom. He is replaced by Zhou Ziyang, another reformer. Hu Yaobang became known as "the Soul of China" after he freed many Chinese unjustly imprisoned during the Cultural Revolution and then fought against corruption in the Party. In April, China and Portugal sign a Joint Declaration on Macao, which also pledges application of the policy of "one country, two systems." At the CCP Thirteenth National Congress, which meets from October 25 to November 1, Deng and all other "Second Generation" CCP leaders officially retire from their active position and "Third Generation" members (led by Zhao) hold all the key CCP positions. In practice, Deng controls everything from behind the scenes.

1988 The price reform launched in May results in high inflation, rampant corruption, and soon growing urban discontent.

1989   In February, 40 scholars send a signed petition to the government,
        demanding freedom of the press, release of political prisoners, and greater
        democracy. In March, riots take place in Lhasa following the death of
        Panchen Lama, compelling the government to declare martial law in
        Tibet. The sudden death of Hu Yaobang on April 15 leads students in
        Beijing and other parts of China to make speeches voicing discontent
        with corruption, inflation, press restrictions, university conditions, and
        the continued informal rule of Party "elders." The students occupy
        Tiananmen Square and are joined daily by thousands of other Chinese,
        including journalists and factory workers. Many others cheer on the street
        demonstrators from their apartment balconies. Party, state, and military
        leaders divide on how to respond to the unprecedented mass demonstra-
        tions, whose members establish camp at Tiananmen but also begin to di-
        vide on tactics. The student leaders organize mass hunger strikes and
        benefit from widespread media coverage because, before the protests
        began, the Chinese government had invited journalists to Beijing to cover
        the visit of Soviet President Michael Gorbachev to China in a summit
        that was supposed to mark the end of the Sino-Soviet confrontation. After
        weeks of internal debate and infighting, the hard-line faction within the
        PRC leadership—led by Premier Li Peng, President Yang Shangkun,
        and Deng—warns of mass disorders as during the Cultural Revolution
        and secures support for Li to declare martial law on May 20. Jiang Zemin
        replaces Zhao Ziyang, who refuses to support the crackdown, as CCP
        general secretary. After a show of force fails to end the protests, Deng
        orders fresh PLA units to use force to end the demonstrations, which they
        did beginning on the evening of June 3. The PLA kills hundreds, perhaps
        thousands, of people, including Beijing residents who are simply traveling
        in Beijing. Only a few of the student leaders manage to escape the sub-
        sequent police dragnet and reach political asylum in the West. Western
        governments impose economic sanctions, arms embargoes, and other
        measures against the PRC.

1990   The PRC's first stock market opens in Shanghai. The government aban-
        dons martial law and other emergency measures. Iraq's invasion of Kuwait
        in August 1990 forces Western governments to engage with PRC leaders
        to prevent China's vetoing UN Security Council actions against Iraq.
        Unsafe medical practices lead tens of thousands of peasants who donate
        blood plasma to contracting HIV.

1991   China authorizes UN military action to use force to expel Iraqi forces from
        occupied Kuwait. Beijing then participates in the Paris Peace Agreements end-
        ing the Cambodian civil war.

1992   In January, President Yang Shangkun visits Malaysia and Singapore to strengthen Beijing's ties with Southeast Asia despite conflicting territorial claims over the South China Sea. The 10-nation Association of Southeast Asian Nations (ASEAN) issues a "Declaration on the South China Sea" on July 22, urging the peaceful resolution of territorial disputes. China signs the Nuclear Nonproliferation Treaty and later pledges to adhere to the Missile Technology Control Regime. The United States waives sanctions on state-owned PRC companies that had been imposed for their shipping of nuclear-capable missile technologies to Pakistan. The International Monetary Fund ranks China as the world's third-largest economy. Although 87 years old and technically retired, Deng tours the south and calls for more reforms to promote a "socialist market economy." Deng's successor, Jiang Zemin, supports the same goals. In August, Seoul recognizes Beijing rather than Taipei as "China," stripping Taiwan of its last major Asian ally. In September, however, France and the United States announce they will sell Taiwan new warplanes. In October 1992, the 14th National Party Congress reaffirms Deng's policy of economic reform and international engagement. In December, Boris Yeltsin, the president of the new Russian Federation, signs a declaration of friendship in Beijing. China establishes formal diplomatic relations with Israel.

1993   Construction on the controversial Three Gorges Dam begins despite international environmental protests. The newly elected Bill Clinton administration resumes high-level political exchanges with China, a sign that tensions provoked by the 1989 Tiananmen Square incident were easing. Clinton attempts to make China's Most Favored Nation (MFN) trade status contingent on the PRC's improving its human rights record, but China denounces the effort as unwarrantable intrusion into its internal affairs. Faced also with protests from U.S. business groups, Clinton grants China a one-year extension of MFN status on May 28, but makes further renewals dependent on significant human rights progress. Secretary of State Warren Christopher expresses his willingness to help China make a peaceful transition to democracy, which Chinese officials interpret as a Western threat to change their governmental system. Deng Xiaoping effectively forces Yang Shangkun to retire as president, making way for Deng's protégé, Jiang Zemin. Although Jiang was the first Chinese leader who had not risen to power explicitly through the PLA, he was already CMC chairman. In April, Wang Daohan of the Chinese Association for Relations Across the Taiwan Straits (ARATS) and Koo Chen-fu of the Taiwanese Straits Exchange Foundation (SEF) meet in Singapore for their first high-level negotiations. In July, the PRC becomes a member of the

ASEAN Regional Forum, an organization founded to promote peaceful conflict resolution and regional security. Jiang meets Clinton at the Asia-Pacific Economic Cooperation (APEC) organization meeting in Seattle in November, the first formal meeting between a PRC and U.S. heads of state since 1989. Clinton announces a policy of "constructive engagement" with China. However, after Beijing loses its bid to host the 2000 Olympic Games, the PRC authorities detain Wei Jingsheng, a political prisoner since 1979 who had only recently been released.

1994   In January China abolishes the official Renminbi (RMB) controls on currency exchange rates and unifies the exchange rates. Separate and more favorable exchange rates for manufactured exports are abolished. The new consolidated official rate is set at 8.7 yuan per dollar, which is not so different from the previous swaps rate. In March Warren Christopher visits Beijing, continuing U.S. efforts to tie China's MFN status to closer alignment with Western standards of human rights. Despite the failure of this effort, Clinton extends China's MFN status for another year. In October, China finally persuades North Korea to accept an Agreed Framework in which Pyongyang commits to halting its nuclear development program and abide by the Nuclear Non-Proliferation Treaty (NPT) in exchange for U.S. and Japanese fuel oil and civilian reactor technology. Although China did not formally accede to the Missile Technology Control Regime (MTCR), in a joint U.S.-Chinese statement in October, Beijing reiterates a promise to act in accordance with MTCR provisions and not sell missile equipment capable of carrying 500 kilograms for 300 kilometers (a capacity that would allow the equipment to carry nuclear weapons). The USS Kitty Hawk carrier detects a Chinese submarine following it in the South China Sea and U.S. forces track the Chinese submarine with aircraft. Although common practice during the Cold War, the confrontation was completely unfamiliar to the People's Liberation Army Navy (PLAN), which took great offense and threatened to shoot down the next Navy aircraft to conduct similar action. The Russian and Chinese defense ministers agree on measures to reduce the danger of inadvertent military escalation by adopting the policy of no first use for nuclear weapons and retargeting nuclear missiles away from each other's territory. Overall EU trade with China triples in ten years, from US$14.3 billion in 1985 to US$45.6 billion in 1994. China becomes the fourth-largest trading partner of EU countries. The Mongolian-Chinese Treaty of Friendship and Cooperation is signed, which codifies mutual respect for the independence and territorial integrity of both sides, though the Tibet issue remains a sore point in Mongolian-Chinese relations.

1995   China continues to clash with its neighbors over maritime claims. In February, the PRC sends soldiers thinly disguised as fishermen to erect "shelters" on Mischief Reef in territory claimed by both the Philippines and Vietnam. The fishing shelters have machine-gun emplacements. Several difficult political and security issues surface in the bilateral relationship between China and Japan. The PRC's nuclear testing program draws strong protests from Japan, which led to the freezing of some Japanese aid to China. The presidents of China and South Korea hold a joint press conference in Seoul in which they criticized Japan's alleged failure to adequately address its history of aggression. After Taiwanese President Lee Teng Hui makes an unofficial visit to an alumni reunion at Cornell University in June, the PRC recalls its ambassador to the United States and begins conducting military exercises and missile tests off Taiwan's coast.

1996   The PLA conducts more missile tests to intimidate Taiwanese from re-electing President Lee. In response, the United States deploys two aircraft carrier battle groups near Taiwan. If anything, Beijing's intimidation attempt backfires: Lee wins reelection by a wide margin. Nevertheless, the episode galvanizes Chinese military modernization. On February 14, China launches the Long March 3B, a three-stage rocket with liquid rocket boosters from the Xichang Satellite Launch Centre. The rocket crashes into a nearby village soon after its launch. In April, China, Russia, Kazakhstan, Kyrgyzstan, and Tajikistan sign the Treaty on Deepening Military Trust in Border Regions, developing a multilateral forum unofficially named the "Shanghai Five." A Sino-Russian Joint Declaration describes their relationship as a "strategic partnership." In May, Jiang visits Kenya, Egypt, Ethiopia, Mali, Namibia, and Zimbabwe, promoting stronger Sino-African relations. In the first state visit by a Chinese president to New Delhi, Jiang Zemin and Indian Prime Minister H. D. Deve Gowda agree to reduce their military presence in disputed border areas and refrain from cross-border attacks. China ratifies the UN Law of the Sea on June 7, but reaffirms its disputed claim over the South China Sea.

1997   Deng dies in Beijing on February 19, at the age of 92. A new national defense law in March defines the tripartite structure of China's defense forces: the People's Liberation Army (PLA), the People's Armed Police (PAP), and the People's militia. The PLA reduces its size by 500,000 and focuses on strengthening its military technology. Hong Kong reverts to Chinese control under the "one country, two systems" principle. Chinese officials then begin weakening the prodemocracy reforms that Hong Kong's last British governor, Chris Patten, had instituted. On

September 10, Li Peng signs an agreement, reached in 1993, to forbid nuclear exports to any facilities not supervised by the International Atomic Energy Agency (IAEA). Partly in response to international pressure over its human rights record, China signs the United Nations International Covenant on Economic, Social, and Cultural Rights in October, but this legal change brought little improvement in Chinese practice on the ground. In October, Jiang Zemin formally assumes leadership of the Chinese government at the fifteenth National Congress of the Communist Party. His accession brings other political changes to China's seven-member Politburo Standing Committee. Although Li Peng continues to hold the second-highest authority in the Party, Jiang replaces him as premier, promoting the economic reformer Zhu Rongji in his place. Zhu enacts broad reforms of state-owned enterprises, launching the drive to disentangle the "debt chains" of state enterprises. As governor of the Central Bank, Zhu deftly deals with the excessive money supply, and the "overheating" of the economy because of runaway investments. Li Lanqing, whose experience in foreign trade and investment was well suited to China's increasing efforts to modernize its economy, is selected as senior vice-premier in charge of the economy. Li also heads China's efforts to join the WTO, negotiations that would finally conclude in 2000. In October and November, Jiang's state visit to Washington confirms his political leadership to the international community and helps strengthen bilateral economic and political ties. The Asian economic crisis of 1997 also prompts stronger regional cooperation efforts led by South Korea and China under the ASEAN Plus three rubric (APT)—this group becomes the paramount regional grouping in Eastern Asia. At the first meeting of the ASEAN Plus three in Jakarta, China signs a Joint Declaration with ASEAN committing to peaceful resolution of regional territorial disputes, but by this time the conflicting territorial claims in the South China Sea have been overshadowed by the Asian financial crisis. Conversely, China vetoes a UN resolution to support the peacekeeping effort in Haiti because of Haiti's pro-Taiwan foreign policy. About 1,000 people, mostly Uighur farmers and unemployed youths, rampage through Yining near the border with Kazakhstan. State media reports that nine people were killed and at least 198 wounded. Uyghurs in exile said that the real death toll was between 80 and 90.

1998   In May, India responds to growing fears over Chinese nuclear development and delivery of nuclear technology to Pakistan by conducting a series of nuclear tests. China reacts with strong rhetoric against the Indian nuclear bomb tests. Later in the year, North Korea launches a missile over Japanese territory, raising international anxiety over its nuclear capacity.

In June, President Clinton makes a state visit to Beijing, where the United States and China reach an agreement on nontargeting nuclear weapons, although China still refuses to join the MTCR. During this visit, Clinton also explicitly rejects Taiwanese independence or recognition of Taiwan as a nation-state, reiterating U.S. support for Beijing's "One-China policy," but stressing the need for China and Taiwan to resolve their differences peaceably. Diplomacy between China and Taiwan resumes for the first time since the crisis of 1996 with another meeting between Koo Chen-fu and Wang Daohan. The PRC purchases the partially built Soviet aircraft carrier Varyag, which it later refurbishes into China's first aircraft carrier. In November Jiang visits Japan to participate in a Sino-Japanese summit in Tokyo; the two governments are unable to agree on how to conduct of the oil and gas deposits located in the East China Sea.

1999   PRC authorities ban the Falun Gong, a nonviolent religious sect that operates independently of the Chinese Communist Party. On May 8, a NATO airstrike mistakenly attacks the Chinese embassy in Belgrade. Three Chinese nationals are killed in the accident and at least 20 are injured. The Chinese government issues a statement condemning the incident as a "barbaric attack and a gross violation of Chinese sovereignty." Beijing and other Chinese cities see days of mass popular protests, especially near U.S. diplomatic facilities such as the Beijing embassy. Despite apologizing and announcing that it would launch an investigation, the United States and NATO continue the Kosovo campaign. In response, China suspends negotiations with the United States on several issues. By the end of the year, the two countries had reached an agreement concerning China's accession to the WTO, with China promising financial liberalization and a reduction on import tariffs as conditions of membership. China agrees to purchase Russia SU-30 fighters in a continued effort to modernize its military. The U.S. Cox-Dicks Committee accuses China of using espionage to steal U.S. nuclear weapons technology and achieve considerable advancements in its nuclear program over a very short period of time. PRC officials accuse the statements made by the Cox report as being slanderous and of "obvious racial discrimination." Tensions continue to increase after President Lee of Taiwan insists that China and Taipei are separate states. In response, China's defense minister, Chi Haotian, announces that Beijing could use force should Taiwan continue its route of independence. Continuing to alarm its neighbors with its growing nuclear capacities, North Korea threatens to test a long-range missile that could reach the United States, raising Western fears and leading to a revised Japan-U.S. defense agreement that gives the Japanese military more freedom of action in the territory surrounding the Japanese home islands. North Korea's nuclear development program also increases interest in a theater missile defense (TMD) system that the United States could potentially operate in defense of South Korea and Japan. Both of these developments—and especially Taiwan's support for them—concern the Chinese government. On October 1, China celebrates the fiftieth anniversary of People's Republic of China. On December 20, Macao reverts to China from Portugal. China pledges to govern Macao under the policy of "one country, two systems."

2000   China launches its China's Zhongxing-22 communications satellite on January 25. Chinese state media claims that the satellite will be used for civilian telecommunications and broadcasting, whereas Western media agencies report that the U.S. Defense Intelligence Agency assesses the satellite as having military applications. In October, Clinton signs the U.S.-China Relations Act in October, which grants permanent normal trade relation status to China and puts it on the path to becoming a WTO member. As election season in Taiwan approaches again in March, China does not repeat the overt military posturing of 1996. However, Zhu Rongji warns Taiwan that a stubborn commitment to independence would lead to war with its mainland neighbor. On March 20, Taiwanese voters elected Chen Shui-bian, as the first president from the Democratic Progressive Party, which advocates Taiwan's independence. Despite Chen's attempts to soften the party line and his pledge not to declare formal independence unless the PRC attacks Taiwan, Beijing turns to direct negotiations with the losing Kuomintang party in an attempt to secure unification under the "One-China principle." Leaders of 45 African countries meet in Beijing to form the China-Africa Cooperation Forum (CACF). China pursues oil deals, notably with Nigeria, Sudan, and Angola; mineral extraction rights with Congo-Kinshasa and Zambia; exports of textiles, consumer goods, machinery, and other manufactured good to multiple countries and, notably, a multimillion-dollar trade investment package deal with South Africa; arm sales to several African states; and one-China policy affirmation by all African states throughout the continent. In July a new meeting of the "Shanghai Five" is held in Dushanbe, Tajikistan. As stated in the previous summit, the partners determine to deepen their cooperation in politics, diplomacy, economic and trade relations as well as security matters. Chinese authorities execute a former deputy chairman of the National People's Congress for taking bribes in an effort to crackdown on government corruption.

2001   In March, China and the United States continue to clash over U.S. support for Taiwan as Taiwanese Defense Minister Tang Yao-ming meets with U.S. Deputy Defense Secretary Paul Wolfowitz and Assistant Secretary of State James Kelly. This meeting is the highest level of diplomatic exchange between the two countries since Washington switched recognition from Taipei to Beijing. In the same month, Chinese warships confront the USNS Bowditch, a U.S. civilian vessel working for the Navy, near the PRC's coast in the Yellow Sea, claiming that it was violating international law by conducting military survey operations in China's Exclusive Economic Zone (EEZ), which extends 200 nautical miles from the PRC's coast. The U.S. military replies that because the EEZ implies control over commercial resources—rather than military operations—conducting military surveys in Chinese territory is within the boundaries of international law. Although the confrontation did not lead to open hostilities, it continued the Chinese pattern of aggressively defending its territorial claims against any attempt at international interference. In April, U.S.-Chinese relations worsen when a U.S. Navy EP-3E Aries II surveillance plane collides in midair with a F-8 Chinese fighter jet inside China's EEZ but outside the PRC's territorial airspace. Weeks of tense negotiations are needed to secure the release of the American crew, which crashed landed on China's Hainan Island, and the wrecked plane. Tensions between China and Taiwan also rise when China begins military exercises, simulating an invasion of Taiwan, and Taiwan tests their defense capabilities against a possible missile attack from China. In June, Uzbekistan joins the Shanghai Five; and the group is renamed the Shanghai Cooperation Organization (SCO). In July, an annual U.S. report to Congress concerning PRC military power suggests that China is embarking on a "long-term military modernization effort to develop capabilities to fight and win short-duration, high-intensity conflicts along its periphery." The report claims that the PLA had accelerated the modernization of its military in direct response to Beijing's concern that developments on the other side of the Taiwan Strait could jeopardize its objective of a reunification with Taipei. The authors warned that "the PLA is focused on developing a variety of credible military options to deter moves by Taiwan toward permanent separation or, if required, to compel by force the integration of Taiwan under mainland authority"; a second assumed objective of the PLA is to develop the capability to deter, delay, and disrupt third party intervention, such as by the United States. Although subsequent U.S. reports on China's military power repeat these assertions, PRC officials insist that China's military modernization is purely for defensive purposes. Later, China and Russia sign a 20-year Treaty of Friendship and Cooperation, aimed at increasing bilateral cooperation and mutual assistance in the economic, military, diplomatic, energy, and environmental spheres. China and Russia also agree on a new border treaty between the two countries. At the end of July, Beijing is chosen to host the 2008 Summer Olympics, a sign of China's increasing international influence and respect. The September 11 terrorist attacks in the United States allow the Chinese government to position itself as a U.S. ally in the global war on terrorism, despite Americans' unease at China's repressive domestic policies that punish peaceful opponents of Beijing's policies as terrorists. In November, both China and Taiwan enters the World Trade Organization.

2002   The Chinese Communist Party allows private entrepreneurs to become members. In February, President George W. Bush visits China on the 30th anniversary of President Nixon's visit to China. That same month, China publishes its missile export control regulations modeled on the MTCR, despite China's exclusion from the regime itself. In March, China ratifies the IAEA Additional Protocol, granting IAEA inspectors further access to its civilian nuclear facilities. In November, Vice President Hu Jintao is named head of the ruling Communist Party, replacing outgoing President Jiang, who is re-elected head of the influential Central Military Commission, which oversees the armed forces. In November, China agrees with ASEAN to draft a Declaration of Conduct governing the disputed waters in the South China Sea. The Severe Acute Respiratory Syndrome (SARS) Virus quietly spreads in Guangdong province. In October, China successfully launches astronaut Yang Liwei in orbit for the first time with a Long March 2F rocket. The Bush administration's 2002 U.S. National Security Strategy report calls for better relations with China. Concessions and gestures, mainly from the Chinese side dealing with proliferation, Iraq, the release of dissidents, U.S. agricultural imports, Tibet and Taiwan facilitate the positive Crawford summit.

2003   In January, North Korea withdraws from the NPT, citing U.S. threats to its national security. The resulting talks with China and the United States fail to find a solution to the North Korean nuclear problem. China refuses to join the Proliferation Security Initiative announced by President Bush on May 31, citing concerns about "military interception." Between January and June, SARS becomes an epidemic. The PRC authorities impose strict quarantine measures to contain the epidemic. In June Hong Kong becomes free of SARS and the World Health Organization cancels its SARS-related travel warning for Beijing. Between July and August, around 500,000 people march in Hong Kong against Article 23, an anti-subversion bill that aims to increase security in Hong Kong, deeming it excessively authoritarian. Two key Hong Kong government officials resign, and the government freezes the bill. In November, the PRC seeks to improve relations in Southeast Asia by signing a landmark trade agreement with ASEAN to remove tariffs on goods and develop a system to solve trade disputes. India formally recognizes the Tibetan autonomous region as a part of China. The historic decision came in response to Beijing's agreement to begin border trade through the northeast Indian state of Sikkim, an action largely seen as China's acceptance of India's claim to the region. Since the 1980s, the two countries had failed to resolve the boundary disagreements in fifteen separate attempts. They discuss plans to increase cooperative efforts in science, technology, commerce, and education; ease visa rules; set up joint infrastructure development projects focusing on energy resources; and develop cultural centers in each other's countries. More than 500,000 civilians march in Hong Kong against Article 23, an antisubversion bill, which they see as restricting their freedom of speech. The unrest forces the PRC to withdraw the bill and leads two Hong Kong government officials, Financial Secretary Antony Leung and Security for Security Regina Ip, to resign. China launches its first manned spacecraft; Astronaut Yang Liwei is sent to space.

2004   Faced with the reelection of proindependence Taiwanese President Chen Shui-bian, Hu continues to insist on Chinese sovereignty over Taiwan; in a May 17 statement, China urges Taiwan to accept the One-China principle as a matter of national interest, citing economic benefits and urging cross-Strait communication. In mid-September, Jiang relinquishes his CMC chairmanship three years ahead of schedule. President Hu now controls the PLA as well as the Chinese state and the ruling Communist Party. In November, China dispatches a nuclear-powered submarine to Guam, to highlight its growing military reach. On December 24, Hu also announces a change to the PLA's "historic missions" to extend them beyond China's borders and to emphasize the PLA's noncombat activities, such as disaster relief and international peacekeeping. China becomes the EU's second-largest trade partner, following the United States. The PRC government agrees to buy large quantities of Iranian natural gas over a twenty-five-year period. Meanwhile, Chinese firms become deeply involved in developing the Tehran subway, electricity, dams, and other industries and infrastructure. China signs a landmark trade agreement with the Association of Southeast Asian Nations.

2005   The first direct flights between China and Taiwan since 1949 occur. In January, Japanese forces near the Chunxiao gas and oil field in the East China Sea spot a Chinese maritime force deployed to the region to stake out China's territorial claim. On March 14, the PRC's tenth National People's Congress enacts an Anti-Secession Law that again threatens use of "non-peaceful means" against Taiwan's independence movement.

KMT leader Lien Chien visits China in early May for the first meeting between Nationalist and Communist leaders since 1949. A series of anti-Japan protests lasting several weeks in China mark the lowest point in diplomatic relations between the two countries since they were established 30 years earlier. They follow Tokyo's approval of a new scholarly textbook that many Chinese believe whitewashes Japan's wartime atrocities. In September, Deputy Secretary of State Robert B. Zoellick calls on China to use its growing international influence to serve as a "responsible stakeholder" in managing global challenges. In October China conducts its second manned space flight, with two astronauts circling Earth in the Shenzhou VI capsule. In November, an explosion occurs at a chemical plant in Jillin province that poisons the Songhua River with 100 tons of chemicals including benzene. China joins with Russia and other SCO members and calls for NATO to set a deadline for withdrawing its military force from Central Asia. Some 10,000 Chinese and Russian forces hold "Peace Mission 2005" military exercises, ostensibly under the SCO's auspices.

2006   Leaders of more than 40 African countries meet in Beijing at the third Forum on China-Africa Cooperation (FOCAC). They sign almost $2 billion in business deals and China promises billions of dollars' worth of loans and credits. During the 2000–2005 period, trade between China and Africa increased 400 percent, to $40 billion. China swiftly increased its investment in Africa, investing $900 million in 2004, a 300 percent increase from the previous year, with a focus on developing the African continent's oil and natural resources. Formerly the world's largest oil exporter, in 2006 China became the second-largest oil importer, with 30 percent of its oil coming from Africa. The PRC's economic expansion in Africa has been heavily criticized by Western governments, accusing Beijing of undermining attempts to reduce corruption in government responsible for severe human rights violations; for instance, the West has accused China of ignoring the genocide in Sudan. Meanwhile, China surpasses Mexico as the United States' second-largest trading partner, after Canada, while its foreign currency reserves exceed $1 trillion. President Hu and Indian leaders meet in New Delhi and establish the goal of $40 billion in bilateral trade in 2010. In August, 18 million people are affected by China's worst drought in 50 years. Russian President Vladimir Putin's visit to Beijing initiates the "year of Russia" celebrations in China that would be reciprocated with the "year of China" celebrations in Russia in 2007. During the visit, Russia and China sign several major agreements in the energy field. Work is completed on the Three Gorges Dam, the world's largest hydropower project.

2007   In January, the PLA successfully tested an antisatellite weapon by maneu-
       vering a Chinese ground-launched missile to fly into the path of a non-
       functioning Chinese weather satellite. Later in the year, China
       successfully launches its first moon orbiter. In March 2007, China
       announces yet another double-digit increase in its military budget, by
       17.8 percent. China's improving defense industries results in the PRC's
       reducing its purchases of Russian military equipment, with China now
       able to build many of the weapons systems that it used to buy from
       Russia. China surpasses Germany as world's third-largest economy.
       President Hu Jintao visits eight African countries to negotiate enhanced
       trade and investment relations, but Western governments criticize China
       for supporting corrupt and abusive regimes. Prime Minister Wen Jiabao
       becomes the first PRC prime minister to address Japan's parliament. Both
       the PRC and Japan agree to try to ease tensions regarding their shared
       past but not breakthrough results. Hundreds of men and boys are found
       working as slaves in Chinese factories. As a result, the Standing Commit-
       tee of the National People's Congress, in the face of opposition from
       foreign investors, introduces a new labor law, enhancing the role of the
       CCP-controlled unions and allowing collective bargaining. Food and
       drug scandals and growing international fears about the safety of Chinese
       products induces PRC authorities to prosecute officials responsible for
       their safety for taking bribes. In September, the first China-based Roman
       Catholic Bishop is consecrated with the Pope's approval in over fifty years.

2008   The U.S. Justice Department announces in February that a Defense
       Department analyst and former engineer for Boeing Co. are being
       charged with spying for China. Furthermore, the FBI detains two immi-
       grants from China and Taiwan accused of aiding the alleged spy. In
       March, anti-Han violence erupts in the Tibetan capital of Lhasa, as civi-
       lians skirmish with Chinese security forces. In some of the worst violence
       reported in 20 years, crowds burn shops, vehicles, and military equip-
       ment. The Beijing government accuses the Dalai Lama of inciting the
       violence, but anti-Beijing protests occur throughout the world, though
       calls on world leaders to boycott the 2008 Summer Olympics in Beijing
       are widely ignored. Taiwan's election of the KMT candidate, Ma Ying-
       jeou, in the May presidential elections eases cross-Strait tensions, though
       Beijing continues to block Taiwan's bids for UN membership and decry
       U.S. arms sales to Taiwan. Beijing and Taipei hold formal talks in
       June—the first since 1999. The talks produce an agreement for both sides
       to set up offices in each other's territory. In May, Hu Jintao visits Japan,
       where he and Japanese Prime Minister Yasuo Fukuda agreed on various
       cooperative measures, including the joint development of a gas field in

the East China Sea. A massive earthquake hits Sichuan province, killing tens of thousands of Chinese people. A devastating snowstorm affects up to 100 million people; the storm is one of the worst in decades. An outbreak of mass ethnic violence occurs in Xinjiang between Muslim Uyghurs and Han Chinese. In July, China and Russia end their last remaining border dispute. Nearly 53,000 Chinese children fall ill after drinking tainted milk, leading Prime Minister Wen to apologize for the scandal. A lot of countries cancel the import of baby formulas from China. In response to the deepening global financial crisis, the PRC government announces a $586-billion stimulus package in November. The naval deployment to the Gulf of Aden in December marks the first PLAN combat mission to foreign territory, demonstrating the increasing global reach of the Chinese Navy. Chinese Astronaut Zhai Zhigang completes China's first spacewalk during space mission Shenzhou VII.

2009   The leaders of Beijing and Taiwan exchange the first direct messages since the Communist Party came into office. Russia and China sign an extensive deal supplying China with access to Russian oil supplies (roughly 15 million tons per year) in exchange for $25 billion in loans over the next 20 years. On her first overseas tour as Secretary of State, Hillary Clinton calls for a stronger U.S.-China partnership to manage the global recession. The United States and China continue to clash over the U.S. Navy's presence in the South China Sea. On March 8, several Chinese ships confront the USS Impeccable, an acoustic surveillance vessel conducting routine survey operations twelve miles off the Chinese coast. Beijing objects to the intrusion on its territorial waters and claims that the USS Impeccable was operating illegally according to the statutes of international law; U.S. officials deny the charges of illegality and criticize what they describe as harassment. In April, North Korea leaves the Six-Party Talks and tests a nuclear device, prompting condemnation from the UN Security Council and the other five members of the talks, including China. In July riots break out in Urumqi between Uyghurs and Han Chinese. They spread to other parts if China. PRC sources estimate that 197 people died and 1721 were wounded, as well as many burnt vehicles and destroyed buildings. Uyghur claims place the number of victims much higher. Human Rights Watch documents 73 cases of Uyghur disappearances during police raids in the days following the riots. Subsequently six men are sentenced to death for involvement in ethnic violence in Xinjiang. As China continues efforts to modernize its military, Hu Jintao uses the 60th anniversary of the PLA air force to stress the need for continued technological development. To celebrate the 60th anniversary of the PLA Navy, China also hosts an international fleet review in Qingdao;

many foreign militaries attend the maritime parade, marking another step towards international acceptance of China as a major maritime power. Clinton delivers a speech calling for greater Internet freedoms in China and for the PRC authorities to investigate Google's claim of a cyber campaign originating from China to collect personal information on Chinese human rights activists. On her first visit to China as secretary of state in 2009, Clinton emphasized other issues besides human rights, stating that, "We have to continue to press, but our pressing on those issues can't interfere with the global economic crisis, the global climate change crisis and the security crises." From November 15 to 18, President Barack Obama visits Shanghai and Beijing in a trip that saw no major breakthroughs on Iran, climate change, or any of the other major issues dividing the two countries. The PRC authorities relax their one-child policy, encouraging parents in Shanghai to have a second child in an effort to counteract the aging population.

2010   Google redirects web searches to Hong Kong after cyberattacks occur on its Chinese users' accounts, particularly human rights activists. China and the United States clash again over Taiwan, when China suspends Sino-American military-to-military contacts over a $6 billion U.S. arms sale to Taiwan. Nevertheless, China and Taiwan reach a landmark economic agreement later in the year. After several rounds of talks in Taipei and Beijing, the parties sign the Economic Cooperation Framework Agreement (ECFA) in June. The ECFA provides for tariff reductions and greater commerce between Taiwan and the mainland. Although the ECFA brought economic benefits to both sides of the Strait, it was significantly more advantageous to Taiwan, prompting many Taiwanese citizens to protest that it was nothing but a Chinese lure, designed to make Taiwan economically dependent on the mainland. China continues to defend its territorial claims in East Asia, heightening tensions with many countries. In April, the PLAN conducts exercises close to Japanese territory, while in September, Japan arrests a Chinese trawler crew in the East China Sea, near a group of uninhabited islands that both countries claim. The Japanese authorities claim that the Chinese captain deliberately rammed Japanese Coast Guard ships, but Chinese Foreign Minister Wang Guangya insists that Japan was acting illegally. Following Chinese economic pressure and the arrest of several Japanese nationals in China, Japan frees the crew, but refuses to apologize. In October the imprisoned dissident Liu Xiaobo becomes the first Chinese citizen to win the Nobel Peace Prize, "for his nonviolent efforts to protect human rights in China." PRC pressure succeeds in persuading many foreign governments from sending high-level representatives to attend the ceremony. In

October, Xi Jinping is named vice chairman of the Central Military Commission in a move widely seen as a step toward succeeding President Hu Jintao. Vice Premier Li Keqiang headed a commission that ends a short-term crisis over the safety of China's food. The PRC surpasses Japan as the world's second-largest economy after it is valued at $1.33 trillion for the second quarter of 2010, slightly above Japan's US$1.28 trillion. If present trends continue, China will overtake the United States as the world's number one economy in approximately two decades.

2011   The PLA unveils its new J-20 stealth fighter in January, when U.S. Defense Secretary Robert Gates is in Beijing. Both sides paper over the incident, and Hu Jintao makes a successful state visit to the United States later in the month. Clashes over the South China Sea continue as other countries, backed by the United States, resist Beijing's claims. In an essay for *Foreign Policy* magazine entitled "America's Pacific Century," Secretary of State Clinton describes the Barack Obama administration's new "pivot" from the Middle East to Asia to promote U.S. interests better in the Pacific region. Although Clinton and other senior U.S. representatives deny any attempt to contain China, PRC analysts see the move as a potential effort to counter China's rising economic and military power in the region. That month, at the Asia-Pacific Economic Cooperation summit in Hawaii, Obama announces the United States and eight other countries have reached an agreement on the Trans-Pacific Partnership whose free-trade provisions would likely exclude China. In his November trip to the region, Obama announces plans to deploy 2,500 U.S. marines in Australia. PRC police detain dissident artist Ai Weiwei for two months for "tax evasion." In November, the authorities present Ai with a $2.3 million tax demand, which was then paid in full by his supporters. The increasingly good relations with Taiwan do not prevent China from objecting to another U.S. arms sale announcement in September. In October, however, Ma Ying-jeou suggests that Taiwan and China might sign a peace treaty within ten years, a statement that draws praise from PRC leaders but intense criticism from his Taiwanese political opponents. In December residents of Wukan, a village in Guangdong province, protest for days claiming that they were robbed of their farmlands by corrupt officials. China becomes increasingly uncomfortable with NATO's use of force to assist the rebels seeking to overthrow the Libyan government. The U.S. trade deficit with China rises to an all-time high of $295.5 billion in 2011.

2012   China's rate of economic growth continues to slow, due partly to the global economic slowdown. In January, according to a report by Chinese Academy of Social Sciences (CASS), for the first time in history of China, there are more people living in urban areas than the countryside. In February, Chongqing's ex–police chief Wang Lijun, a close aide to Chongqing Party leader Bo Xilai, seeks political asylum in the U.S. Consulate in Chengdu, where he reveals information about Xilai's crimes. Later he voluntarily leaves the consulate and is taken by Chinese national security officials. In March Bo Xilai and his wife are placed under investigation for causing the death of British businessman Neil Heywood in November 2011. She confesses to the murder, but her death sentence is later suspended. In April the Chinese Central Bank widens the fluctuation of the yuan against the U.S. dollar. Previously Chinese currency could fluctuate only within +/− 0.5 percent. Instead new rules allowed the currency to fluctuate up to +/− 1 percent. The Bank of China also commits itself to maintain a stable exchange rate. The general director of the International Monetary Fund (IMF), Christine Lagarde, welcomes the decision, but foreign government leaders call for further Chinese currency reform measures. In April, Chen Guangcheng, a blind legal activist best known for denouncing forced abortions, flees house arrest in his rural Chinese village and takes shelter in the U.S. Embassy in Beijing. Chinese and U.S. officials avert a crisis by agreeing to a face-saving deal that allows Chen to study law in the United States. Throughout the year, China becomes increasingly uncomfortable with rising Western pressure to change the Syrian government but, besides joining Russia and vetoing for several anti-Assad UN Security Council resolutions, adopts a generally low profile during the growing civil war there. The Philippines and China escalate their confrontation in the South China Sea over their competing territorial claims over the Scarborough Shoal. The territory's seabed is thought to contain billions of dollars' worth of natural resources, including oil and gas. The PLA launches its first aircraft carrier, the Liaoning.

On November 15, the 18th Party Congress announces the members of the Political Bureau Standing Committee of the 18th CCP Central Committee. These seven men mark the transition from the fourth generation of CCP leaders, led by outgoing President Hu Jintao, to the fifth generation leadership, under CCP General Secretary Xi.

Bibliography

Abramowitz, Morton, Funabashi Yoichi, and Wang Jisi. *China-Japan-U.S. Relations: Meeting New Challenges*. Tokyo: Japan Center for International Exchange, 2002.

Agence-France Presse. "China Takes Aim At US Over Claims Chinese Missiles Are In Iraq." *Sino Daily*, July 26, 2007. http://www.spacewar.com/reports/China_Takes_Aim_At_US _Over_Claims_Chinese_Missiles_Are_In_Iraq_999.html.

Agence-France Presse. "Obama Urged to Pressure China on Human Rights." *Sino Daily*, January 27, 2009. http://www.sinodaily.com/reports/Obama_urged_to_pressure_China _on_human_rights_999.html.

Agence-France Presse. "Seychelles Invites China to Set Up Anti-Piracy Base." *Defense News*, December 2, 2011. http://www.defensenews.com/article/20111202/DEFSECT03/ 112020302/Seychelles-Invites-China-Set-Up-Anti-Piracy-Base.

Airforce-Technology.com. "Shenyang J-11 Multirole Fighter Aircraft." *Airforce-Technology.com*. Accessed February 3, 2013. http://www.airforce-technology.com/projects/ shenyang-j11-multirole-fighter-aircraft-china/.

Akidi, Rachael. "Ask Not What China Wants From Africa, But What Africa Wants From China." *The Huffington Post*, June 11, 2012. http://www.huffingtonpost.co.uk/rachael -akidi/africa-china-ask-not-what-china-wants-_b_1578719.html.

Alessi, Christopher, and Stephanie Hanson. "Expanding China-Africa Oil Ties." *Council on Foreign Relations*, February 8, 2012. http://www.cfr.org/china/expanding-china-africa-oil -ties/p9557.

Allen, Kenneth. "Introduction to the PLA's Administrative and Operational Structure." In *The People's Liberation Army as Organization*, edited by James C. Mulvenon and Andrew N.D. Yang. Arlington, VA: RAND Corporation, 2002.

Amnesty International. "Arms Trade Fuels Violations in Sudan Conflict." *Amnesty International*, July 8, 2011. http://www.amnesty.org/en/news-and-updates/arms-trade -fuels-violations-sudan-conflict-2011-07-08.

Amnesty International. "China—Amnesty International Report 2008." *Amnesty International*, 2008. http://www.amnesty.org/en/region/china/report-2008#.

Anshan, Li. "China and Africa: Policy and Challenges." *China Security* 3, no. 3 (2007). http://www.chinasecurity.us/index.php?option=com_content&view=article&id=105.

Archick, Kristin, Richard Grimmett, and Shirley Kan. *European Union's Arms Embargo on China: Implications and Options for U.S. Policy.* CRS Report for Congress. Congressional Research Service, April 15, 2005. http://fpc.state.gov/documents/organization/45458.pdf.

Armacost, Michael. "The Mismatch Between Northeast Asian Change and American Distractions." *NBR Analysis*, January 2007. http://www.nbr.org/publications/nbranalysis/pdf/vol18no1.pdf.

Ashley J. Tellis. *Punching the U.S. Military's "Soft Ribs": China's Antisatellite Weapon Test in Strategic Perspective.* Policy Brief. Carnegie Endowment for International Peace, June 2007. http://www.carnegieendowment.org/files/pb_51_tellis_final.pdf.

Associated Press. "China Nationals Missing After Attack in Sudan." *Yahoo! News*, January 29, 2012. http://news.yahoo.com/china-nationals-missing-attack-sudan-091802031.html.

Associated Press. "Zimbabwe Buys Six Fighter Jets." *The Guardian*, April 14, 2005. http://www.guardian.co.uk/world/2005/apr/14/zimbabwe.

Axe, David. "China's Navy—Good for Us All?" *The Diplomat*, February 12, 2010. http://thediplomat.com/2010/02/12/china%e2%80%99s-navy-good-for-us-all/.

Bader, Jeffery. "Rising China and Rising Oil Demand: Real and Imagined Problems for the International System." In *The Global Politics of Energy*, edited by Kurt Campbell and Price. Washington, DC: The Aspen Institute, 2008.

Bajoria, Jayshree. "The Question of Tibet." *Council on Foreign Relations*, December 5, 2008. http://www.cfr.org/china/question-tibet/p15965.

Banks, Martin. "EU Arms Embargo Against China Dismissed as 'Unimportant.'" *TheParliament.com*, August 2, 2011. http://www.theparliament.com/latest-news/article/newsarticle/eu-arms-embargo-against-china-dismissed-as-unimportant/.

Banks, Martin. "EU Urged to Scrap Arms Embargo Against China." *TheParliament.com*, April 2, 2012. http://www.theparliament.com/latest-news/article/newsarticle/eu-urged-to-scrap-arms-embargo-against-china/#.UQw7heibZlo.

BBC. "African Union Opens Chinese-funded HQ in Ethiopia." *BBC*, January 28, 2012, sec. Africa. http://www.bbc.co.uk/news/world-africa-16770932.

BBC. "Anger over Guantanamo Bay Ruling." *BBC*, October 7, 2008, sec. Americas. http://news.bbc.co.uk/2/hi/americas/7658045.stm.

Becker, Jasper. "China in an Energy Quandary." *Asia Times Online*, August 28, 2003. http://www.atimes.com/atimes/China/EH28Ad01.html.

Beresford, David. "Chinese Ship Carries Arms Cargo to Mugabe Regime." *The Guardian*, April 18, 2008. http://www.guardian.co.uk/world/2008/apr/18/china.armstrade.

Bergsten, Fred C., Charles Freeman, Nicholas R. Lardy, and Derek J. Mitchell. *China's Rise: Challenges and Opportunities.* Washington, DC: Peterson Institute for International Economics and the Center for Strategic and International Studies, 2008.

Berteau, David J., Guy Ben-Ari, Joachim Hofbauer, Priscilla Hermann, and Sneha Raghavan. *Asian Defense Spending, 2000–2011.* Washington, DC: Center for Strategic and International Studies, October 2012. http://csis.org/publication/asian-defense-spending-2000-2011.

Bhattacharji, Preeti. "Uighurs and China's Xinjiang Region." *Council on Foreign Relations*, May 29, 2012. http://www.cfr.org/china/uighurs-chinas-xinjiang-region/p16870.

Blasko, Dennis. "PLA Self-Assessments and the Direction of Modernization." Presented at the 2012 China Defense and Security Conference, Jamestown Foundation, Washington, DC, February 16, 2012.

Blumenthal, Dan. "America and Japan Approach a Rising China." *AEI Asian Outlook*, December 2006. http://www.aei.org/files/2006/12/11/20061208_200612AOg.pdf.

Bradsher, Keith. "Security Tops the Environment in China's Energy Plan." *New York Times*, June 17, 2010, sec. Business / Global Business. http://www.nytimes.com/2010/06/18/business/global/18yuan.html.

Buckley, Chris. "Chinese Anger and Terror Warnings Cloud Olympics." *Reuters*, April 12, 2008. http://uk.reuters.com/article/2008/04/11/uk-china-tibet-idUKPEK2036492 0080411?feedType=RSS&feedName=topNews.

Bush, Richard. "Abe Foreign Policy: A Good Start but Challenges Ahead." *Japan Economic Currents* no. 64 (Winter 2007). http://www.brookings.edu/research/articles/2007/01/winter-japan-bush.

Butts, Kent Hughes, and Brent Bankus. "China's Pursuit of Africa's Natural Resources." In *Understanding Africa: A Geographical Perspective*, edited by Amy Richmond Krakowka and Laurel J. Hummel. U.S. Army War College Center for Strategic Leadership, 2009. http://www.csl.army.mil/usacsl/publications/understanding_africa.pdf.

Calabrese, John. *China and Iran: Mismatched Partners.* Occasional Paper. Jamestown Foundation, August 2006. http://www.jamestown.org/uploads/media/Jamestown-China IranMismatch.pdf.

Campbell, Kurt, Nirav Patel, and Vikram Singh. *The Power of Balance: America in Asia.* Washington, DC: Center for a New American Security, 2008.

Casarini, Nicola. *The Evolution of the EU-China Relationship: From Constructive Engagement to Strategic Partnership.* Occasional Paper. Condé-sur-Noireau, France: EU Institute for Security Studies, October 2006. http://www.iss.europa.eu/uploads/media/occ64.pdf.

"Chinese Mainland Official Slams Referendum Promoted by Taiwan Separatists." *Xinhua*, June 13, 2007. http://www.china.org.cn/english/government/213753.htm.

Cendrowicz, Leo. "Should Europe Lift Its Arms Embargo on China?" *Time*, February 10, 2010. http://www.time.com/time/world/article/0,8599,1961947,00.html.

Central Intelligence Agency. "Africa." *The World Factbook*, August 5, 2011. https://www.cia .gov/library/publications/the-world-factbook/wfbExt/region_afr.html.

Central Intelligence Agency. "China." *The World Factbook*. Accessed February 2, 2013. https://www.cia.gov/library/publications/the-world-factbook/geos/ch.html.

Chandler, Clay. "China Threatens Voters in Taiwan: Premier Issues Warning Near Election." *Washington Post*, March 16, 2000. http://www.washingtonpost.com/wp-srv/WPcap/2000-03/16/032r-031600-idx.html.

Cheng, Dean. "China's C4ISR Modernization: Problems, Progress, and Prospects." Presented at the 2012 China Defense and Security Conference, Jamestown Foundation, Washington, DC, February 16, 2012.

Cheung, Tai Ming. "The Influence of the Gun: China's Central Military Commission and Its Relationship with the Military, Party, and State Decision-Making Systems." In *The Making of Chinese Foreign and Security Policy in the Era of Reform*, edited by David M. Lampton. Stanford: Stanford University Press, 2001.

China Daily. "Avoiding Civil War in Syria." *China Daily*, February 6, 2012. http://www .chinadaily.com.cn/cndy/2012-02/06/content_14540573.htm.

China Daily. "EU Arms Ban a 'Prejudice Against China.'" *China Daily*, January 29, 2010. www.chinadaily.com.cn/china/2010-01/29/content_9396856.htm.

China Defense Blog. "China Navy, Welcomed." *China Defense Blog*, December 2, 2011. http://china-defense.blogspot.com/2011/12/china-navy-welcomed.html.

China Defense Blog. "Rebranded in China, Exported to Africa." *China Defense Blog*, December 16, 2011. http://china-defense.blogspot.com/2011/12/rebranded-in-china-exported-to-africa.html.

China Post. "Next Chiang-Chen Meeting Crucial." *China Post*, October 27, 2008. http://www.chinapost.com.tw/taiwan/china-taiwan-relations/2008/10/27/180482/Next-Chiang-Chen.htm.

China Radio International. "Jiang Zemin's Eight-point Proposal." *China Radio International*, January 11, 2007. http://english.cri.cn/4426/2007/01/11/167@184028.htm.

Chinese Defence. "Project 956/EM Sovremenny Class Missile Destroyer." *Chinese Defence*, April 15, 2012. http://www.chinesedefence.com/forums/chinese-navy/2872-project-956-em-sovremenny-class-missile-destroyer.html.

Chinese Military Review. "New Ambush Protected Vehicles For Peoples Liberation Army (PLA)." *Chinese Military Review*, February 25, 2012. http://chinesemilitaryreview.blogspot.com/2012/02/new-ambush-protected-vehicles-for.html.

Chu, Henry. "In Rebuke of Taiwan, China Raises Specter of Military Clash." *Los Angeles Times*, August 8, 2002. http://articles.latimes.com/2002/aug/08/world/fg-chitai8.

Chunshan, Mu. "China's Nimble Libya Pullout." *The Diplomat*, March 22, 2011. http://thediplomat.com/china-power/china%e2%80%99s-nimble-libya-pullout/.

Cole, Bernard. "China's Evolving Naval Strategy." Presented at the 2012 China Defense and Security Conference, Jamestown Foundation, Washington, DC, February 16, 2012.

Collins, Gabe, and Andrew Erickson. " 'Flying Shark' Gaining Altitude: How Might New J-15 Strike Fighter Improve China's Maritime Air Warfare Ability?" *China SignPost*, June 8, 2011. http://www.chinasignpost.com/2011/06/flying-shark%E2%80%9D-gaining-altitude-how-might-new-j-15-strike-fighter-improve-china%E2%80%99s-maritime-air-warfare-ability/.

Collins, Gabe, and Andrew Erickson. "Implications of China's Military Evacuation of Citizens from Libya." *China Brief* 11, no. 4 (March 10, 2011). http://www.jamestown.org/programs/chinabrief/single/?tx_ttnews%5Btt_news%5D=37633&cHash=7278cfd21e6fb19afe8a823c5cf88f07.

Connell, Dan, and Tom Killion. *Historical Dictionary of Eritrea*. Lanham, MD: Scarecrow Press, 2011.

Cooke, Jennifer G. "China's Soft Power in Africa." In *Chinese Soft Power and Its Implications for the United States: Competition and Cooperation in the Developing World*, edited by Carola McGiffert. Center for Strategic and International Studies, 2009. http://csis.org/files/media/csis/pubs/090403_mcgiffert_chinesesoftpower_web.pdf.

Crane, Keith, Roger Cliff, Evan S. Medeiros, William Mulvenon, and William H. Overholt. *Modernizing China's Military: Opportunities and Constraints*. Santa Monica: RAND Corporation, 2005. http://www.rand.org/content/dam/rand/pubs/monographs/2005/RAND_MG260-1.pdf.

Dasgupta, Saibal. "China Wants More Aircraft Carriers to Compete with India." *Times Of India*, July 30, 2011. http://articles.timesofindia.indiatimes.com/2011-07-30/china/29832885_1_aircraft-carriers-geng-yansheng-experiments-and-training.

Dobson, Hugo. *Japan and the G7/8: 1975-2002*. London: Routledge, 2004.

Eisenman, Joshua, and Joshua Kurlantzick. "China's Africa Strategy." *Current History* (May 2006). http://www.carnegieendowment.org/files/Africa.pdf.

Ellis, R. Evan. *China-Latin America Military Engagement: Good Will, Good Business, and Strategic Position*. Strategic Studies Institute, U.S. Army War College, August 2011. http://www.strategicstudiesinstitute.army.mil/pubs/download.cfm?q=1077.

Erikson, Andrew W., and Michael Chase. "China's SSBN Forces: Transitioning to the Next Generation." *China Brief* 9, no. 12 (June 12, 2009). http://www.jamestown.org/single/?no_cache=1&tx_ttnews[tt_news]=35120.

Erikson, Andrew W., and Michael Chase. "Information Technology and China's Naval Modernization." *Joint Forces Quarterly* no. 50 (3rd quarter 2008): 24–30.

Europe China Research and Advice Network. "The High-Level Economic and Trade Dialogue." *ECRAN*, April 2008. http://www.euecran.eu/high-level-economic-and-trade-dialogue.

European Commission. "China." *European Commission*. Accessed February 3, 2013. http://ec.europa.eu/trade/creating-opportunities/bilateral-relations/countries/china/.

Fan, Maureen. "China Moves to Tighten Control Over Religion in Tibet." *Washington Post*, March 26, 2008, sec. Religion. http://www.washingtonpost.com/wp-dyn/content/article/2008/03/25/AR2008032501665.html.

Federation of American Scientists. "Third Department–PLA—Chinese Intelligence Agencies." *Federation of American Scientists*, April 15, 2000. https://www.fas.org/irp/world/china/pla/dept_3.htm.

Feldman, Harvey, Balbina Hwang, John Tkacik, and Dana Dillon. "Asia's Security Challenges." *The Heritage Foundation*, April 4, 2005. http://www.heritage.org/research/reports/2005/04/asias-security-challenges/.

Finkelstein, David. "China's National Security Policymaking Capacity." Presented at the 2012 China Defense and Security Conference, Jamestown Foundation, Washington, DC, February 16, 2012.

Fisher Jr, Richard. "China's Aviation Sector: Building Toward World Class Capabilities." *International Assessment and Strategy Center*, May 20, 2010. http://www.strategycenter.net/research/pubID.199/pub_detail.asp.

Fisher Jr, Richard. "Plan for Growth: China's Surface Fleet Modernization Fits Beijing's Appetite for Sea Power." *Armed Forces Journal*, April 2006. http://www.armedforcesjournal.com/2006/04/1813798/.

Fisher Jr, Richard. "The Implications of China's Naval Modernization for the United States." *International Assessment and Strategy Center*, June 11, 2009. http://www.strategycenter.net/research/pubID.199/pub_detail.asp.

Ford, Peter. "The New Face of Chinese Diplomacy: Who is Wang Yi?" *Christian Science Monitor*, March 18, 2013. http://csmonitor.com/World/Asia-Pacific/2013/0318/The-new-face-of-Chinese-diplomacy-Who-is-Wang-Yi.

Foreign Policy. "The Chinese-African Union." *Foreign Policy*, March 19, 2012. http://www.foreignpolicy.com/articles/2012/03/19/african_union_addis_ababa.

Friedberg, Aaron L. "Ripe for Rivalry: Prospects for Peace in a Multipolar Asia." *International Security* 18, no. 3 (Winter/94 1993): 5–33.

G7. "Declaration on China." *University of Toronto*, July 15, 1989. http://www.g7.utoronto.ca/summit/1989paris/china.html.

Gangopadhyay, Abhrajit, and Anant Vijay Kala. "Brics Wants World Bank, IMF Reforms." *Wall Street Journal*, March 29, 2012, sec. Business. http://online.wsj.com/article/SB10001424052702303816504577311012331186378.html.

Garrett, Banning, and Jonathan Adams. *U.S.-China Cooperation on the Problem of Failing States and Transnational Threats*. Special Report. United States Institute of Peace, September 2004. http://www.usip.org/publications/us-china-cooperation-problem-failing-states-and-transnational-threats.

Garthoff, Raymond L. *Détente and Confrontation: American-Soviet Relations from Nixon to Reagan*. Washington, DC: Brookings Institution, 1994.

Gill, Bates, and Chin-hao Huang. *China's Expanding Peacekeeping Role: It's Significance and the Policy Implications*. Policy Brief. Stockholm International Peace Research Institute, 2009. http://books.sipri.org/files/misc/SIPRIPB0902.pdf.

Gill, Bates, and Martin Kleiber. "China's Space Odyssey: What the Antisatellite Test Reveals About Decision-Making in Beijing." *Foreign Affairs*, May 1, 2007. http://www.foreignaffairs.com/articles/62602/bates-gill-and-martin-kleiber/chinas-space-odyssey-what-the-antisatellite-test-reveals-about-d.

Global Times. "Respecting Africa's Decisions Will Benefit China." *Global Times*, November 3, 2011. http://www.globaltimes.cn/NEWS/tabid/99/ID/682394/Respecting-Africas-decisions-will-benefit-China.aspx.

GlobalSecurity.org. "General Armament Department." *GlobalSecurity.org*. Accessed February 2, 2013. http://www.globalsecurity.org/military/world/china/gad.htm.

GlobalSecurity.org. "General Logistics Department." *GlobalSecurity.org*. Accessed February 2, 2013. http://www.globalsecurity.org/military/world/china/gld.htm.

GlobalSecurity.org. "HangZhou Type 956 Sovremenny." *GlobalSecurity.org*, June 6, 2009. http://www.globalsecurity.org/military/world/china/haizhou.htm.

GlobalSecurity.org. "PLA History." *GlobalSecurity.org*, August 7, 2007. http://www.globalsecurity.org/military/world/china/pla-history.htm.

Goldstein, Lyle J. "Cold Wars at Sea." *Armed Forces Journal*, April 2008. http://www.armedforcesjournal.com/2008/04/3373649/.

Goodman, Peter S. "Big Shift in China's Oil Policy." *Washington Post*, July 13, 2005, sec. Business. http://www.washingtonpost.com/wp-dyn/content/article/2005/07/12/AR2005071201546.html.

Gries, Peter Hays. "Nationalism, Indignation, and China's Japan Policy." *SAIS Review* 25, no. 2 (2005): 105–114. doi:10.1353/sais.2005.0034.

Griffin, Christopher, and Dan Blumenthal. "China's Defense White Paper: What It Does (and Doesn't) Tell Us." *China Brief*, January 24, 2007. http://www.jamestown.org/programs/chinabrief/single/?tx_ttnews%5Btt_news%5D=32421&tx_ttnews%5BbackPid%5D=197&no_cache=1.

La Guardia, Anton. "US Fury over EU Weapons for China." *The Telegraph*, January 15, 2005, sec. worldnews. http://www.telegraph.co.uk/news/worldnews/1481253/US-fury-over-EU-weapons-for-China.html.

Gunness, Kristen. "China's Military Diplomacy in an Era of Change." Presented at the National Defense University symposium on China's Global Activism: Implications for U.S. Security Interests, Fort Lesley J. McNair, June 20, 2006. http://www.ndu.edu/inss/symposia/pacific2006/Gunnesspaper.pdf.

Hachigian, Nina, Michael Schiffer, and Winny Chen. *A Global Imperative: A Progressive Approach to U.S.-China Relations in the 21st Century*. Washington, DC: Center for American Progress, August 2008. http://www.americanprogress.org/wp-content/uploads/issues/2008/08/pdf/china_report.pdf.

Harding, Thomas. "Chinese Nuclear Submarine Base." *The Telegraph*, May 1, 2008, sec. World News. http://www.telegraph.co.uk/news/worldnews/asia/china/1917167/Chinese-nuclear-submarine-base.html.

Harris, Shane. "China's Cyber-Militia." *NationalJournal.com*, May 31, 2008. http://www.nationaljournal.com/magazine/china-s-cyber-militia-20080531.

Hevi, Emmanuel John. *The Dragon's Embrace: The Chinese Communists and Africa*. New York: F.A. Praeger, 1966.

Hills, Clara A., Dennis C. Blair, and Frank Sampson Jannuzi. *U.S.-China Relations: An Affirmative Agenda, A Responsible Course*. Council on Foreign Relations Press, April 2007. http://i.cfr.org/content/publications/attachments/ChinaTaskForce.pdf.

Holtom, Paul, Mark Bromley, Pieter D. Wezeman, and Siemon T. Wezeman. *Trends in International Arms Transfers, 2011*, SIPRI Fact Sheet. Stockholm International Peace Research Institute, March 2012.

Hooker, Jake. "Quake Revealed Deficiencies of China's Military." *New York Times*, July 2, 2008, sec. International / Asia Pacific. http://www.nytimes.com/2008/07/02/world/asia/02china.html.

Hu Jintao. "Hold High the Great Banner of Socialism with Chinese Characteristics and Strive for New Victories in Building a Moderately Prosperous Society in All Respects." Speech presented at the 17th National Congress of the Communist Party of China, Beijing, Great Hall of the People, October 15, 2007. http://www.chinadaily.com.cn/china/2007-10/25/content_6204667_10.htm.

Huaheng, Zhao. "China, Russia, and the United States: Prospects for Cooperation in Central Asia." *CEF Quarterly* (February 2005). http://www.silkroadstudies.org/new/docs/CEF/CEF_Quarterly_Winter_2005.doc.pdf.

International Committee of the Red Cross. "Sudan: ICRC Organizes Transfer of Released Chinese Citizens." *International Committee of the Red Cross*, February 7, 2012. http://www.icrc.org/eng/resources/documents/news-release/2012/sudan-news-2012-02-07.htm.

International Crisis Group. *China's Growing Role in UN Peacekeeping* 166. Asia Report. International Crisis Group, April 17, 2009. http://www.crisisgroup.org/~/media/Files/asia/north-east-asia/166_chinas_growing_role_in_un_peacekeeping.pdf.

International Institute for Strategic Studies. "China's three-point naval strategy." *International Institute for Strategic Studies*, October 2010. http://www.iiss.org/publications/strategic-comments/past-issues/volume-16-2010/october/chinas-three-point-naval-strategy/.

International Institute for Strategic Studies. "Long March of China's Military Reform." *Real Clear World*, September 19, 2010. http://www.realclearworld.com/articles/2010/09/19/long_march_of_chinas_military_reform_99189.html.

International Maritime Organization. "IMO Adopts Comprehensive Maritime Security Measures." International Maritime Organization, December 13, 2002. http://www.imo.org/blast/mainframe.asp?topic_id=583&doc_id=2689.

International Monetary Fund. "Factsheet—IMF Quotas." *IMF.org*, March 30, 2012. http://www.imf.org/external/np/exr/facts/quotas.htm.

Jakobson, Linda, and Dean Knox. *New Foreign Policy Actors in China*. Policy Paper. Stockholm International Peace Research Institute, September 2010. http://books.sipri.org/files/PP/SIPRIPP26.pdf.

Japan Defense Agency. *Defense of Japan 2005 (Summary/Tentative Translation)*. Tokyo, 2005. http://www.mod.go.jp/e/publ/w_paper/2005.html.

Jencks, Harlan. "The General Armaments Department." In *The People's Liberation Army as Organization*, edited by James C. Mulvenon and Andrew N.D. Yang. Arlington, VA: RAND Corporation, 2002.

Kamphausen, Roy. "China's New Military Leadership and the Challenges It Faces." Interview by Greg Chaffin, January 18, 2013. http://www.nbr.org/research/activity.aspx?id=303.

Kardon, Isaac. "The PLA as an Interest Group in Chinese Politics." Presented at the 2012 China Defense and Security Conference, Jamestown Foundation, Washington, DC, February 16, 2012.

Karnozov, Vladimir. "Russian Officials Reveal J-31 Engine and Describe Sales to China." *AINonline*, November 23, 2012. http://www.ainonline.com/aviation-news/ain-defense -perspective/2012-11-23/russian-officials-reveal-j-31-engine-and-describe-sales-china.

Kristof, Nicholas D. "China and Taiwan Have First Talks." *New York Times*, April 28, 1993. http://www.nytimes.com/1993/04/28/world/china-and-taiwan-have-first-talks.html.

Kupchan, Charles, Jason Davidson, and Mira Sucharov. *Power in Transition: The Peaceful Change of International Order*. Tokyo: United Nations University Press, 2001.

Kurlantzick, Joshua. *Charm Offensive*. New Haven: A New Republic Book, 2007.

Lam, Willy. "Communist Youth League Clique Maintains Clout Despite Congress Setback." *China Brief* 12, no. 23 (November 30, 2012). http://www.jamestown.org/single/?no _cache=1&tx_ttnews%5Btt_news%5D=40180&tx_ttnews%5BbackPid%5D=589.

Landler, Mark. "Offering to Aid Talks, U.S. Challenges China on Disputed Islands." *New York Times*, July 23, 2010, sec. World / Asia Pacific. http://www.nytimes.com/2010/07/24/ world/asia/24diplo.html.

Lee, John. "EU Not on China's Chessboard." *The Diplomat*, May 13, 2010. http:// thediplomat.com/2010/05/13/eu-not-on-china%e2%80%99s-chessboard/.

Lee, John. "Structural Flaws Will Limit China's Rise." *World Politics Review*, November 10, 2009. http://www.worldpoliticsreview.com/articles/4868/structural-flaws-will-limit -chinas-rise.

Lexian, Fang. "Arms Ban Tarnishes EU Image." *China Daily*, February 9, 2010. http://www .chinadaily.com.cn/opinion/2010-02/09/content_9448894.htm.

Li, Cheng. "China's Top Future Leaders to Watch." *The Brookings Institution*, November 15, 2012. http://www.brookings.edu/about/centers/china/top-future-leaders.

Ling, Bonny. "China's Peacekeeping Diplomacy." *International Relations and Institutions* (November 1, 2007). http://hrichina.org/sites/default/files/oldsite/PDFs/CRF.1.2007/ CRF-2007-1_Peacekeeping.pdf.

Lubold, Gordon. "After Earthquake, China Welcomes U.S. Military." *Christian Science Monitor*, May 30, 2008. http://www.csmonitor.com/USA/Military/2008/0530/p02s01 -usmi.html.

Lynch, Colum. "Russia, China Veto Resolution On Burma." *Washington Post*, January 13, 2007. http://www.washingtonpost.com/wp-dyn/content/article/2007/01/12/AR200 7011201115.html.

Lynch, Daniel. "Chinese Thinking on the Future of International Relations: Realism as the Ti, Rationalism as the Yong?" *The China Quarterly* 197 (March 2009): 87–107.

MacDonald, Bruce W. *China, Space Weapons, and U.S. Security*. Council on Foreign Relations Press, September 2008. http://i.cfr.org/content/publications/attachments/China_Space _CSR38.pdf.

Martinot, Eric. "Renewable Power for China: Past, Present, and Future." *Frontiers of Energy and Power Engineering in China* (2010). http://www.martinot.info/Martinot_FEP4 _prepub.pdf.

Mattis, Peter. "New Departments and Research Centers Highlight Military's Concerns for the Future." *China Brief* 12, no. 1 (January 6, 2012).

Mbaye, Sanou. "Matching China's Activities with Africa's Needs." In *Chinese and African Perspectives on China in Africa*, edited by Axel Harneit-Sievers, Stephen Marks, and Sanusha Naidu. Capetown: Pambazuka Press, 2010.

Medeiros, Evan S. *China's International Behavior: Activism, Opportunism, and Diversification*. Santa Monica: RAND Corporation, 2009.

Milbank, Dana, and Glenn Kessler. "President Warns Taiwan on Independence Efforts." *Washington Post*, December 10, 2003.

Miles, Donna. "Priorities Set U.S. Africa Command's Agenda." *United States Africa Command*, June 12, 2012. http://www.africom.mil/NEWSROOM/Article/9017/priorities-set-us-africa-commands-agenda.

Miller, Alice L. "The Politburo Standing Committee Under Hu Jintao." *China Leadership Monitor* no. 35 (Summer 2011). http://media.hoover.org/sites/default/files/documents/CLM35AM.pdf.

Ministry of Commerce, PRC. "Mission." *Ministry of Commerce, PRC*, December 7, 2010. http://english.mofcom.gov.cn/column/mission2010.shtml.

Ministry of Foreign Affairs (PRC). "Departments." *Ministry of Foreign Affairs (PRC)*. Accessed February 2, 2013. http://www.fmprc.gov.cn/eng/wjb/zzjg/.

Ministry of Foreign Affairs (PRC). "Foreign Ministry Spokesperson Jiang Yu's Regular Press Conference on May 26, 2011." *Ministry of Foreign Affairs (PRC)*, May 27, 2011. http://www.fmprc.gov.cn/eng/xwfw/s2510/t826007.htm.

Ministry of Foreign Affairs (PRC). "Joint Statement Between the People's Republic of China and the Russian Federation," April 6, 2007. http://www.fmprc.gov.cn/eng/wjdt/2649/t309361.shtml.

Ministry of Foreign Affairs (PRC). "The Minister." Accessed February 2, 2013. http://www.fmprc.gov.cn/eng/wjb/wjbz/.

Ministry of Foreign Affairs (PRC). "Treaty of Good-Neighborliness and Friendly Cooperation Between the People's Republic of China and the Russian Federation," July 24, 2001. http://www.fmprc.gov.cn/eng/wjdt/2649/t15771.htm.

Ministry of Foreign Affairs (Russia). "Transcript of Remarks and Response to Media Questions by Russian Minister of Foreign Affairs Sergey Lavrov Following Talks with Chinese Minister of Foreign Affairs Yang Jiechi," April 27, 2009. http://www.mid.ru/bdomp/brp_4.nsf/e78a48070f128a7b43256999005bcbb3/9da17eb2ca6711d7c32575a600255d45!OpenDocument.

Ministry of National Defense (PRC). "Central Military Commission of Communist Party of China." *Ministry of National Defense (PRC)*. Accessed February 3, 2013. http://eng.mod.gov.cn/Database/Leadership/index.htm.

Minnick, Wendell. "Russia Admits China Illegally Copied Its Fighter." *Defense News*, February 13, 2009. http://minnickarticles.blogspot.com/2009/10/russia-admits-china-illegally-copied.html.

MSNBC.com. "Chinese Anti-satellite Test Sparks Concern." *MSNBC.com*, January 18, 2007. http://www.msnbc.msn.com/id/16689558/ns/technology_and_science-space/t/chinese-anti-satellite-test-sparks-concern/.

Myers, Ramon H. "The Divided China Problem: Conflict Avoidance and Resolution." *Hoover Institution*, June 1, 2000. http://www.hoover.org/publications/monographs/27162.

Nathan, Andrew J., and Andrew Scobell. *China's Search for Security*. New York: Columbia University Press, 2012.

National Development and Reform Commission. "Brief Introduction of the NDRC." *National Development and Reform Commission*. Accessed February 3, 2013. http://en.ndrc.gov.cn/brief/default.htm.

Nebehay, Stephanie. "China, Russia to Offer Treaty to Ban Arms in Space." *Reuters*. Geneva, January 25, 2008. http://www.reuters.com/article/2008/01/25/us-arms-space-idUSL2578979020080125.

Nelson, Craig. "China's Naval Base Proposal May Raise Suspicion." *The National*, January 3, 2010. http://www.thenational.ae/news/world/chinas-naval-base-proposal-may-raise-suspicion.

Ning, Lu. "The Central Leadership, Supraministry Coordinating Bodies, State Council Ministries, and Party Departments." In *The Making of Chinese Foreign and Security Policy in the Era of Reform*, edited by David M. Lampton. Stanford: Stanford University Press, 2001.

Norling, Nicklas. "The Emerging China-Afghanistan Relationship." *Central Asia-Caucasus Institute Analyst*, May 14, 2008. http://www.cacianalyst.org/?q=node/4858.

Nuclear Threat Initiative. "State Administration for Science, Technology and Industry for National Defense (SASTIND)." *NTI*, July 13, 2012. http://www.nti.org/facilities/781/.

O'Rourke, Ronald. *China Naval Modernization: Implications for U.S. Navy Capabilities: Background and Issues for Congress*. Washington, DC: Congressional Research Service, April 9, 2010. http://www.fas.org/sgp/crs/row/RL33153.pdf.

Ogunsanwo, Alaba. *China's Policy in Africa, 1958-1971*. Cambridge: Cambridge University Press, 1974.

Organisation for Economic Co-operation and Development. "Reforms Could Boost China's Ability to Attract Foreign Investment." *Organisation for Economic Co-operation and Development*, July 3, 2003. http://www.oecd.org/industry/internationalinvestment/investmentstatisticsandanalysis/reformscouldboostchinasabilitytoattractforeigninvestment.htm.

Organisation for Economic Co-operation and Development. "The OECD Welcomes Policy Advances at China's 2007 National People's Congress Session." Organisation for Economic Co-operation and Development, March 27, 2007. http://www.oecd.org/investment/investmentfordevelopment/38309228.pdf.

Page, Jeremy, and Tom Wright. "Chinese Military Considers New Indian Ocean Presence." *Wall Street Journal*, December 14, 2011. http://online.wsj.com/article/SB100014240529702035184045770962610611550538.html.

Pan, Philip P. "China Warns Taiwan Again on Issue of Independence." *Washington Post*, November 27, 2003.

Pan, Philip P., and John Pomfret. "Bin Laden Network's China Connection: Beijing Estimates 1,000 Muslims Have Received Training in Al Qaeda Camps." *Washington Post*, November 11, 2001.

Parello-Plesner, Jonas. "Civis Sinicus Sum: China's Great Power Burdens in Libya." *World Politics Review*, March 3, 2011. http://www.worldpoliticsreview.com/articles/8072/civis-sinicus-sum-chinas-great-power-burdens-in-libya.

Pehrson, Christopher. *String of Pearls: Meeting the Challenge of China's Rising Power Across the Asian Littoral*. Strategic Studies Institute, U.S. Army War College, 2006. http://www.strategicstudiesinstitute.army.mil/pdffiles/pub721.pdf.

Penttilä, Risto E.J. *The Role of the G8 in International Peace and Security*. New York: Oxford University Press, 2003.

People's Daily Online. "The Five Principles of Peaceful Co-existence." *People's Daily Online*, June 28, 2004. http://english.peopledaily.com.cn/200406/28/eng20040628_147763.html.

Pew Charitable Trust. *Who's Winning the Clean Energy Race?* Pew Charitable Trust, 2010. http://www.pewtrusts.org/uploadedFiles/wwwpewtrustsorg/Reports/Global_warming/G-20%20Report.pdf.

Pham, J. Peter. "Hu's Selling Guns to Africa." *World Defense Review*, June 28, 2007. http://worlddefensereview.com/pham062807.shtml.

Pham, J. Peter. "Pandas in the Heart of Darkness: Chinese Peacekeepers in Africa." *World Defense Review*, October 25, 2007. http://worlddefensereview.com/pham102507.shtml.

Pierson, David. "Libyan Strife Exposes China's Risks in Global Quest for Oil." *Los Angeles Times*, March 9, 2011. http://articles.latimes.com/2011/mar/09/business/la-fi-china-oil -20110310.

Pollpeter, Kevin. "Informationization and Joint Operations." Presented at the 2012 China Defense and Security Conference, Jamestown Foundation, Washington, DC, February 16, 2012.

Puska, Susan. "Military Backs China's Africa Adventure." *Asia Times Online*, June 8, 2007. http://www.atimes.com/atimes/China/IF08Ad03.html.

Pyle, Kenneth. *Japan Rising: The Resurgence of Japanese Power and Purpose*. New York: Public Affairs, 2007.

Qiu, Jin. "The Politics of History and Historical Memory in China-Japan Relations." *Journal of Chinese Political Science* 11, no. 1 (2006).

Reid, Tim. "China's Cyber Army Is Preparing to March on America, Says Pentagon." *Times Online*, September 8, 2007. http://chinadigitaltimes.net/2007/09/chinas-cyber-army-is -preparing-to-march-on-america-says-pentagon-tim-reid/.

Rettman, Andrew. "EU to Keep China Arms Embargo Despite Massive Investments." *Euobserver.com*, May 1, 2011. http://euobserver.com/china/31592.

Rettman, Andrew. "EU-China Diplomacy Fails to Convince Sceptics." *EUobserver.com*, April 30, 2010. http://euobserver.com/china/29981.

Reuters. "Chinese Admiral Floats Idea of Overseas Naval Bases." *Reuters*. Beijing, December 30, 2008. http://www.reuters.com/article/2009/12/30/us-china-navy-idUSTRE 5BT0P020091230.

Reuters. "France's Sarkozy Says Not Reasonable to Meet as G8." *Reuters*. Paris, July 5, 2009. http://www.reuters.com/article/2008/07/05/us-g8-france-sarkozy- idUSPAC00963220080705.

RIA Novosti. "President Medvedev's Interview with China Central Television." *RIA Novosti*, June 15, 2009. http://en.rian.ru/analysis/20090615/155252094.html.

Richburg, Keith B. "China, After Abstaining in U.N. Vote, Criticizes Airstrikes on Gaddafi Forces." *Washington Post*, March 22, 2011, sec. World. http://www.washingtonpost.com/ world/china_after_abstaining_in_un_vote_criticizes_airstrikes_on_gaddafi_forces/2011/ 03/21/ABwL4M7_story.html?wprss=rss_homepage.

Robert L. Worden, Andrea Matles Savada, and Ronald E. Dolan. *China: A Country Study*. Washington, DC: GPO for the Library of Congress, 1987. http://countrystudies.us/ china/126.htm.

Rosen, Daniel H., and Trevor Houser. *China Energy: A Guide for the Perplexed*. Peterson Institute for International Economics, May 2007. http://www.petersoninstitute.org/ publications/papers/rosen0507.pdf.

Rotberg, Robert I. *China Into Africa: Trade, Aid, and Influence*. Cambridge, MA: World Peace Foundation, 2008.

Rothkopf, David. "New Energy Paradigm, New Foreign Policy Paradigm." In *The Global Politics of Energy*, edited by Kurt Campbell and Price. Washington, DC: Aspen Institute, 2008.

Roy, Denny. "China and the War on Terrorism." *Orbis* 46, no. 3 (Summer 2002): 511–521.

Russian Federation and People's Republic of China. "Treaty of Good-Neighborliness and Friendly Cooperation Between the People's Republic of China and the Russian Federation." Signed at Moscow, July 16, 2001, http://www.fmprc.gov.cn/eng/wjdt/2649/ t15771.htm.

Sanchez, Alex. "Arm Sales, Especially By Russia And China, Continue To Penetrate Latin America." *Eurasia Review*, February 22, 2011. http://www.eurasiareview.com/22022011 -arm-sales-especially-by-russia-and-china-continue-to-penetrate-latin-america/.

Sanger, David E., and Joseph Kahn. "U.S. Tries to Interpret China's Silence Over Test." *New York Times*, January 22, 2007, sec. International / Asia Pacific. http://www.nytimes.com/ 2007/01/22/world/asia/22missile.html.

Schulz, William F. *Strategic Persistence: How the United States Can Help Improve Human Rights in China*. Washington, DC: Center for American Progress, January 2009. http://www .americanprogress.org/issues/2009/01/pdf/china_human_rights.pdf.

Scobell, Andrew. "PLA Professionalization and the Civil-Military Gap." Presented at the 2012 China Defense and Security Conference, Jamestown Foundation, Washington, DC, February 16, 2012.

Scobell, Andrew, and Andrew J. Nathan. "China's Overstreched Military." *Washington Quarterly* (Fall 2012).

Seth, S. P. "VIEW: US-China Strategic Competition." *Daily Times*, August 15, 2010. http:// www.dailytimes.com.pk/default.asp?page=2010%5C08%5C15%5Cstory_15-8-2010 _pg3_4.

Sevastopulo, Demetri. "US Concerns over China Weapons in Iraq." *Financial Times*, July 6, 2007. http://www.ft.com/cms/s/82ce0740-2c03-11dc-b498-000b5df10621,Authorised =false.html?_i_location=http%3A%2F%2Fwww.ft.com%2Fcms%2Fs%2F0%2F82ce0740 -2c03-11dc-b498-000b5df10621.html&_i_referer=#axzz2JaM4Jw1Q.

Shambaugh, David. "Don't Lift the Arms Embargo on China." *International Herald Tribune*, February 23, 2005. http://www.nytimes.com/2005/02/22/opinion/22iht-edshambaugh. html?_r=0.

Shambaugh, David. *Modernizing China's Military: Progress, Problems and Prospects*. Berkeley: University of California Press, 2004.

Shambaugh, David. "The Pinnacle of the Pyramid: The Central Military Commission." In *The People's Liberation Army as Organization*, edited by James C. Mulvenon and Andrew N.D. Yang. Arlington, VA: RAND Corporation, 2002.

Shaplen, Jason T., and James Laney. "Washington's Eastern Sunset." *Foreign Affairs*, November 1, 2007. http://www.foreignaffairs.com/articles/63012/jason-t-shaplen-and-james-laney/ washingtons-eastern-sunset.

Shi, Tianjian, and Meredith Wen. *Avoiding Mutual Misunderstanding: Sino-U.S. Relations and the New Administration*. Washington, DC: Carnegie Endowment for International Peace, January 2009. http://carnegieendowment.org/files/china_us_relations.pdf.

Shinn, David H. *China's Growing Role in Africa: Implications for U.S. Policy*. Washington, DC, 2011. http://www.foreign.senate.gov/imo/media/doc/David_Shinn_Testimony.pdf.

Shirk, Susan. "Changing Media, Changing Foreign Policy in China." *Japanese Journal of Political Science* 8, no. 1 (2007): 43–70.

Shirk, Susan. *China: Fragile Superpower*. New York: Oxford University Press, 2007.

Shirouzo, Norihiko. "China's Auto Sale Run Hot." *The Wall Street Journal*, October 23, 2010.

Simon, Sheldon. "US-Southeast Asia Relations: Growing Enmeshment in Regional Affairs." *Comparative Connections* (October 2010). http://csis.org/files/publication/1003qus_seasia.pdf.

Smith-Spark, Laura. "Chinese Product Scares Prompt US Fears." *BBC*, July 10, 2007, sec. Americas. http://news.bbc.co.uk/2/hi/americas/6275758.stm.

Snyder, Scott, and See-won Byun. "China-Korea Relations: China's Post-Kim Jong Il Debate." *Comparative Connections* (January 2012). http://csis.org/files/publication/1103qchina _korea.pdf.

State Council Information Office (PRC). *China's Foreign Aid*. Beijing: State Council Information Office (PRC), 2011. http://english.gov.cn/official/2011-04/21/content_1849913. htm.

State Council Information Office (PRC). *China's National Defense in 2008*. Beijing: State Council Information Office (PRC), 2009. http://english.gov.cn/official/2009-01/20/content_1210227.htm.

State Council Information Office (PRC). *China's Peaceful Development*. Beijing: State Council Information Office (PRC), 2011. http://english.gov.cn/official/2011-09/06/content_1941354.htm.

Stephen Herzog. *The Dilemma Between Deterrence and Disarmament: Moving Beyond the Perception of China as a Nuclear Threat*. British American Security Information Council, July 31, 2008. http://www.basicint.org/sites/default/files/BP57.pdf.

Stewart, Devin T., and Joshua Eisenman. "China's New-Rich and Global Responsibility." *Carnegie Council*, October 13, 2006. http://www.carnegiecouncil.org/publications/ethics_online/0002.html.

Stockholm International Peace Research Institute. "SIPRI Arms Transfers Database." *Stockholm International Peace Research Institute*. Accessed May 7, 2012. http://www.sipri.org/databases/armstransfers.

Stokes, Mark. "China's Space-Based Intelligence, Surveillance and Reconnaissance." Presented at the 2012 China Defense and Security Conference, Jamestown Foundation, Washington, DC, February 16, 2012.

Storey, Ian. "Trouble and Strife in the South China Sea: Vietnam and China." *China Brief*, April 16, 2008. http://www.jamestown.org/single/?no_cache=1&tx_ttnews%5Btt_news%5D=4854.

Sukhoi Corporation. "Su-30MK2." *Komsomolsk-on-Amur Aircraft Production Association*, March 30, 2010. http://www.knaapo.ru/eng/products/su-30mk2/index.wbp.

Sutter, Robert, and Chin-Hao Huang. "China-Southeast Asia Relations: US Interventions Complicate China's Advances." *Comparative Connections* (October 2010). http://csis.org/files/publication/1003qchina_seasia.pdf.

Swami, Praveen, and Malcolm Moore. "Japans Warns West Against Lifting China Arms Embargo." *The Telegraph*, November 18, 2010, sec. worldnews. http://www.telegraph.co.uk/news/worldnews/asia/china/8144383/Japans-warns-West-against-lifting-China-arms-embargo.html.

Synovitz, Ron. "Afghanistan: China's Winning Bid For Copper Rights Includes Power Plant, Railroad." *RadioFreeEurope/RadioLiberty*, November 24, 2007, sec. Afghanistan. http://www.rferl.org/content/article/1079190.html.

Synovitz, Ron. "China: Afghan Investment Reveals Larger Strategy." *RadioFreeEurope/RadioLiberty*, May 29, 2008, sec. Afghanistan. http://www.rferl.org/content/article/1144514.html.

Taipei Times. "Ma's 'No War' Mantra Is Capitulation." *Taipei Times*, October 27, 2008. http://www.taipeitimes.com/News/editorials/archives/2008/10/27/2003427063.

Task Force on Foreign Relations for the Prime Minister. "Basic Strategies for Japan's Foreign Policy in the 21st Century: New Era, New Vision, New Diplomacy," November 28, 2002. http://www.kantei.go.jp/foreign/policy/2002/1128tf_e.html.

Task Force on Foreign Relations for the Prime Minister (Japan). "Basic Strategies for Japan's Foreign Policy in the 21st Century New Era, New Vision, New Diplomacy." *Prime Minister of Japan*, November 28, 2002. http://www.kantei.go.jp/foreign/policy/2002/1128tf_e.html.

Taylor, Guy. "China's Caribbean Mission Shows Growing Naval Capability." *World Politics Review*, November 7, 2011. http://www.worldpoliticsreview.com/trend-lines/10586/chinas-carribbean-mission-shows-growing-naval-capability.

Taylor, Ian. *China's New Role in Africa*. Boulder, CO: Lynne Rienner Publishers, 2009.

Teng-hui, Lee. "Understanding Taiwan: Bridging the Perception Gap." *Foreign Affairs*, November 1, 1999. http://www.foreignaffairs.com/articles/55598/lee-teng-hui/understanding-taiwan-bridging-the-perception-gap.

Thomas, Timothy L. "Chinese and American Network Warfare." *Joint Force Quarterly* (July 2005). http://www.dtic.mil/cgi-bin/GetTRDoc?AD=ADA530848.

Tillemann, Levi. "Blowback from Zimbabwe: China's Faltering Strategy on Arms Exports." *China Brief*, June 24, 2008. http://www.jamestown.org/single/?no_cache=1&tx_ttnews%5Btt_news%5D=5000.

Times Of India. "French Prez Wants India in G8." *Times Of India*, August 31, 2007. http://articles.timesofindia.indiatimes.com/2007-08-31/india/27989683_1_french-president-nicolas-sarkozy-g13-nicholas-sarkozy.

Tomkins, Damien. "China-India Relations: An Unresolved Border and 60,000 Troops Deployed." *Atlantic Council*, June 23, 2009. http://www.acus.org/new_atlanticist/china-india-relations-unresolved-border-and-60000-military-personnel-deployed.

U.K. Foreign and Commonwealth Office. "Unrest in Xinjiang Province China." *British Embassy in Washington*, July 8, 2009. http://ukinusa.fco.gov.uk/en/news/?view=News&id=20541202.

U.S. Department of Defense. "DOD Press Briefing on the 2011 Annual Report to Congress: Military and Developments Involving the People's Republic of China." *U.S. Department of Defense*, August 24, 2011. http://www.defense.gov/transcripts/transcript.aspx?transcriptid=4868.

U.S. Department of Defense. *Military and Security Developments Involving the People's Republic of China 2011*. Washington, DC: U.S. Department of Defense, 2011.

U.S. Department of Defense. *Military and Security Developments Involving the People's Republic of China 2012*. Washington, DC: U.S. Department of Defense, 2012. http://www.defense.gov/pubs/pdfs/2012_CMPR_Final.pdf.

U.S. Department of Defense. *Military Power of the People's Republic of China 2008*. Washington, DC: U.S. Department of Defense, 2008. http://www.defense.gov/pubs/pdfs/China_Military_Report_08.pdf.

U.S. Department of Defense. *Military Power of the People's Republic of China 2009*. Washington, DC: U.S. Department of Defense, 2009. http://www.defense.gov/pubs/pdfs/China_Military_Power_Report_2009.pdf.

U.S. Department of Defense, Office of the Secretary of Defense. *Military and Security Developments Involving the People's Republic of China: 2010*. Washington, DC: U.S. Department of Defense, August 2010. http://www.defense.gov/pubs/pdfs/2010_CMPR_Final.pdf.

U.S. Department of State. "Joint Statement of U.S.-Japan Security Consultative Committee," February 19, 2005. http://2001-2009.state.gov/r/pa/prs/ps/2005/42490.htm.

U.S. Department of State. "Taiwan U.N. Membership Referendum Opposed by United States." http://iipdigital.usembassy.gov/st/english/article/2007/06/20070625135742zjsredna0.3750421.html#axzz2PYAOI2Le.

U.S. Energy Information Administration. "China: Background." *U.S. Energy Information Administration*, November 2010.

U.S. Energy Information Administration. *International Energy Outlook 2010*. U.S. Energy Information Administration, 2010. http://www.eia.gov/forecasts/archive/ieo10/pdf/0484(2010).pdf.

U.S. Energy Information Administration. "International Energy Outlook 2010—Highlights." *U.S. Energy Information Administration*, May 2010. http://www.eia.gov/forecasts/archive/ieo10/highlights.html.

U.S. National Intelligence Council. *Global Trends 2025: A Transformed World*. Washington, DC: U.S. Government Printing Office, 2008. http://www.dni.gov/files/documents/Newsroom/Reports%20and%20Pubs/2025_Global_Trends_Final_Report.pdf.

U.S. National Intelligence Council. *Global Trends 2030: Alternative Worlds*. Washington, DC: U.S. National Intelligence Council, 2012. http://www.dni.gov/files/documents/GlobalTrends_2030.pdf.

U.S. Navy, Office of Naval Intelligence. *China's Navy 2007*. U.S. Navy, Office of Naval Intelligence, n.d. http://www.fas.org/irp/agency/oni/chinanavy2007.pdf.

U.S. Navy, Office of Naval Intelligence. *The People's Liberation Army Navy: A Modern Navy with Chinese Characteristics*. Suitland, Maryland: U.S. Navy, Office of Naval Intelligence, August 2009. http://www.fas.org/irp/agency/oni/pla-navy.pdf.

U.S.-China Economic and Security Review Commission. *2008 Report to Congress of the U.S.–China Economic and Security Review Commission*. Washington, DC: U.S. Government Printing Office, November 2008. http://www.uscc.gov/Annual_Reports/2008-annual-report-congress.

U.S.-China Economic and Security Review Commission. *2012 Report to Congress of the U.S.–China Economic and Security Review Commission*. Washington, DC: U.S. Government Printing Office, November 2012. http://www.uscc.gov/Annual_Reports/2012-annual-report-congress.

United Nations. "Monthly Summary of Contributions (Police, UN Military Experts on Mission and Troops)." United Nations, March 31, 2012. http://www.un.org/en/peacekeeping/contributors/2012/March12_1.pdf.

United Nations. "Peacekeeping Fact Sheet." *United Nations*, March 31, 2012. http://www.un.org/en/peacekeeping/resources/statistics/factsheet.shtml.

United Nations Security Council, "Russian-Chinese Joint Declaration on a Multipolar World and the Establishment of a New International Order." United Nations Security Council, April 23, 1997, http://www.fas.org/news/russia/1997/a52—153en.htm.

United Press International. "Chinese Army's Quake Response Said Lacking." *UPI.com*, July 2, 2008. http://www.upi.com/Top_News/2008/07/02/Chinese-armys-quake-response-said-lacking/UPI-43621215001044/.

Varljen, Peter J. "Leadership: More Than Mission Accomplished." *Military Review* (April 2003). http://usacac.leavenworth.army.mil/cac/milreview/download/English/MarApr03/varljen.pdf.

Vogel, Augustus. "Navies Versus Coast Guards: Defining the Roles of African Maritime Security Forces." *Africa Center for Strategic Studies*, December 2009. http://www.ndu.edu/press/lib/pdf/Africa-Security-Brief/ASB-2.pdf.

Voice of America. "US-China Tensions Flare Over South China Sea Dispute." *VOA*, July 28, 2010. http://www.voanews.com/content/us-china-tensions-flare-over-south-china-sea-dispute-99538694/166117.html.

Walton, Julie. "China Must Push Through Reforms in Its Energy Sector—Especially Price Reform." *China Business Review* (October 2005).

Wang, Fei-ling. "Preservation, Prosperity and Power: What Motivates China's Foreign Policy?" *Journal of Contemporary China* 14, no. 45 (November 2005).

Wang, Fei-ling. "To Incorporate China: a New Policy for a New Era." *The Washington Quarterly* 21, no. 1 (1998): 67–81.

Wayne, Martin I. "Five Lessons from China's War on Terror." *Joint Force Quarterly* 47 (October 2007): 42–47.

What's On Xiamen. "China Yangtze Power Signs with EuroSibEnergo to Invest in Russia." *What's On Xiamen*, October 14, 2010. http://www.whatsonxiamen.com/invest326.html.

Willis, Andrew. "Japan: Ashton Was Wrong on China Arms Ban." *EUobserver.com*, May 19, 2011. http://euobserver.com/news/32360.

Wong, Edward. "Arrests Increased in Muslim Region of China." *New York Times*, January 5, 2009. http://www.nytimes.com/2009/01/05/world/asia/05iht-06china.19097680.html?_r=0.

Wong, Edward. "China Hedges Over Whether South China Sea Is a 'Core Interest' Worth War." *New York Times*, March 30, 2011, sec. World / Asia Pacific. http://www.nytimes.com/2011/03/31/world/asia/31beijing.html.

World Bank. *Doing Business 2013: Smarter Regulations for Small and Medium-Size Enterprises.* Washington, DC: World Bank Group, October 2012. http://www.doingbusiness.org/~/media/GIAWB/Doing%20Business/Documents/Annual-Reports/English/DB13-full-report.pdf.

World Coal Association. "Coal Statistics." *World Coal Association*, August 2012. http://www.worldcoal.org/resources/coal-statistics/.

World Energy Council. *2010 Survey of Energy Resources*, November 2010. http://www.worldenergy.org/documents/ser_2010_report_1.pdf.

Wortzel, Larry. "The General Political Department and the Evolution of the Political Commissar System." In *The People's Liberation Army as Organization*, edited by James C. Mulvenon and Andrew N.D. Yang. Arlington, VA: RAND Corporation, 2002.

Xinhua. "China Denies Arm Sales to Syria." *China Radio International*, February 11, 2012. http://english.cri.cn/6909/2012/02/11/53s680485.htm.

Xinhua. "China Focus: New Features Highlight Sino-African Relations." *Sina.com*, July 18, 2012. http://english.sina.com/china/2012/0718/487414.html.

Xinhua. "China to Adhere to 'Mutual Benefits and Win-win' Strategy." *Embassy of the People's Republic of China in the Republic of South Africa*, August 24, 2006. http://www.chinese-embassy.org.za/eng/zt/pd/t268890.htm.

Xinhua. "China Urges U.S. Companies Stop Arms Sales to Taiwan." *People's Daily Online*, February 2, 2010. http://english.peopledaily.com.cn/90001/90776/90883/6885977.html.

Xinhua. "China's Clean Energy Sector Protests Against U.S. Probe into Chinese New Energy Industry." *People's Daily Online*, October 20, 2010. http://english.peopledaily.com.cn/90001/90776/90883/7171353.html.

Xinhua. "Cooperation Framework Key to Further Promote China-Africa Relations," December 24, 2010. http://www.focac.org/eng/zt/10th/t781406.htm.

Xinhua. "EU Arms Embargo Against China Is Political Prejudice." *China Radio International*, November 29, 2011. http://english.cri.cn/6909/2011/11/29/2743s669477.htm.

Xinhua. "FM: China, Major World Powers Ties Growing in Cooperation, Win-win Direction." *Consulate-General of the People's Republic of China in Vancouver*, March 4, 2008. http://vancouver.china-consulate.org/eng/news/t412078.htm.

Xinhua. "Wen: China-Indonesia Relations Moving Toward Maturity." *Xinhuanet*, October 30, 2006. http://news.xinhuanet.com/english/2006-10/30/content_5268705.htm.

Xinhua. "Yang Jiechi Appointed China's New Foreign Minister." *Xinhuanet*, April 27, 2007. http://news.xinhuanet.com/english/2007-04/27/content_6034725.htm.

Xinhua. "Four-point Guidelines on cross-Straits Relations Set Forth by President Hu (Full Text)." *Xinhuanet*, March 4, 2005. http://news.xinhuanet.com/english/2005-03/04/content_2651270.htm.

Xinhua. "Top CPC Leadership." *Xinhuanet*, 2013. http://www.xinhuanet.com/english/special/topcpcleadership/index.htm.

Yaakov, Katz. "Latest Rockets Manufactured in China." *Jerusalem Post*, January 1, 2009. http://www.jpost.com/Israel/Article.aspx?id=127179.

Yihe, Xu. "China Energy Watch: Onshore Depletion Problems Loom." Dow Jones Energy Service, April 2, 2002. Dow Jones Factiva.

Ying, Ding. "The Sum of All Summits." *Beijing Review* no. 25 (June 18, 2007). http://www.bjreview.com/world/txt/2007-06/18/content_66532.htm.

Yunjie, Cheng, and Xu Jinzhang. "PLA Continues Long March of Logistics Reform." *Xinhuanet*, July 29, 2007. http://news.xinhuanet.com/english/2007-07/28/content_6441943..htm.

Zambelis, Chris, and Brandon Gentry. "China Through Arab Eyes." *Parameters* 38, no. 1 (Spring 2008): 60–72.

Zhou, Hao. "29 Chinese Abducted by Sudan Rebels." *Global Times*, January 30, 2012. http://www.globaltimes.cn/NEWS/tabid/99/ID/693721/29-Chinese-abducted-by-Sudan-rebels.aspx.

Index

          Index

133, 137, 138, 146, 153, 154, 155, 157;
    in Taiwan, 64
Democratic People's Republic of Korea. *See*
    Korea, North
Democratic Progressive Party (DPP), 62,
    65, 66, 68, 160
Democratic Republic of Congo, 97,
    98, 99, 160
Demography, 5, 48, 167
Deng Yingchao, 135
Development Research Center, 148
Diaoyu Islands. *See* Senkaku Islands
Diplomatic Service Bureau, 14
Djibouti, 108n
Dongshan Island, 143
DPP. *See* Democratic Progressive
    Party (DPP)
DPRK. *See* Korea, North
DRC. *See* Democratic Republic of Congo
drugs. *See* narcotics
Dvorchak, Eleanor, 145

East China Sea, 3, 39, 49, 58, 59, 60–61,
    159, 163, 166
East Turkestan Independence Movement
    (ETIM), 116
Ebermann, Klaus, 88
economic aid, 9, 18, 69, 70, 71, 75, 77
economic challenges, 4, 5, 6, 7, 55, 61, 70,
    89, 119, 120, 142, 148, 158, 167
economic cooperation, 65, 66, 67,
    68, 69, 72, 75, 77, 83, 84, 90,
    92, 93, 94, 95, 96, 98, 107, 116,
    122, 125, 140, 152, 158
Economic Cooperation Framework
    Agreement (ECFA) between China and
    Taiwan, 66–67, 167
economic growth, 2, 3, 4, 5, 6, 7, 9,
    11, 18, 25, 26, 37, 55, 60, 73, 74, 75,
    78, 98, 104, 135, 138, 139, 140, 146,
    147, 164, 168
economic institutions, 1, 75
economic power, 2, 3, 6, 27, 73,
    112, 114, 115, 168; of the West, 3
economic reforms, 1, 25, 62, 63,
    69, 71, 136, 137, 138, 139, 143, 144,
    146, 155, 158

economic rights, 6
economic zones, 59, 137, 152, 153
economy; of the DPRK, 71; of Japan, 59;
    of the PRC, 1, 2, 4, 11, 19, 25, 38, 55,
    73, 86, 88, 98, 103, 117, 118, 120, 124,
    133, 135, 137, 147, 155, 158, 165, 168;
    of the Soviet Union, 75; of Taiwan, 66
Ecuador, 103
Egypt, 95, 157
Elections; China (2008), 68; Free and fair,
    5, 6, 13, 56, 63; Taiwan (2000), 65;
    Taiwan May (2008), 66, 165; US
    (2008), 66; Zimbabwe, 126–27
Environment, 117, 119, 139
Equatorial Guinea, 101–2
Eritrea, 97, 98, 101–2
Espionage, 42, 44, 45, 141, 159, 165
Ethiopia, 101–2, 157
EU Commission. *See* European
    Commission
EU-China High-Level Economic and
    Trade Dialogue, 87
EU. *See* European Commission
Europe, 2, 6, 55, 78, 92, 93, 103,
    105, 114, 119,
European Commission, 87–88
European Union, 86–92; EU arms
    embargo on China, 87–89, 90–92, 101;
    trade with China, 93, 156, 163
EuroSibEnergo PLC, 124
Exclusive Economic Zone (EEZ), 57, 61,
    85, 161
Export-Import Bank of China,
    96, 122
Exports, 2, 4, 17, 18, 26, 56, 67, 74, 75,
    84, 88, 89, 91, 92, 93, 96, 98, 101, 120,
    121, 123, 125, 126, 127, 156, 158, 160,
    162, 164

Falun Gong, 25, 149, 159
FARC, 104
FBI, 165
Five Principles of Peaceful Coexistence, 72,
    111–12, 135
Foreign Policy (magazine), 168
Forum on China-Africa Cooperation
    (FOCAC), 98, 100, 101, 160, 164

About the Author

RICHARD WEITZ is Senior Fellow and Director of the Center for Political-Military Analysis at Hudson Institute. His current research includes regional security developments relating to Europe, Eurasia, and East Asia as well as U.S. foreign, defense, and Homeland Security policies. Dr. Weitz is also an Expert at Wikistrat and a nonresident Senior Fellow at the Center for a New American Security (CNAS), where he contributes to various defense projects.

Before joining Hudson in 2003, Dr. Weitz worked for the Institute for Foreign Policy Analysis; Center for Strategic and International Studies; Defense Science Board; DFI International, Inc.; Center for Strategic Studies; Harvard University's Kennedy School of Government; and the U.S. Department of Defense. Dr. Weitz is a graduate of Harvard College (B.A. with Highest Honors in Government), the London School of Economics (M.Sc. in International Relations), Oxford University (M.Phil. in Politics), and Harvard University (Ph.D. in Political Science), where he was elected to Phi Beta Kappa. He is proficient in Russian, French, and German.

Dr. Weitz has published or edited several books and monographs, including two volumes of *National Security Case Studies* (Project on National Security Reform; 2012 and 2008); *Can We Manage a Declining Russia?* (Hudson, 2011); *War and Governance: International Security in a Changing World Order* (Praeger, 2011); *The Russian Military Today and Tomorrow* (Strategic Studies Institute, 2010); *Global Security Watch-Russia* (Praeger, 2009); *China-Russia Security Relations* (Strategic Studies Institute of the U.S. Army War College, 2008); *Kazakhstan and the New International Politics of Eurasia* (Central Asia-Caucasus Institute, 2008); *Mismanaging Mayhem: How Washington Responds to Crisis* (Praeger, 2008); *The Reserve Policies of Nations: A Comparative Analysis* (Strategic Studies Institute, 2007); and *Revitalising US–Russian Security Cooperation: Practical Measures* (International Institute for Strategic Studies, 2005).

Dr. Weitz has also published in such journals as *Global Asia, Survival, Jane's Intelligence Review, Jane's Islamic Affairs Analyst, The Washington Quarterly, The National Interest, NATO Review, Studies in Conflict and Terrorism, Defense Concepts, Pacific Focus, Journal of Defence Studies, Small Wars Journal, WMD Insights, World Affairs, Political Science Quarterly, The Journal of Strategic Studies*, and *Yale Journal of international Affairs*. The commentaries of Dr. Weitz have appeared in the *International Herald Tribune, Baltimore Sun, The Guardian, Christian Science Monitor, Washington Times, Wall Street Journal* (Europe), *Japan Times*, and many Internet-based publications such as those of the WashingtonPost.com, ForeignPolicy.Com, Yale Global, The Diplomat, EurasiaNet, Project Syndicate, Middle East Times, Eurasia Daily Monitor, and World Politics Review, where he is Senior Editor. Dr. Weitz has appeared on the BBC, CNN, C-SPAN, PBS, ABC, FOX, MSNBC, VOA, NHK, UK Channel 4, ITN, France 24, Deutsche Welle, CBC, CTV, RT, ARD, KSA, Al-Hurra, Al-Arabiya, Al-Jazeera, Al-Alam, Kuwait TV, Dubai TV, PressTV, CCTV, IHA TV, Pacifica Radio, and additional broadcast media. He has delivered numerous presentations at conferences, panels, and other events.

CPSIA information can be obtained
at www.ICGtesting.com
Printed in the USA
BVHW040744060620
580614BV00030B/202